Operationalizing Culturally Relevant Leadership Lea
on leadership learning in critical ways. It was suc
just," "intentional opportunities" "contextualizing .... dimensions"
and "educators and learners" in one model. I am excited to see how this work
transform research and practice.

—**Dr. Scott J. Allen**, Dr. James S. Reid Chair in Management
John Carroll University

As we continue to reel from the devastating events of 2020—COVID-19 pandemic, racial inequity, widening economic gaps, and threats to American democracy—Beatty and Guthrie's new book is a timely resource for leadership educators. This deeper exploration of the culturally relevant leadership learning (CRLL) model guides leadership educators in reconstructing not only what and how we teach, but who needs be included and why. Narratives from scholars and practitioners utilizing the model are weaved throughout to demonstrate how CRLL supports the development of individual leader identity, capacity, and efficacy, and the development and implementation of co-curricular and academic programs. At the cusp of the next phase of leadership education, this book is an invitation to deeply explore CRLL and its place in changing the direction of how we define, teach, practice, and embody leadership.

—**Christie Navarro** (she/her/hers), Director
Center for Leadership Learning, Office of Undergraduate Education
University of California, Davis

Operationalizing Culturally Relevant Leadership Learning offers an essential guide for leadership educators. The need for culturally relevant work is critical, and the authors have provided the roadmap to follow to ensure that we are engaging all students in ways that honor their whole selves. The narratives and examples provided are the tools necessary for educators to immediately apply the CRLL to their own contexts. An essential addition to the literature!

—**Dr. Jackie Bruce** (she/her/hers), Associate Professor
Director of the Oaks Leadership Scholars Program, NC State University
and Editor, *Journal of Leadership Education*

This text is a must-read for leadership educators. The authors have developed a resource that has utility whether applying the culturally relevant leadership learning framework for the first time or considering ways to integrate into programs further. The authors strike an artful balance of theoretical framework and first-person reflection of educators. This text is a call-to-action for leadership educators to continue the important work of creating inclusive environments for students' authentic leadership voices to emerge.

—**Dr. Michael C. Gleason** (he/him/his)
Irving R. Burling Distinguished Professor of Leadership
Wartburg College

Beatty, Guthrie, and the contributing narratives beautifully connect context and content in the work of culturally relevant leadership learning. They offer entry points to intentionally engage leadership while centering identity, efficacy and capacity. The collection of conceptual knowledge, insight and storytelling provides practical strategies in the invitation to develop meaningful learning opportunities in socially just and conscious ways.

—**dr. becky martinez** (she/her/hers)
Infinity Martinez Consulting, Inc.
and Faculty, Social Justice Training Institute

Operationalizing Culturally Relevant Leadership Learning uses storytelling to provide guidance on systemic, programmatic, and personal application of the CRLL framework. The diverse leadership educator experiences woven throughout the text successfully illustrate how CRLL can be used as a strategic design tool across educational contexts and functions. Any educator exploring how to broaden leadership beliefs and practices in their work beyond dominant cultural narratives will find this an insightful and useful resource.

—**Dr. Melissa Rocco** (she/her/hers)
Lecturer and Program Manager for Leadership Studies and Development
University of Maryland, College Park

Leadership education needs to address culturally relevant leadership in order to prepare students for the 21st century. This text establishes the significance of culturally relevant leadership and prepares leadership educators to apply CRLL intentionally in their contexts. This text guides educators in the development of CRLL academic and co-curricular programs—a necessary step in supporting the work educators do.

—**Dr. Katherine E. McKee** (she/her/hers), Assistant Professor
Agricultural and Human Sciences, NC State University

Operationalizing Culturally Relevant Leadership Learning

A volume in
Contemporary Perspectives on Leadership Learning
Kathy L. Guthrie, *Series Editor*

Contemporary Perspectives on Leadership Learning

Kathy L. Guthrie, *Series Editor*

Operationalizing Culturally Relevant Leadership Learning

Cameron C. Beatty
Florida State University

Kathy L. Guthrie
Florida State University

INFORMATION AGE PUBLISHING, INC.
Charlotte, NC • www.infoagepub.com

Library of Congress Cataloging-in-Publication Data

A CIP record for this book is available from the Library of Congress
http://www.loc.gov

ISBN: 978-1-64802-658-4 (Paperback)
      978-1-64802-659-1 (Hardcover)
      978-1-64802-660-7 (E-Book)

Copyright © 2021 Information Age Publishing Inc.

All rights reserved. No part of this publication may be reproduced, stored in a
retrieval system, or transmitted, in any form or by any means, electronic, mechanical,
photocopying, microfilming, recording or otherwise, without written permission
from the publisher.

Printed in the United States of America

To those committed to the lifelong work of making leadership education more socially just, equitable, and inclusive for all identities and cultures, especially those who have been historically marginalized and erased from leadership education.

Contents

vii

Narrative Overview

Operationalizing Culturally Relevant Leadership Learning, pages xi–xiv
Copyright © 2021 by Information Age Publishing
All rights of reproduction in any form reserved.
xi

Preface

When we decided to write this book, we knew it would be challenging, but we felt a conviction that we could not just share the knowledge without also demonstrating how culturally relevant leadership learning (CRLL) can be leveraged, and also interrogated. The CRLL model is a relatively new framework for teaching and developing curriculum for leadership programs. The goal of CRLL is to support leadership educators as they critically challenge the programs they design and facilitate (Bertrand Jones et al., 2016). The beginning of the book highlights the CRLL model, which is grounded in Ladson-Billings' (1992, 1995) culturally relevant pedagogy. For pedagogy to be culturally relevant, educators must implement an assets-based approach to teaching and learning with students of various cultural backgrounds. Ladson-Billings highlighted how the lived experiences, knowledge, and skills of students of color are often seen as a deficit in a classroom setting rather than an asset. But how do leadership educators take an assets-based approach in leadership education? What does centering the lived experiences, knowledge, and skills of students of color look like in leadership learning? How do leadership educators understand their own biases and socialization in leadership learning in order to design more equitable and just learning spaces for the purpose of transforming how learners engage in leadership? When we facilitate workshops or present at conferences on the CRLL model, we are oftentimes asked, "But how do you do this? What are the steps to revamp my curriculum? How do I make the leadership program I coordinate more culturally relevant?" We felt it was

Operationalizing Culturally Relevant Leadership Learning, pages xv–xx
Copyright © 2021 by Information Age Publishing
All rights of reproduction in any form reserved.

important to offer leadership educators a practical resource and guide with diverse voices and experiences in implementing this model within their work. We wanted to dig deeper, focusing on all the components of CRLL, and explore the operationalization of the model.

As we began to outline the book, we had to reflect on the assumptions, leadership theories and practices, underlying cultural competence, relevance, and pedagogy. We had to incorporate the ways leadership educators teach, conduct research, consult, and engage in socially just outcomes and how they evolve and change given environment and context. In doing so, we explored how our own work at the Leadership Learning Research Center at Florida State University, as well the broader field of leadership education within higher education, has evolved and become more plentiful, complex, and dynamic.

Underlying Assumptions

For us, it is important to be explicit about our assumptions underlying this book and define key terms we use. While the first few chapters will explore leadership, leadership learning, leadership education, context, and campus climate, we will highlight a few terms and assumptions that guide our meaning making for the book. According to Bertrand Jones et al. (2016), the CRLL model "seeks to compel leadership educators to challenge old paradigms of leadership and learning, in order to consider new ways to educate students and develop leaders capable of challenging inequity to create social change" (p. 10). The model acknowledges the prevalence of all forms of oppression, such as racism, classism, and sexism. Leadership learning that is culturally relevant recognizes the concept and influence of power (Bertrand Jones et al., 2016). It acknowledges power in leadership, language, and campus climate as well as the influences and dynamics of power on a leader and their ability to produce social change.

With regard to the power of language and words, CRLL acknowledges the importance of how certain words are defined or described, particularly the words *leader* and *leadership*. Not everyone defines these words the same. How these words are conceptualized is personal and reliant on the social and cultural norms and ideologies that have influenced what these terms mean to people from various backgrounds (Bertrand Jones et al., 2016). It is important to remember and understand this when facilitating leadership learning for people with different cultural backgrounds and experiences. The language of leadership and the social construction of leader and leadership will be explored more in Chapter 1.

The CRLL model is centered on the development of three aspects: identity, capacity, and efficacy. The first aspect is the individual—the person who is being developed. The second aspect is the leadership process, which illuminates the idea that leadership is a process and not a destination. The third aspect (see Chapter 2, Figure 2.2) of the development is a vibrant and continuous interaction between the individual and the leadership process through their leader identity, capacity, and efficacy. The researchers who created the CRLL model understood that leadership learning does not occur in a bubble, especially on a college campus. These three aspects will be explored in more detail in early chapters of the book.

We center our work on CRLL through social justice pedagogy. The social justice definition that guides our work is from Adams et al. (2000), which acknowledges social justice as both a goal and a process. "Socially just leadership education is the intersection of leadership education and social justice work" (Guthrie & Chunoo, 2018, p. 2). Without insight into the belief system of the authors, readers can sometimes be encouraged to view academic writing as neutral or unbiased. We strongly disagree with this notion, and we want to be intentional in acknowledging our core beliefs that leadership education should always center equity and justice, which birthed and actualized the idea for this book. Next, we offer our individual positionalities in approaching the work of leadership education and writing this book.

Our Positionality Statements

In *Decolonizing Educational Research: From Ownership to Answerability*, Patel (2016) called on researchers to adopt a different way of framing and explaining their positionality in the research process. Patel called on researchers to critically reflect and ask themselves three questions: "Why me/us?"; "Why this particular study?"; and "Why now?" We felt acknowledging our positionalities as leadership educators and researchers using this format was important in order to understand how we approached organizing this book for the purpose of advancing CRLL in leadership education.

For me (Cameron), the "Why me?" is because as a leadership educator I feel passionate that leadership education should be inclusive, transformative, and liberating. As a highly educated, middle-class, Black, gay, cisman, I have seen and experienced how leadership education can be demoralizing and not represent my identities and lived experiences. I have also attempted to cultivate learning spaces where leadership education can be a transformative space for learners to want to enact change. To address the question of *why this particular book*, I feel strongly that leadership educators have the capacity to create more culturally relevant spaces for leadership learners if they only had the tools and resources. I offer this book in partnership with Kathy in order to continue to move the leadership education field forward in enacting more socially just leadership learning. My actions as an educator must match my values of social justice and equity.

For me (Kathy), the "Why me?" is something of constant reflection. As a White, highly educated ciswoman from a low-income farming background, I acknowledge the privileges I hold. I have witnessed how the dominant narrative of White culture has excluded and silenced diverse individuals in all settings, but especially in leadership education. I have worked to disrupt these environments in and out of the classroom but know greater need to continue and enhance disruption is essential. In reflection of "Why this particular book?" there is a lack of tools to develop and implement programs in culturally relevant and socially just ways. Leadership educators have a great influence in developing future leaders, who can shift the tides to centering humanity and diverse lived experiences in leadership learning.

The "Why now?" for both authors (Cameron and Kathy) is rooted in the current political, cultural, and educational climate we are navigating in the United States and globally. This book was written during the global pandemic of COVID-19, during a time the country is continuing to reckon with the histories of racism and anti-Blackness, and during a divisive presidential campaign and insurrection of the U.S. Capitol on January 6, 2021. All of these contexts have significant implications for us, as leadership educators, and how we teach and frame leadership for learners. If we are not framing leadership from a socially just and culturally relevant lens, then we are not preparing learners to address compound issues of systemic injustices.

Purpose of the Book

The primary purpose of this book is to expand our understanding of CRLL and how to operationalize it in personal and professional development, curricular and co-curricular programs, and leadership education research and scholarship. Specifically, this book will (a) offer the CRLL model as a framework for leadership educators that infuses socially just leadership outcomes, (b) present specific examples and narratives of how leadership educators have put the CRLL model into action, and (c) provide readers with reflective questions and tools to get them started in applying the CRLL model in their own context. The book provides leadership educators with a substantive and comprehensive approach to the topic, offering personal narratives from leadership educators who have operationalized the model in their own personal and professional contexts. We believe that reframing leadership education with the CRLL model, leadership educators will be able to integrate new insights into their own pedagogy and practice and move towards action.

Audience

The primary audience for this book is leadership educators who work in both curricular and co-curricular programs in higher education. This book is meant to be a practical resource, which raises leadership educators' understanding of culturally relevant leadership pedagogy and learning for the purpose of creating inclusive learning spaces that are socially just for students from all cultural backgrounds. This book could also be for personal and professional development to assist in building and enhancing one's level of cultural competence in leadership education. Ultimately, this book could serve leadership educators from new and entry-level roles to senior scholars in leadership education.

Overview of the Contents

The book is designed to introduce the model to those who may be new to CRLL and expand the application of the model to those who might be familiar to CRLL. This book illustrates how leadership educators can shift the way they experience and facilitate leadership learning. Readers of this text are encouraged to actively engage in the content and questions each chapter poses and consider for themselves how CRLL can be implemented in their own context. In this book, we offer operationalizing the CRLL model in a why, who, what, where, when, how framework. chapters 1–3 explore in more detail the answers to the five W's and one H in relation to operationalizing the CRLL model through a socially just leadership education lens:

- Why? (socially just leadership education),
- Who? (leadership educators and learners),
- What? (leadership identity, capacity, and efficacy development),
- Where/When? (contextualizing environmental dimensions of CRLL), and
- How? (creating intentional opportunities for leadership learning).

Chapter 1 defines the language of leadership, leadership education, and the leadership learning framework. The chapter also addresses what socially just leadership is. The chapter is also critical in framing the operationalization of CRLL and discusses the why, who, what, where, when, and how of developing culturally relevant and socially just leadership education. Chapter 2 describes the components of the CRLL model and breaks down the aspects of identity, capacity, and efficacy. Chapter 3 explores leadership as a process in relation to context and the five dimensions of campus climate.

In the next section of the book, narratives are embedded in the chapter as examples for how leadership educators have operationalized CRLL in different contexts with various goals. Chapter 4 begins with addressing the importance of personal reflection and development by highlighting how leadership educators navigated doing their own self-work in relation to the CRLL model. Similarly, Chapter 5 shares narratives of application of the CRLL model in professional development for leadership educators engaged in both curricular and co-curricular programs. Chapter 6 offers how in co-curricular contexts, leadership educators can support individual student contributions in order to empower and encourage leader identity, capacity, and efficacy (Guthrie & Rodriguez, 2018). The narratives in Chapter 7 provide rich illustrations of how CRLL has been used to fuel a variety of co-curricular leadership learning experiences. Chapter 8 considers the various contexts interdisciplinary and multidisciplinary academic programs provide, using the CRLL model. Chapter 9 offers narratives of several approaches to consider for aligning pedagogical strategies with learning outcomes using CRLL as a supporting framework. Finally, Chapters 10 and 11 close this section of the book, highlighting how leadership educators have applied CRLL to their own positionalities, theoretical frameworks, and research methods.

Following the chapters focused on leadership educators' narratives, Chapters 12 and 13 conclude the book and offer processing questions for leadership educators to consider when operationalizing CRLL. These chapters provide resources for personal and professional development, curriculum design for curricular and co-curricular programs, and leadership education research. The book concludes that the application of the CRLL model can assist leadership educators in fulfilling their personal, institutional, and professional objectives to create and maintain inclusive, equitable, and just leadership learning environments.

Acknowledgments

We know our vision of a more equitable world is not ours alone. To collectively do this challenging work we must continually engage in conversations, thinking, reflecting, learning, and co-creating knowledge of how to move forward. We thank all of those who continue to participate in these processes with us. Especially, the diverse educators who shared their narratives in how they are operationalizing culturally relevant leadership learning (CRLL) in this book. We feel fortunate to have the opportunity to continue to learn from and with you all. Although there are countless individuals who continue to inform our work in creating culturally relevant and socially just leadership learning opportunities, we do want to thank some individuals specifically for their help with this book. Destiny Caldwell, thank you for your assistance with the early conceptualization of this book. Brittany Devies, Darius Robinson, Derrick Pacheco, Ross Allbritton, Anna Van Gurp, and Sarah Aguilar, we appreciate your invaluable feedback (yes, feedback = love) and energy in getting us to the finish line. Julie LeBlanc, thank you for your reference and APA formatting knowledge. Jessica Chung, your artistry continues to inspire us, thank you for sharing your talent for the cover. We also want to thank all the professionals in the Leadership Learning Research Center at Florida State University. Even during pandemics and the complexity of constant change, we are grateful to work with such an intelligent, passionate, and fun group of people.

Cameron wants to thank his guardian angels, his late mother Carmen T. Taylor and godfather Fr. Chester P. Smith, SVD. Your spirits pushed me to

Operationalizing Culturally Relevant Leadership Learning, pages xxi–xxii
Copyright © 2021 by Information Age Publishing
All rights of reproduction in any form reserved. **xxi**

put words on the screen often when I felt I had nothing left to say. I strive to make you both proud of me daily. Thinking about you both shining down on me gives me strength to continue to strive to leave this world better than I found it. Thank you, Dr. Kathy Guthrie, for your love, understanding, support, friendship and for your ongoing cheerleading. You have not only been a friend and colleague, but you have been a mentor and confidant. Thank you for being a co-conspirator in doing this work. I want to especially thank each student I have had the privilege to learn from and be in community with, both in and out of the classroom. Thank you to my family, friends, and Zora Neale Beatty (my fur baby) for loving me unconditionally and encouraging me to press on in this work.

Kathy wants to thank Dr. Susan R. Komives for her endless support, love, advocacy, and mentorship over the years. I am overflowing with gratitude to have such a dynamic woman in my life. I also want to thank my co-author, Dr. Cameron Beatty. I feel lucky every day to be able to learn from and with you. Your brilliance, passion, thoughtfulness, and friendship mean more than I could ever express in words. You are truly a gift, not only to me, but this world. I am also thankful for Team Guthrie; I am nothing without you. Brian, you have always been the love of my life, my biggest fan, and the greatest partner I could ask for. Kinley, you have sharpened my focus, given me purpose, and motivate me every day to be the best version of myself. You are my *why* and my hope is this work will be seen for your generation to have more equitable ways of being and to carry forward towards humanity being at the center of all we know, be, and do.

—**Cameron C. Beatty** & **Kathy L. Guthrie**

1

Interrogating Culturally Relevant Leadership Learning

It has been well established that leadership learning is critical to the purpose of higher education (Bok, 2011; Chunoo & Osteen, 2016; Kezar et al., 2005). However, leadership education as a field and profession is still in its infancy. Leadership educators are still discovering how to intentionally develop leadership learning opportunities, especially in culturally relevant and socially just ways. In this chapter, we begin our journey of exploring the why, who, what, where, when, and how of culturally relevant leadership learning. We start this journey by discussing the language of leadership and how this complex concept emerged. Although higher education's purpose is increasingly seen to include leadership learning there is still confusion in the use of the language of leadership (Guthrie et al., 2013), which includes how leadership is defined, discussed, and practiced. After establishing how we frame leadership and our work in this book, we create the framework of operationalizing culturally relevant leadership learning focusing on why we engage in this work, who does this work, what our intended outcome is,

Operationalizing Culturally Relevant Leadership Learning, pages 1–14
Copyright © 2021 by Information Age Publishing
All rights of reproduction in any form reserved. **1**

environmental dimensions of the where and when of the work, and how leadership learning is created.

Language of Leadership

Leadership scholars and practitioners have discussed the importance of the language of leadership for years (Bertrand Jones et al., 2016; Dugan, 2017; Guthrie et al., 2013; Komives, 2011). In discussions on how leadership is defined, many look to Kellerman's (2012) meta-analysis of leadership literature that emerged with over 1,500 definitions and 40 models of leadership. As Dugan and Komives (2011) state, the definition of leadership has become more debated than agreed upon. Defining leadership spans from concepts rooted in "Great Men" to serving others to moving toward social change (Guthrie & Jenkins, 2018).

In fact, Rost (1991) attempted to develop a definition of leadership after exploring the historical evolution of the concept and how others defined it. After years of work, Rost (1991) settled on a definition that met the criteria of being "clear, concise, understandable by scholars and practitioners, researchable, practically relevant, and persuasive" (p. 99). The definition Rost (1991) proposed was that "leadership is an influence relationship among leaders and followers who intend real change that reflects their mutual purposes" (p. 102). One of the strong aspects of Rost's definition is that it is accessible for everyone engaged in the process of leadership. This includes leaders and followers who want to create change, and not just for a chosen few or those with titles. However, Rost's definition does not mention who those leaders and followers may be. Inclusion of such language gives signals to learners about who may be included or excluded from the leadership process. This goes back to the importance of language used regarding leadership. As Guthrie et al. (2017) discuss, language provides insight to individual and collective worldviews, but also how one constructs knowledge. This is especially salient in the social construction of leadership.

Social Construction

Individuals may define the complex concept of leadership differently based on personal experiences, social identities, or various worldviews. This means leadership is socially constructed and holds different meanings to various individuals (Dugan, 2017, Guthrie et al., 2013, Guthrie & Jenkins, 2018). Social construction means that an understanding of an idea (leadership in this case) is jointly created over time and develops into a shared assumption. Shared assumptions have significant cultural influence as they become central to the meanings developed with others. Jones et al. (2013) point out constructivism and constructionism are often used interchangeably; however, they hold different meanings. While constructivism indicates developing individual meaning, social constructionism takes social cultural influence to generate and transmit meaning (Crotty, 1998). This is important to note when defining leadership. Honoring the complexity and nuances of context is critical in centering cultural relevance in leadership learning. Chapter 3 will explore social constructions more deeply, especially in regard to the context of leadership learning.

Leader and Leadership

Put in simple terms, leader is the individual and leadership is the process. As Dugan and Komives (2011) discuss, common phrasing and writing on leadership often interchange leader and leadership with little distinction. However, when they are carelessly interchanged, "leadership becomes the work of one versus all, which is not in alignment with postindustrial models of leadership" (Guthrie & Jenkins, 2018, p. 5). Unfortunately, this is not a new challenge, as scholars and educators continue to develop and deliver leadership development programs without clarifying the meaning. This lack of clarity has not only confused learners, but continues to exclude diverse students who may not see themselves represented in the language used, and does not acknowledge social construction and lived experiences as part of being a leader and engaging in the leadership process.

Follower and Followership

When discussing the language of leadership, it is essential to consider the terms follower and followership. As Guthrie et al. (2021) share "a follower is an individual who engages in behaviors while interacting with leaders in an effort to make change and meet needed objectives alongside leaders" (p. 5). Antiquated notions of followers include people unequivocally following others in positions of authority. Even though this may still be true in some situations, followers also work independently, take initiative over necessary tasks that need to be accomplished, and have a reciprocal relationship with leaders. Followership can be described as an intentional practice of followers to improve the collaborative exchange between them and a leader. Just as leadership, followership is a social construct that is essential to the leadership process and can be developed. Hurwitz and Thompson (2020) examine not only the concept of followership, but the development of followership. To further the idea of followership, Riggio (2020) offers citizenship as an alternative way to conceptualize it and states that many qualities of exemplary followers align with influential and engaged citizens.

Leadership and Management

Although leadership and management both involve relationships, working with others, and pursuing effective goals, they are different processes. An individual can be both a great leader and manager, but because they are different concepts that require different skills. Leadership has been around for centuries, but the Industrial Revolution helped the expansion of management, both as a concept and as a practice (Kotter, 1990). Leadership and management differ in four areas: relationship, roles, changes, and overall purposes (Rost, 1991). Influential relationships are central to leadership, where authoritative relationships are the focus of management. Roles of leader and follower emerge in leadership, but positional roles of manager and subordinate exist in the management process. Real change is the intention of leadership whereas producing something tangible is management's focus. Overall purposes are another difference between leadership and management. Leadership reflects mutual purposes, where management focuses on the coordinated activities to produce goods and services.

Interdisciplinary, Multidisciplinary, and Transdisciplinary

It has been long considered that leadership learning and practice benefits from including diverse perspectives, constructs, and contexts (Riggio et al., 2003). Harvey and Riggio (2011) named various perspectives such as historical, psychological, sociological, political, linguistic, and cultural as perspectives that enhance students' understandings of various leadership approaches. If leadership learning is enhanced by various constructs, then leadership education should not only be drawn from multiple disciplines but integrated across disciplines. Leadership being interdisciplinary and multidisciplinary has been a part of the conversation for years (Guthrie et al., 2013; Sowcik & Komives, 2020). However, to understand leadership and leadership learning even better within higher education, we must also explore how it is transdisciplinary.

Introduced by Piaget (1972), transdisciplinarity suggests an integration of ideas (Nicolescu, 2008) and is across and between disciplines. The goal is to create a holistic approach that can provide a better understanding of the present world (Bernstein, 2015). Transdisciplinary education brings this integration of ideas to construct new knowledge and elevate learning to more complex cognitive abilities. Transdisciplinarity connects with leadership

(Francovich, 2020) and provides a stronger framework because of the integration of ideas and brings it into the present world, which is where leadership and leadership learning is situated.

Framework to Interrogate Culturally Relevant Leadership Learning

In this text, we are not only highlighting how to operationalize culturally relevant leadership learning, but we are also interrogating it. We feel it is imperative to continue to question all aspects of cultural relevance in leadership learning opportunities. As leadership educators, we need to continue growing and developing in this work of leadership education, as our effectiveness relies on our continual growth and development. Using the interrogative pronouns of why, who, what, where, when, and how will help guide us in deconstructing and reformulating leadership education by using various means in culturally relevant and socially just ways. Figure 1.1 offers a quick overview of our interrogation strategy that will guide this book and our work.

Starting With Why: Socially Just Leadership Education

When discussing the interrogation of culturally relevant leadership learning, we must start with why. "Why do we engage in this work?" Brought into mainstream consciousness, Sinek (2009) proposes that starting with establishing your *why* allows us to focus our work and begin with purpose. Starting with this one-word question helps us make sense of the things around us and leads to other questions that can help us progress in not

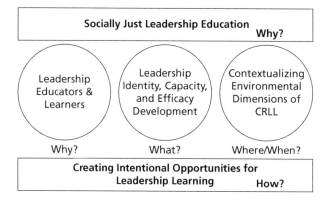

Figure 1.1 Interrogation of culturally relevant leadership learning framework.

only working from a place of passion and purpose, but also creating innovative and influential programs that have the power of developing the future leaders our world needs.

As Sinek (2009) introduces with the golden circle, which are three concentric circles with why in the middle, how in the center circle and what in the outside circle. Although the golden circle (Sinek, 2009) is a simple illustration, the metaphor is complex as it was inspired by the golden ratio, which is a mathematical concept that has been used throughout history in various ways (Sinek, 2009). The golden circle provides perspective to current assumptions about why some leaders have high levels of influence. Although Sinek describes the golden circle through a context of organizations, there is acknowledgment of application to this in personal journeys. We encourage you to not only interrogate your program's why, but also your own personal why in engaging in this work. The questions throughout this book can be used to guide you throughout your personal exploration of your *why.*

The visual of the golden circle is of three concentric circles. At the center circle sits the why, which Sinek (2009) proclaims very few know. The reason of why we engage in certain activities or work is often overlooked and rarely communicated. Oftentimes it is assumed individuals and others just know why we are engaging in certain activities. The next circle represents the how, which some know how the work is done. Whether you are interrogating this through a personal lens or organizational lens, details in the how might not be as clear as they should or could be. Finally, the outer circle is what is being done, which Sinek (2009) proclaims everyone typically knows. It is through engaging in the work of leadership education and our need to not only market and assess it, but we also need to be well versed at what the work is.

In our interrogation of leadership education, we expand beyond the interrogative questions of why, how, and what, and include who, when, and where as well. However, we do believe that starting with why we do this work, personally and in programs, is critical in grounding the conversation for operationalizing culturally relevant leadership learning. The why for us is to move towards leadership education that is socially just to yield more leaders driven by social justice, which is desperately needed in our world. Throughout this text, you will find how the culturally relevant leadership learning model is one tool towards the path of socially just leadership education.

The Who: Leadership Educators and Learners

Leadership educators are the *who* in creating and delivering intentional culturally relevant leadership learning opportunities. We subscribe to Guthrie and Jenkins's (2018) assertion that "anyone who intentionally develops and delivers leadership initiatives" is a leadership educator (p. 4). We honor that leadership educators are not just professionals who work in dedicated leadership development offices. Rather, we believe anyone who works with students can be considered a leadership educator, regardless of position or context. Priest and Jenkins (2019) consider "leadership education to represent a professional community of practice within the larger field of leadership studies, as well as a pedagogical approach to facilitating leadership learning and development." (p. 10). As Priest and Jenkins (2019) state, leadership educators' practice is in various contexts such as teaching, research, service, administration, community outreach, and programming. Throughout this text, we wish to situate ourselves in this work, specifically in relation to creating culturally relevant and socially just leadership education. We view the culturally relevant leadership learning model as a tool to help us position ourselves in the work as leadership educators.

From a phenomenological study, Jenkins (2019) reported that reflection from participants' journey of becoming a leadership educator comprise four key points: impact, serendipity, feeling as if they are faking it, and developing others. Participants explained the importance of making a positive impact on students and how this inspired their chosen career path. Reflection of serendipity surfaced regarding participants' pathway into the leadership educator profession. Since most leadership educators have little to no formal training prior to taking on this role, another emergent theme from Jenkins (2019) study is a feeling of faking competence. Study participants also reflected on the importance of entering the leadership educator profession to be able to develop others. These points are important to consider in how leadership educators enter the profession in and out of higher education.

Educators Bringing Self to Learning Environment

As Rosch and Anthony (2012) discuss, it is important for leadership educators to model the skills and values they are teaching. Inconsistencies on educator practices and delivery of content would create an overall disconnected leadership learning experience (Guthrie & Jenkins, 2018). In reflecting on how educators must bring their whole selves to leadership learning environments, complexity of how educators show up in delivering leadership programs is realized. As educators, we need to spend time reflecting on how we not only enter leadership learning spaces, but also the space we take up in learning environments. Simply put, as educators, we have an incredible amount of responsibility for creating a learning environment where all students feel not only welcomed, but also validated in their personal leadership learning journey. Both majority and minoritized populations must bring their whole selves to leadership learning environments and processes.

At the core of our own teaching journey, Harding (2011) reminds us that our own identity influences how we engage students, teach leadership, and create intentional leadership learning opportunities and environments. The complexity of bringing our whole selves to the leadership educator role while guiding students through the journey, all while continuing to increase our own self-awareness, is not only acknowledged but honored. Just as our students are evolving and growing, so are we as educators (Guthrie & Jenkins, 2018). Constant deep reflection is needed for growth in our engagement with concepts of leadership (Volpe White et al., 2019) and teaching as a profession.

Leadership Educator Professional Identity

In the last decade, more attention has been given to the development of a leadership educators professional identity. As Harding (2011) offered, "Identities of leadership educators would be expected to develop as they participate in a community of practice with the students and their colleagues" (p. 93). Communities of practice can support new educators and allow them to engage with seasoned educators to create spaces and opportunities for mentoring, offer professional development experiences, and share resources (Seemiller & Priest, 2017). Exploring how to best develop leadership educators is vital to continued development of our leadership programs and therefore students' growth. Offered through narratives in Chapters 4–6, culturally relevant leadership learning (CRLL) supports the personal and professional development of leadership educators.

By synthesizing professional development literature, Seemiller and Priest (2015) developed the leadership educator professional identity development (LEPID) model. Identity spaces, influences, and critical incidents are aspects of this model. Exploration, experimentation, validation, and confirmation are four identity spaces in which leadership educators are situated within. From analysis of professional leadership educator developmental experiences stories, Seemiller and Priest (2017) found that prior leadership experience was an instrumental part of their professional journey. Whether it was through serving in a formal leadership position or making mistakes as a leader, both positive and negative experiences were foundational to the development of professional identity development of leadership educators. This confirms Harding's (2011) findings, "leadership educators shared that their interests in leadership, which eventually led to their interest in teaching leadership" (p. 94).

Honoring Leadership Educator Social Identities

It has been established that social identities are significant in conceptualizing leadership as a process of not only understanding self, but others (Beatty, Irwin et al., 2020; Guthrie et al., 2013; Ostick & Wall, 2011). Our personal identity is a significant part of how we engage as leadership educators. How we involve our leadership educator identities while honoring our social identities and their intersections is essential in creating leadership learning opportunities. Which of these identities become more salient when teaching to different student populations allows us to develop into the best leadership educators we can be. As Mahoney (2017) reminds us, leadership educators need to reflect on how they show up in the context of influencing student learning.

Beatty, Irwin et al. (2020) extend this conversation to the importance of researchers in leadership education to interrogate how past research perpetuates the lack of scholarship about educator identity. This will push scholars to work towards reimagining leadership education. By placing identities and power at the center of leadership learning, scholars can examine the challenges and opportunities, as well as provide recommendations for leadership practice. This not only honors social identities but also appropriately centers it in the work of leadership education and learning.

Palmer (2007) discusses the "hidden wholeness" (p. 68) of being an educator. The paradox of separating teacher and learner is one we need to reconsider so the wholeness of an educator can be honored. This wholeness is acknowledging and honoring that we all are both teachers and learners. In the discipline of leadership, educators are urged and often inspired to join students' journeys of learning. Discussing this need, especially in the context of how social identities, the intersectionality of our various identities influences our role as leadership educators. In working towards socially just leadership education, we not only need to discuss leadership educators, but focus on the purpose of *why* educators do what they do, which is for the learners. Although we did not discuss learners, they are a part of the who. However, they are the focus of the *what* we do, which is leadership identity, capacity, and efficacy development.

The What: Leadership Identity, Capacity, and Efficacy Development

Focusing on the development of leadership identity, capacity, and efficacy is critical to leadership learning and student growth. This is the *what* in working towards culturally relevant and socially just leadership education. Although discussed in more depth in Chapter 2, we introduce the concepts of identity, capacity, and efficacy here.

As previously discussed, leadership educator identities directly influence how we teach leadership. Just like leadership, identity is a socially constructed concept that is influenced greatly by language. As personal identities continue to evolve, working with students to reflect on various identities and how they intersect is critical for their development. As Guthrie et al. (2013) assert, one's thoughts about who they are as a leader is their leader identity. Students' growth in better understanding their identity impacts capacity and efficacy development.

Dugan (2017) defines leadership capacity as the incorporation of knowledge, skills, and attitudes, which lead to an overall ability to engage effectively in the leadership process. Guthrie et al. (2021) highlight that capacity should not be confused with potential. Where leadership potential is realizing one's ability to be a leader, leadership capacity is already possessing the ability to be a leader and receiving and absorbing knowledge, skills, values, and attitude to be a leader. Leadership potential does need to be realized before leadership capacity can be enhanced, which is part of identity development.

Efficacy is how one can produce a desired result. Put differently, it is the belief one can be successful at specific activities. Specifically, in the context of leadership, efficacy is situated in effectively engaging in the leadership process using knowledge, skills, and values learned. As capacity continues to be developed, one's self-confidence is essential and centers belief in the ability to work towards common goals with others in the leadership process. The interplay of identity, capacity, and efficacy are crucial to understanding the leadership learning journey. This interplay along with the environmental dimensions of culturally relevant leadership learning will be discussed further in Chapter 2.

The Where and When: Contextualizing Environmental Dimensions of CRLL

Foundational to our thinking and our continued interrogation of leadership education, cultural relevance is essential in learning leadership and critical in developing as a leader. CRLL assists in putting this thinking into practice by considering diverse student perspectives. This model encourages examination of what diverse students contribute to learning spaces with their identities, capacities, and efficacies (Guthrie et al., 2021). The acknowledgment of oppression and power in leadership and how it influences student leaders' confidence to create and lead social change is critical in understanding the CRLL model (Bertrand Jones et al., 2016).

With this at the core, CRLL considers five critical dimensions of leadership learning environment, which are the where and when of developing culturally relevant and socially just leadership education. These dimensions include: (a) historical legacy of inclusion and exclusion, (b) compositional diversity, (c) psychological climate, (d) behavioral climate, and (e) organizational/structural aspects (Bertrand Jones et al., 2016).

Historical legacy of inclusion and exclusion creates space for us to examine who has traditionally participated in programs and who has engaged in the leadership process, as well as how. Compositional diversity signifies the proportion of various populations who are represented in learning education programs. Attitudes about difference and perceptions of discrimination is the psychological dimension. Interactions and the quality of exchanges across differences is part of the behavioral dimension. Lastly, the organizational/structural dimension focuses on what processes guide the organizational operation from which programs take place.

The intention of the five dimensions of the culturally relevant leadership learning model is to consider the importance of individual experiences and how we work with students to engage in the leadership learning context. These dimensions of the environment highlight the *when* and *where* of leadership education. These aspects will be explored more in Chapter 2 and Chapter 3.

The How: Creating Intentional Leadership Learning Opportunities

As we continue to interrogate culturally relevant leadership learning in efforts to expand *how* we operationalize it, we must think about how we create intentional leadership learning opportunities. How educators should approach leadership learning has been a part of the discussion for decades. Beginning this conversation, Roberts and Ullom (1989) provided one model of training, education, and development, also known as the TED model. Proposing to expand on the TED model, Guthrie and Osteen (2012) proposed adding engagement as a critical part to learning leadership. Although terms such as training, education, development, and engagement are often used interchangeably (Ayman et al., 2003), each has distinctive function and implication. Honoring these early conversations about how leadership learning opportunities are created, Guthrie and Jenkins (2018) expanded and reimagined a framework to support how leadership educators can intentionally connect pedagogy with learning outcomes and critically think about learning assessment for potential leadership learning.

Guthrie and Jenkins (2018) propose six aspects of leadership learning in the leadership learning framework. These aspects of learning are knowledge, development, training, observation, engagement, and metacognition, all within the context of leadership learning. As seen in Figure 1.2, Guthrie and Jenkins (2018) use the metaphor of a steering wheel in which educators can provide a means for students to steer their own learning, as well as better understand the various ways students learn.

As seen in Figure 1.2, encompassing the entire wheel is leadership knowledge, which is foundational for all leadership learning and needs to be connected to all its aspects. Learning leadership knowledge can happen in programs, including sharing language about leadership, as well as new theories, concepts, and constructs. Working in from the rim of the framework, the four aspects of development, training, observation, and engagement all contribute to metacognition.

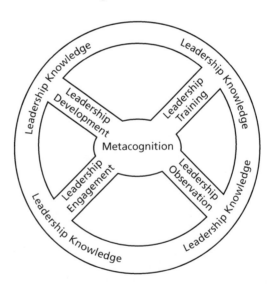

Figure 1.2 Leadership learning framework. *Source:* Reprinted with permission from Guthrie & Jenkins, 2018, p. 58.

Leadership development refers to the human and intrapersonal aspects of leadership learning. The individual is the focus of learning through this aspect, including their needs (Maslow, 1970), readiness to lead (Avolio & Hannah, 2008), identity (Komvies et al., 2005), and multiple dimensions of self (Allen & Shehane, 2016). As Allen and Shehane (2016) provide, leadership development is "characterized by new insights and progression, which can include an individual's motivations, values, identity, emotions, and potential in relation to the activity of leadership" (p. 43). Although it is described as leadership development, leader development is also included. Day (2001) defines leadership development as "expanding the collective capacity of organizational members to engage effectively in leadership roles and processes" (p. 582); whereas leader development focuses on the individual's opportunity for self-understanding and intrapersonal growth (Day, 2001). One can build human capital as a leader through increasing one's knowledge, skills, and values (Guthrie & Jenkins, 2018) in the leadership development aspect of learning.

Focus on skill and competency-based leadership learning is addressed in the leadership training aspect of leadership learning. This type of learning places emphasis on practicing previous skills learned from scaffolded previous lessons. As Allen and Shehane (2016) state, leadership training is the space where "proficiency in demonstrating specific tasks associated with the activity of leadership" (p. 43) is achieved. The training approach allows for educators to work towards student mastery and behavioral changes through development and practicing of skills. As emphasized in Guthrie and Jenkins (2018), this is the most often used aspect of leadership learning in programs created for student leaders holding specific positions.

Leadership observation refers to the social, cultural, and observational aspects of leadership learning (Guthrie & Jenkins, 2018). The learner in this aspect is a passive recipient and allows them to make meaning from how leaders and followers act in relation to others in social and cultural contexts. Bandura (1977) asserts that context and culture are key to learning, which observation has abundant opportunities to learn from context and culture. Just as Merriam and Caffarella (1999) note, learning is culturally bound, which supports this notion, and is powerful when observing how leadership is enacted in different cultures. Mitra (2011) introduces how ways of observing or, "looking with intentionality" (p. 185), both in inductive and deductive ways, can enhance leadership learning greatly.

Experiential, relational, interactional, and interpersonal aspects of leadership learning are seen in the leadership engagement aspect. Just as in leadership observation, leadership engagement is constructed from the learner's experience. The difference between the two, however, is that the learner is an active participant in leadership engagement. Learners can construct meaning in response to experiences and encounters with the process of leadership. Allen and Shehane (2016) state the purpose of leadership engagement "is to provide the learner with new experiences, and the role of the educator is often to help individuals capture and make sense of planned or naturalistic experiences (constructivism) following an activity" (p. 44).

Metacognition sits at the heart of leadership learning. Without critical reflection and thought, one cannot make meaning of or apply and ultimately adapt what is learned. Leadership metacognition refers to the organizational, reflective, evaluative, adaptive, analytical, mindful, and complex aspects of leadership learning. Metacognition is the mindfulness of one's knowledge and the capability to recognize, control, and use one's intellectual processes (Meichenbaum, 1985). This awareness includes knowing when, where, and why to use certain strategies for decision-making, problem solving, and ultimately learning. Simply put, in this aspect, the learner is critically aware and understands their thoughts about the leadership process and the learning of leadership. Considering aspects of leadership learning offered here assists in framing how leadership educators intentionally develop and deliver leadership programs.

Summary

In interrogating leadership education, we discussed the why, who, what, where, when, and how of developing culturally relevant and socially just leadership education. We focused on why educators do this work, who does this work, what is the focus, the where and when in relation to the environment of the work, and how leadership learning is created. As shared previously, the visual reminds us of how we are interrogating leadership education and providing thoughtful narratives, discussion, and resources on the what, where, and how of this work. In continuing with this learning journey, Chapter 2 expands the discussion of culturally relevant leadership learning model constructs, which is focused on the what, where, and when. Next, Chapter 3 investigates even further the where and when and the significance of context in creating culturally relevant and socially just leadership learning opportunities.

2

Constructs of the Culturally Relevant Leadership Learning Model

To operationalize culturally relevant leadership learning (CRLL), one must not only learn foundational aspects of leadership learning, but how to integrate culturally relevant aspects into creating intentional learning opportunities. As we work to integrate CRLL in expanding its usefulness, having a working knowledge of the model's constructs is key in understanding not only how it has evolved, but what the future potential may be. This chapter provides a historical snapshot of the evolution of the CRLL model and how it has been operationalized and put into practice, as well as where it is headed.

Evolution of the Culturally Relevant Leadership Learning Model

Leadership development of diverse students has been a part of the leadership education conversation (Komives et al., 2011), but the first publication

Operationalizing Culturally Relevant Leadership Learning, pages 15–27
Copyright © 2021 by Information Age Publishing
All rights of reproduction in any form reserved.

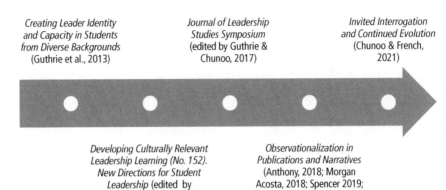

Figure 2.1 Timeline of culturally relevant leadership learning model evolution.

that situated identity at the heart of leadership learning was published in an Association for the Study of Higher Education (ASHE) monograph in 2013. The 2013 monograph started the conversation around the need for social identities and leader identity development to be at the core of our work regarding the future of leadership education. From that first publication, it was acknowledged there was more work to be done, especially regarding an evolved model and tools leadership educators could use to center leadership learning in cultural relevance. From that point, the model has continued to evolve, and model collaborators have invited others to not only join in the work, but to question the constructs and how to fully operationalize CRLL. This is in an effort to strengthen its usefulness in supporting leadership educators' implementation of socially just leadership education and to develop future leaders that will ultimately create and lead a more socially just global world. Figure 2.1 provides a brief timeline of this evolution to help understand how CRLL is situated in the leadership learning literature.

Beginning With Identity and Capacity

In 2013, Kathy L. Guthrie, Tamara Bertrand Jones, Laura Osteen, and Shouping Hu wrote a publication published through the Association for the Study of Higher Education titled *Creating Leader Identity and Capacity in Students from Diverse Backgrounds*. This publication started by making the case that because higher education is tasked with educating the next generation of leaders and because our world is becoming increasingly more diverse, there needs to be a focus on not only developing leaders from diverse backgrounds, but for leaders to be able to lead diverse people and organizations. Guthrie et al. spent a considerable amount of time establishing what leader and leadership development meant in higher education and how campus administrators and educators are called upon to create opportunities and environments where students can develop their leadership knowledge, skills, and values; in other words, students' leadership capacity.

This publication centered on enhancing collegiate environments to increase diverse students' capacity to lead. The I-E-O model (Astin, 1993) provided a conceptual framework for discussion in how students' precollege inputs and elements of the college environment interact to produce outcomes, specifically students' ability to lead after college. Although there are many precollege inputs, experiences, and attitudes, this publication focused on the identity and demographics of diverse students. Once situating students' leadership development in higher education and establishing how critical environments were for maximizing leadership learning, this publication included programmatic ideas, recommendations for institutional improvement, and provided opportunities for further research.

The intersection of diverse college students and undergraduate leadership development provided insight on effective program creation and implementation with as many students as possible in mind throughout this publication. It acknowledged the difficulty in encompassing all identities in leadership education, although that should be the ultimate goal and what educators strive to do. The 2013 monograph started the conversation on developing diverse students' identity and capacity while enhancing higher education institutions' ability to educate leaders prepared to create positive, sustainable, and global change.

Culturally Relevant Leadership Learning Model Named

Building off the 2013 publication on developing leader identity and capacity of diverse students, the 2016 *New Directions for Student Leadership* (NDSL) issue titled *Developing Culturally Relevant Leadership Learning* named the model and outlined the model's constructs. As stated in the issue's notes from the editors, Kathy L. Guthrie, Tamara Bertrand Jones, and Laura Osteen, CRLL "proposes infusing the leadership development process with an understanding of how systemic oppression influences educational contexts and with an engagement in and across cultural differences" (Guthrie et al., 2016, p. 6). This NDSL issue argues leadership development programs that are culturally relevant equip all students with the skills to navigate complex, diverse settings and the abilities to better lead culturally diverse groups and organizations.

The editors acknowledged how emotional this work became for them and how important it was to call others into action as incidents continued to show the necessity of creating spaces for all students to be able to engage in leadership development (Guthrie et al., 2016). Although this NDSL publication was released several years prior to what you are reading now, this statement is even more true in our current times:

> The societal issues we face cannot be solved by a few, individual leaders or by the narrow, dominant leadership narratives that often inform leadership development programs. It is the collective and pluralistic ability across our diverse perspectives to create shared understanding and responses in order to solve our seemingly intractable societal issues. (Guthrie et al., 2016, p. 6)

With this at the heart of the publication's purpose, eight chapters from diverse authors shared what CRLL was and how it could be used. Below is a brief overview of the chapters in the NDSL publication, but we encourage you to read each of these chapters to get a more in-depth look at and understanding of CRLL.

- Chapter 1 was *Critical Domains of Culturally Relevant Leadership Learning: A Call to Transform Leadership Programs* by Tamara Bertrand Jones, Kathy L. Guthrie, and Laura Osteen. This chapter introduced the constructs of the CRLL model (Bertrand Jones et al., 2016).
- Chapter 2 was *Authenticity in Leadership: Intersectionality of Identities* by Susan R. Jones. This chapter situated leadership and the process of becoming a leader within an understanding of intersecting social identities (Jones, 2016).
- Chapter 3 was *The Practice of Freedom: Leading through Controversy* by Sherry K. Watt. It shared specific skills for leaders to effectively work with others across differences and practice freedom to facilitate transformational social movements (Watt, 2016).
- Chapter 4 was *Culturally Responsive Integrative Learning Environments: A Critical Displacement Approach* by Antron D. Mahoney. It provided a critical framework for developing culturally responsive integrative learning environments in leadership education (Mahoney, 2016).
- Chapter 5 was *Leadership Lessons From Communities of Color: Stewardship and Collective Action* by Juana Bordas. Building off her earlier texts, this chapter proposed a multicultural leadership model that reflects practices and principles from Black, Latino, and American Indian communities (Bordas, 2016).
- Chapter 6 was *Preparing Interfaith Leaders: Knowledge Base and Skill Set for Interfaith Leaders* by Eboo Patel. It explored interfaith leader-

ship as practical and critical ways for creating CRLL in higher education through religious literacy and active listening (Patel, 2016).

▪ Chapter 7 *Internationalization of Dominance and Subordination: Barriers to Creative and Intellectual Fullness* by Tanya O. Williams. This chapter focused on exploring the ways in which identities and positions of dominance or subordination in a societal system of power and privilege impact the way in which leadership is enacted (Williams, 2016).

▪ Finally, Chapter 8 was *Leading to Transgress: Critical Questions for Transforming Leadership Learning* by Laura Osteen, Kathy L. Guthrie, and Tamara Bertrand Jones. This chapter shared critical questions for guiding leadership educators in the ongoing process of transforming leadership programs through CRLL (Osteen et al., 2016).

The NDSL issue was built off the earlier publication (Guthrie et al., 2013). The diverse authors created the conversation in how the model and its constructs assist in moving towards socially just leadership education.

Application of Culturally Relevant Leadership Learning Model

A year after the NDSL issue was published and the CRLL model was named, Guthrie and Chunoo (2017) edited a symposium in the *Journal of Leadership Studies* titled *Transforming Leadership Learning for Inclusion and Cultural Relevance*. This symposium included four articles focused on teaching and learning from a culturally relevant pedagogical perspective. The publication called greater attention to the context within and the factors influencing the development of leadership learning programs. Recognizing how leadership development programs and initiatives often replicate dominant narratives and oversimplify methods to engaging across differences (Dugan, 2017; Ospina & Foldy, 2009), this publication provided ways to develop new ways of teaching, learning, and being with CRLL at the heart of it.

In the symposium's first article, *Pedagogy in Action: Teaching Culturally Relevant Leadership*, authors Vivechkanand S. Chunoo and Kathleen Callahan (2017) examined critical considerations for teaching culturally relevant leadership in both curricular and cocurricular settings. In their symposium article titled *Culturally Relevant Leadership Learning: Identity, Capacity, and Efficacy*, Julie E. Owen, Sharrell Hassell-Goodman, and Aoi Yamanaka (Owen et al., 2017) provided examples of how campus environment shapes leadership learning differently and strategies for creating inclusive leadership learning environments. Framing it in identity, capacity, and efficacy strengthens how the model is operationalized in various contexts.

Antron D. Mahoney (2017) discussed how emotions and storytelling are effective tools in applying CRLL. In his article, *Being at the Heart of the Matter: Culturally Relevant Leadership Learning, Emotions and Storytelling*, he claims storytelling is necessary for a culturally relevant leadership educator and learner. In the last article of this symposium, Kathy L. Guthrie, Tamara Bertrand Jones, and Laura Osteen (Guthrie et al., 2017) integrate teaching, learning, and being where systems thinking is essential to CRLL being successfully implemented. Their article, *The Teaching, Learning, and Being of Leadership: Exploring Context and Practice of the Culturally Relevant Leadership Learning Model*, provided a place to reflect how we can begin implementing pedagogy and assessment strategies in culturally relevant ways.

▬▬▬▬

Operationalization, Invited Interrogation, and Continued Evolution

As seen in Figure 2.1, starting in 2018, publications citing CRLL supporting scholarship (Spencer, 2019; Torres, 2019), applied to educational contexts (Morgan Acosta, 2018; Wiborg, 2018), and as a practical framework (Anthony, 2018) began to emerge and continues today with needed ongoing interrogation. The 50 narratives collected for this book, highlighted in Chapters 4–11, opened our eyes, hearts, and minds to how CRLL was influencing the way educators were not only discussing the importance of culturally relevant leadership education, but creating space and dedicating resources to developing leadership learning programs and initiatives.

With CRLL beginning to operationalize, we continue to invite constant interrogation of the model and welcome continued evolution. Our hopes are that in collective conversations and work in developing culturally relevant and socially just leadership learning opportunities, we can maximize the usefulness of it. We acknowledge the intent of CRLL was never to be everything to everyone in creating leadership learning opportunities, but to offer constructs to situate the work in. Depending on demographics of learners, context of environment, intended learning outcomes, and content being delivered, only certain constructs might be useful, or perhaps using it as a process rather than an outcome makes the most sense. Continued evolution and thinking can be seen in new publications where motivation and enactment, influenced by Dugan (2017), are added as pathways of leadership along with identity, capacity, and efficacy (Chunoo & French, 2021). This type of interrogation and expansion will only enhance the conversation and keep us moving towards our *why* in delivering socially just leadership education. Now that you have a better sense of the evolution of CRLL, we will now explore the constructs that make up the model.

Overview of the Culturally Relevant Leadership Learning Model

The CRLL model (Bertrand Jones et al., 2016; Guthrie et al., 2017) is grounded in two foundational areas: culturally relevant pedagogy (Ladson-Billings, 2014) and campus climate (Hurtado et al., 1999; Milem et al., 2005). CRLL incorporates leader identity, capacity, and efficacy along the environmental dimensions of a campus culture and climate. As mentioned, CRLL seeks to challenge previous and oftentimes current paradigms of leadership learning. This model "confronts the myriad ways racism, sexism, religious oppression, heterosexism/cisgenderism, and classism advantages and disadvantages individuals' lives" (Guthrie et al., 2017, p. 62).

Critical to CRLL are individuals' pathways to understanding the process of leadership through their own identity, capacity, and efficacy. The interconnection of identity, capacity, and efficacy (Reichard & Walker, 2016) inspires students to engage in the leadership process. As individuals engage in the process of leadership, their identity, capacity, and efficacy are enhanced, further encouraging and motivating more engagement in the leadership process. This interconnection continues to grow when environmental dimensions are created to where all students feel welcome and validated in the leadership learning opportunity.

Considering the broader organizational climate and how one engages in the leadership learning context is the critical piece to creating the inclusive space for all to learn. The environmental domains in CRLL include: (a) historical legacy of inclusion/exclusion, (b) compositional diversity, (c) psychological climate, (d) behavioral climate, and (e) organizational/structural aspects. These environmental dimensions push educators to consider the significance of individuals' lived experiences of broader organizational and program climates and how that influences engagement and potential growth from the leadership learning context.

The pathways of understanding self while contextualizing the environmental dimensions together form CRLL. As seen in Figure 2.2, the CRLL model provides an approach to identifying and reformulating the leadership learning environments for enhanced effectiveness for student learning. The eight constructs used in CRLL will be discussed in more detail and will be the focus of the remainder of this chapter.

Figure 2.2 Culturally relevant leadership learning model. *Source:* Reprinted with permission from Guthrie, Bertrand Jones, & Osteen, 2019.

Identity, Capacity, and Efficacy

To fully understand CRLL, discussion on the importance of identity, capacity, and efficacy in developing leadership learning opportunities is needed. Leadership identity, capacity, and efficacy development is the *what* of our interrogation of CRLL. A critical place to start is leadership identity development. Josselson (1996) stated, "Identity is not just a private, individual matter [but] a complex negotiation between person and society" (p. 31). Just like leadership, identity is a socially constructed concept grounded in cultural, historical, and political norms (Jones & Abes, 2013). Davis and Harrison (2013) help us understand the construction of identity occurs when individuals start to recognize the cultural contexts in which they live and internalize the cultural messages that encompass them. Although identity is constantly evolving, it always comprises multiple dimensions of self; however, each dimension is best appreciated when explored in relation to each other. This intersection is essential in understanding the whole self. When situated in CRLL, it focuses on students exploring their own leader identity through multiple lenses of the complexity of identity (Jones, 2016).

Dugan (2017) explains capacity as the incorporation of students' leadership knowledge, skills, and attitudes, which leads to their overall ability to engage in the process of leadership. As briefly mentioned in Chapter 1, capacity is not the same as potential. Leadership potential is recognizing your ability to be a leader, whereas leadership capacity is already understanding you have the ability to be a leader, but focus your development on knowledge, skills, values, and attitudes to be an effective leader. Capacity development is often the focus of student leader trainings as it focuses on specific knowledge and skills typically associated with a position or specific role. In the dynamic process of learning leadership, identity and capacity inform one another (Guthrie et al., 2013), which leads to efficacy.

Having confidence in your overall ability to act effectively in the leadership process is critical in being able to engage the way you want to is called efficacy (Bandura, 1977). More specifically, leadership efficacy is "a student's beliefs about his or her abilities to exercise their leadership knowledge and skills in a given situation" (Denzine, 1999, p. 3). As Dugan et al. (2013) point out, leadership efficacy has consistently been associated with leadership development and predicts capacity. As an individual's capacity increases and they receive validation for their efforts, self-efficacy increases (Guthrie et al., 2021). Crosby (2017) describes self-efficacy as a meter that increases as you practice and learn from successes and failures.

Together, identity, capacity, and efficacy "describes a student's way of understanding self as an agency of change through interpersonal and intrapersonal development" (Bertrand Jones et al., 2016, p. 12). In the narratives shared in Chapters 4–11, examples of how educators operationalize CRLL by focusing on identity, capacity, and efficacy demonstrate the importance of these pathways of individual development in connection to the leadership process.

Considering the Five Dimensions of Environment

Contextualizing the where and when of CRLL is realized in the environmental dimensions, which include: (a) historical legacy of inclusion/exclusion, (b) compositional diversity, (c) psychological climate, (d) behavioral climate, and (e) organizational/structural aspects. These dimensions drive educators to reflect on the impact diverse students' lived experiences within climates at a program and organizational level have. These lived experiences influence the overall leadership learning and potential for growth. Each dimension should be explored and reflected upon from various perspectives to cultivate environments that are not only welcoming, but maximize learning potential for diverse students.

Historical Legacy of Inclusion and Exclusion Dimension

As seen in the history of higher education, only certain identities could attend institutions in the beginning (Thelin, 2011). Historically, women, people of color, and those from lower income backgrounds were not allowed to attend institutions of higher education. More recently, it has been more widely discussed how leadership studies also has a history of exclusion and how marginalized populations engage in leadership (Bertrand Jones et al., 2016; Guthrie et al., 2013) Oftentimes, leadership in marginalized communities are labeled as service or activism (Martin et al., 2018; Shenberger & Guthrie, 2021). Because of this, voices from marginalized populations were minimized and often hidden throughout leadership learning. Consequentially, diverse students could not see themselves as leaders. This exclusion not only emerges in a hidden curriculum but perpetuates this harmful historical legacy by not developing future leaders.

Bertrand Jones et al. (2016) explain how CRLL requires educators to honestly interrogate the historical legacies of inclusion and exclusion, not only at a broader institutional level related to leadership, but at all contextual levels. Within the CRLL frame, Owen et al. (2021) state, "Leaders must also learn to grapple with larger systemic forces, maintained by power and dominant narratives of exclusion, and their effects on individual agency and action" (p. 92). The use and abuse of power and how dominant narratives have silenced diverse voices, and therefore excluded them from opportunities of leadership learning must not only be examined but changed.

Compositional Diversity Dimension

Milem et al. (2005) defines compositional diversity as the number and proportion of various students' populations. However, as Bertrand Jones et al. (2016) highlight, compositional diversity is more than just numbers of underrepresented students at your university and attending your programs. It moves beyond just recruitment of diverse students, but how diverse students are fully engaging in various leadership programs. Reformulating how diverse students identify with and engage in leadership is the goal.

As representation of diverse students increase, so will the diversity of ideas and opinions which will increase the opportunity for student engagement across differences. As a result, "Experiences and information that challenge the accepted ideology and self-definition" students question their own ways of thinking about leadership and begin to adopt "a new world view" (Hardiman & Jackson, 1997, p. 27). Engaging across differences is a critical outcome for leadership learning (Dugan et al., 2013) and can shape how leaders and followers can engage in change initiatives (Dugan, 2017).

Psychological Dimension

The psychological dimension highlights individual views of group dynamics, perceptions of discrimination, viewpoints about difference, and responses to diversity, equity, and inclusion. Students' cognitive and personal development is also apparent in this dimension. How learning environments are created to both support student learning, but also provide opportunities for dissonance cannot be overlooked for the psychological aspect this holds. As Bertrand Jones et al. (2016) suggest, oftentimes learning environments unintentionally create experiences with great tension for marginalized students. This results in a wall of oppression that Ahmed (2012) describes as becoming juxtaposed with those who have not experienced that wall. Ahmed explains, "To those who do not come up against it, the wall does not appear—the institution is lived and experienced as being open, committed, and diverse" (p. 174).

How one shared experience can be experienced so differently by individuals can cause conflict for all involved. This can cause privileged students to question marginalized students' perception and marginalized students to shut down, creating further mistrust and disagreement. Thus, it is essential for leadership educators to create learning environments built on trust through validation of various thoughts and lived experiences. Educators are also called on to develop opportunities that foster acceptance across differences. Although developing such supportive environments based on trust, especially given how divisive our world is, it is critical for the psychological aspect of leadership learning in culturally relevant ways.

Behavioral Dimension

The behavioral dimension focuses on the everyday interactions between all involved in the learning process. This includes the quality of interactions between individuals, across groups and intragroup, which increases the complexity of this dimension. Personal and individual complexity add to the group dynamics and influence behaviors. Milem et al. (2005) point out that active learning strategies help diverse students engage with others through discussions, group projects, peer teaching, and other pedagogy.

This importance of behavior highlights an essential responsibility of leadership educators to develop students' skill to engage across differences. Helpfully, Dugan and Velázquez (2015) provide three ideas for developing students' capacity to engage across differences. These include sociocultural conversations between and among peers, reformulating leadership education beyond dominant narratives, and development of students' capacities for "critical perspectives and critical self-reflection" (p. 107). Not only cultivating student skill in engaging across difference, but providing support in the behavioral dimension and disrupting microaggressions, discrimination, and oppression is critical to creating more CRLL spaces and more socially just leaders.

Organizational and Structural Dimension

The organizational and structural dimension of the CRLL model represents the "important structures and processes that guide day-to-day 'business' of the institution" (Milem et al., 2005, p. 18). As Bertrand Jones et al. (2016) states, "These structural aspects of higher education institutions are represented by course curricula, budget allocations to support diverse learning opportunities, admissions practices, hiring practices of diverse faculty and staff, tenure and promotion procedures, and rewards structures" (p. 18). These structural aspects influence a campus culture and therefore affects student culture.

Leadership educators must not only critically examine the composition of students who serve in roles, such as teaching assistants and on program committees, but review course readings for diverse authors and ideas that represent a variety of social contexts. Not only is representation critical in organizational structures, but so is the language used. Examining the language used in all facets can shift who has access to leadership learning and whether it is perpetuating the dominant narrative as the only way to be a leader or expanding into socially just ways of engaging in the process of leadership.

Centering Cultural Relevance in Leadership Learning

Metaphors are influential tools in applying complex theories and concepts. Guthrie et al. (2017) uses the metaphor of a house to describe the CRLL model. In this house metaphor, the role of campus and organizational culture creates the structure of the house including the floor, walls, and roof. Fundamentally, the architecture of the house represents the environment of leadership learning and its level of cultural relevance. As when building a house, the structural components need to provide a solid foundation.

Without the foundation of a strong learning environment, the learning activities occurring in the environments (our houses) are more restricted to enhance leadership learning. When a strong culturally relevant learning environment is created, more feel welcome to participate. Acting as doorways to engagement, identity, capacity, and efficacy development provide opportunities for growth.

Mahoney (2017) noted, "Culturally relevant leadership learning harnesses diverse and often-overlooked leadership thought and practice to enhance all students' identity, capacity, and efficacy in leadership development for social change" (p. 57). The CRLL model recognizes the power inherent in leadership and relies on intersectional frameworks of identity development (Guthrie et al., 2013; Jones, 2016; Ostick & Wall, 2011) to create learning environments where everyone can engage in the leadership learning process.

In continuing to interrogate CRLL, we spent months discussing an updated metaphor with various educators, colleagues, friends, family, and students. Although we like the house metaphor Guthrie et al. (2017) provided, we wanted to focus more on context. However, we struggled to find a metaphor that considered multiple contexts and how they were both embedded and interconnected. Several food metaphors came to mind like a layered cake, a 7-layer dip, and even a parfait, in which each layer had a distinct flavor, but when mixed under various conditions, it resulted in different flavors. However, we concluded that in food metaphors you can always pick around the parts you do not like, and that was essentially what exclusion is and that would continue to perpetuate oppressive systems. So, we encourage you to think of what metaphor works for you and your context. Chapter 3 continues to explore context and its importance in centering cultural relevance and social justice in leadership learning.

3

The Where and When of Culturally Relevant Leadership Learning

Understanding Environmental Contexts

Context can be defined as the setting, situation, or role that learners engage with and/or take on when learning and applying new understandings. This is often stated as a real-world application, but often our ideas of a real-world application can vary drastically given our past experiences. When we talk about context or real-world application, we mean that learners are working with or looking at the content from something other than a strictly academic lens, but from lived and cultural experiences. Chapter 3 explores the *where* and *when* and the significance of context in creating culturally relevant and socially just leadership learning opportunities.

The context helps to answer the question, "Why am I learning this?" and "Why is this important?" Context is important because for learners to be able to apply new knowledge and understanding, they must have a grasp of how it can be used. Darling-Hammond et al. (2001) explored in *Lesson for Life: Learning and Transfer,* for applicable learning to occur, learners

Operationalizing Culturally Relevant Leadership Learning, pages 29–39
Copyright © 2021 by Information Age Publishing
All rights of reproduction in any form reserved.

must know how to apply what they have learned to new situations or problems and they must know when it applies. To teach for context, leadership educators must ask, "How do students' identities and background relate to what I am teaching?"; and "Where might this leadership learning be applied?" is fundamental to centering context in leadership education. This chapter interrogates the *where* and *when* of culturally relevant leadership learning (CRLL) in terms of context.

Levels of Context

Leadership educators and learners' understanding of context varies depending on how they are engaged in the leadership process (Roberts, 2007). As Chapter 1 noted, leadership as an engaged process is a socially constructed, cultural phenomenon and varies according to an individual's particular context (Roberts, 2007). Contextual differences in understanding leadership are indicative of the underlying meaning making process. This recognition is critical to appreciating a learner's journey, such that they can simply be and lead from a true place of understanding. Bolman and Deal (2013) contend the ability to understand multiple environments and subsequently reframe context provides a "liberating sense of choice and power" (p. 17).

As institutions of higher education invest in programs to develop student leadership capacity, awareness of the contexts that shape learning environments is vital to successfully educating all students. The layers of collegiate contexts include national, institutional, and curricular and cocurricular. Deconstructing these layers of context leads to better understanding and negotiation of these contexts. Bolman and Deal (2003) argued using multiple frames leads to greater effectiveness as an educator and leader. Consequently, the ability to understand and then reframe context provides a "liberating sense of choice and power" (p. 17). Within the institution, there are multiple contexts to examine, as well as the specific program learning environment (see Figure 3.1). Day-to-day contexts change and influence institutional cultures, campus climates, and learning environments.

Context: National

Terry (1993) explained how identity is shaped by the cultural contexts and are symbolic and ideological aspects. This concept rings true in regard to how one's national identity and context shape an individual's understanding and definition of leadership (Guthrie et al., 2013; House et al., 2004). Historical events of nations, colonized or invaded, can significantly

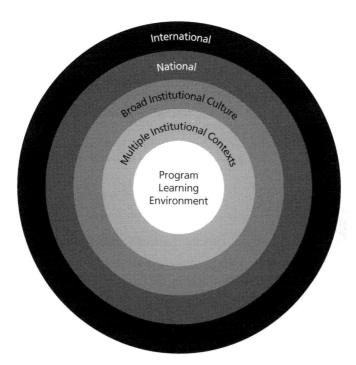

Figure 3.1 Levels of context in higher education. *Source:* Reprinted with permission from Guthrie & Jenkins, 2018.

shape a people's view of leadership, authority, and power (Guthrie et al., 2013). Recognizing the historical legacies and current lived realities of oppression is critical in building inclusive, multicultural leadership voices (Bordas, 2007). "Racism, sexism, and oppression of non-dominant beliefs, behaviors, or cultures are significant adaptive challenges in the United States" (Guthrie et al., 2013, p. 57). The reality is that all forms of oppression are embedded within all aspects of society, including leadership education. The recent national debates on Black Lives Matter, immigration, and trans* rights and protections, illuminates the challenges and imperative for leaders "to be culturally relevant and incorporate the inclusive values and principles inherent in our diverse nation" (Bordas, 2007, p. 6).

Context: Institutional

Astin's (1993) I-E-O model is a well-documented learning framework for researching, understanding, and informing intentional interventions to educate college students engaging in the leadership learning process (Guthrie et al., 2013). The I in Astin's model represents the inputs students bring with them to college (Guthrie et al., 2013). The E in Astin's (1993) model is the educator-influenced environment and programs in which student learning occurs. The O is the collegiate outcomes. Environmental and contextual factors affect student leader development of minoritized students (Zimmerman-Oster & Burkhardt, 1999). While this can be simply stated as environment matters in leader and leadership development, the complexity of multiple contexts and their influences on leadership development is evident. The contexts in which students from diverse backgrounds develop their leader identity and capacity can be explored through the lens of cultural theory.

Engaging with others shapes the understanding of our cultural paradigms, frames understanding of behavior and the interpretation of the others' behavior, and stimulates how we act upon those interpretations (Guthrie et al., 2013). Scholars have argued that the campus climate and its impact involve four connected elements: institutional context, structural diversity, psychological (perceptual) dimensions, and behavioral dimensions (Hurtado et al., 1999). The legacy of segregation in our country continues to affect the campus climate for historically White college campuses to this day. The best example is resistance to desegregation in communities and specific campus settings, the maintenance of old campus policies at predominantly White institutions that best serve a homogeneous population, and attitudes and behaviors that prevent interaction across race and ethnicity (Guthrie et al., 2013; Guthrie & Jenkins, 2018). Because historical legacies of exclusion are embedded in the culture of a campus environment, many campuses sustain long-standing, often unrecognized, benefits for particular groups on campus (Hall, 1983). Cultural context is the undercurrent that structures life; it is learned, interrelated, and defines group boundaries (Hall, 1983).

Context can quickly turn into misconceptions, commonly held assumptions, and prejudices about communities. Contextual differences in understanding leadership reflect the meaning-making process and are critical to recognize so individuals may lead from a place of equity and justice (Guthrie & Chunoo, 2018). Leadership as a socially constructed, cultural phenomenon varies according to one's particular context (Roberts, 2007). Exploring the symbolic roles inherent in cultural contexts of leadership creates educational interactions that foster shared meaning and expectations (Roberts, 2007).

Institutional context influences student leadership programs on campus (Bertrand Jones et al., 2016). Campus context includes the history, traditions, values, mission, student characteristics, and sense of community as you enter the physical or virtual campus. Ahmed (2012) pointed out institutional mission drives a campus's approach to organizational structures. As Osteen (2012) stated, "If an institution has roots as a liberal arts or women's college or has religious affiliation or military purpose, the mission of leadership education will be influenced by the values and beliefs of that foundation" (p. 7). Campus climate and context are factors in the overall campus environment for minoritized students. Understanding the complexities of how campus environments affect the development of diverse student leaders will assist educators as they approach leadership learning from a more culturally relevant practice.

Psychological and behavioral forces influence the campus climate through subtle and overt beliefs and actions. Psychological forces are shaped by the perceptions and attitudes within and across differing groups. Behavioral forces are shaped by the actions and inactions between and among these groups (Guthrie et al., 2013). Consider what is the experience of trans* and gender nonconforming students on campus? Psychologically, do they feel their voices are heard and respected across campus? Psychologically do they feel safe on campus to engage in leadership and leadership learning opportunities? Behaviorally, are they running for positions of influence and trust on campus or relegated to support roles and continuously being marginalized?

How does an institution create an environment that values and seeks diverse leadership voices without relying on structural diversity to recognize, evaluate, and raise the issues connected to history, feeling, and behaviors on a campus? A significant indicator of how a university prioritizes this effort is how it shows up in the budgeting and financial decision-making process (Bertrand Jones et al., 2016; Guthrie et al., 2013). Does a university financially support the growing effort of leadership for all or does it fund small, selective programs that rarely represent the diversity needed for global society? We hope this book is a call to action and you find examples to address these questions. We also hope the narratives in Chapters 4–11 inspire you with ideas of how to address these issues in your own context.

Context: Personal

Scholars have used the term social identity to describe how students make sense of their race, class, gender, and sexuality as aspects of self that exist within a social context. Social identities are understood to influence a student's relationship to others within socially constructed systems of dominance and oppression (Hall, 2004; McEwen, 2003). However, the original definition of social identity by Henry Tajfel described it as both the knowledge of belonging to a certain group and that belonging has a value or significance to the person in some way (Ruderman & Ernst, 2004). Stryker and Burke (2000) also used the term social identity to refer to other social categories or constructed social groups. These definitions would include leadership identity among social identities. The college student development literature refers to this as a social identity in the "global" sense, meaning that it refers to "an overall sense of self or sense of being" (McEwen, 2003, p. 205). The social construction of self and how one defines *self* based on these social spaces is the root of social identity.

Social identity theory is the understanding that each individual has multiple identities (Abes et al., 2007). In applying the leadership models, college educators must also acknowledge the ways leadership identity intersects with other dimensions of identity, such as race, culture, sexual orientation, gender, religion, and social class. A challenge in using leadership models is recognizing intersectionality (Collins, 2000) and how students' multiple identities shift in relative salience, depending on context and relationships (Abes et al., 2007). As social constructionist approaches to identity development have suggested, identity could be socially, historically, politically, and culturally constructed (Weber, 2001). When considering leadership as a social construct, then leadership means something different for each person. Given a person's social identities and context in which they engage with leadership, understanding the distinctions between a leader and leadership might vary.

Different Institutional Contexts

Reflective educators are intentional and deliver programs with multiple contexts in mind. We recognize we are unable to discuss all the varying higher education contexts that are present in a broad institutional context, such as whether institutions are private, public, or religiously affiliated. Contexts that fall within multiple institutional frameworks and are broader than a specific program learning environment are highlighted in Guthrie and Jenkins (2018) text and the report on leadership learning curricular programs (Guthrie et al., 2018). They expand upon the institutional contexts of cocurricular, academic/curricular, undergraduate, graduate, interdisciplinary, integrative, and discipline-specific (see Figure 3.2).

Academic/Curricular-Based Programs

Brungardt et al. (2006), compared undergraduate academic majors focused on leadership in self-identified programs within the United States.

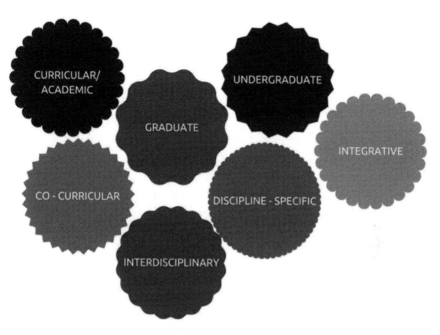

Figure 3.2 Multiple institutional contexts for consideration in leadership programming. *Source:* Reprinted with permission from Guthrie & Jenkins, 2018.

Brungardt et al.'s (2006) examined school profiles, program profiles, mission and program purpose, and curriculum. Notable differences included varied school sizes, host departments, and credit hour requirements. Other variations included the focus of the program, the major scholars evident within the curricula, and the disparity between theory and skill development. Important findings from Brungardt et al.'s (2006) study include: (a) programs are not limited to a particular type or size of institution; (b) careers of graduating students varied greatly, showing occupations in government, social service, religion, business, and industry; (c) an overwhelming majority focusing on both theory and application as well as civic and/or organizational objectives; and (d) several universities focused their learning objectives on cognitive theories while others focused on the development of skills and behaviors. Brungardt et al.'s (2006) study provides an overview of undergraduate academic programs; however, an increasing number of cocurricular programs are being developed on an undergraduate level (Komives et al., 2011). We recognize our biases as authors and the examples we offer here are from a U.S. context. We would encourage you to engage with resources from the International Leadership Association for more of a global context. Some of the narratives offered in Chapters 4–11 highlight a more international perspective from leadership educators who have implemented facilitating, teaching, and research approaches using CRLL.

Cocurricular Programs

With the history of higher education and a philosophy of educational delivery, additional environmental factors emerged. These environmental factors including an increase of women, trans*, non-gender binary, racial, and ethnic minoritized people participating in higher education, the "look" of higher education dramatically changed (Guthrie et al., 2013; Guthrie & Jenkins, 2018; Lucas, 1994). Students participating in activities outside of the classroom (i.e., cocurricular offerings) continued to increase. In 1937, the American Council of Education Studies published a statement, *The Student Personnel Point of View*, addressing the need to view students in higher education in a more holistic way.

As discussed in Chapter 1, leadership programs had a strong beginning in cocurricular programming with student affairs taking the lead on facilitating this type of learning. Oftentimes, part of the job description of student affairs administrators includes providing some type of leadership programming, both in a curricular and cocurricular context. Although still widely absent from graduate student affairs preparation programs, some institutions, such as The Ohio State University, University of Maryland, College Park, and The Florida State University, offer a course on being a leadership educator in order to train future administrators how to develop and deliver leadership programs in a cocurricular format (Guthrie & Jenkins, 2018). Yet, in most of these cases, the courses are contingent on the availability of experienced faculty to teach the courses. These courses provide students with foundational knowledge of theories and concepts in leadership studies. With this knowledge, emerging student affairs professionals will be well-equipped to structure, format, and assess their cocurricular programs in a theoretical context (Guthrie & Jenkins, 2018). These courses also need curriculum with socially just leadership frameworks embedded throughout and grounded in the leadership outcomes.

Environmental Contexts as Five Dimensions of Culturally Relevant Leadership Learning

The CRLL model represents an invitation for leadership educators to assess the context in which leadership education is taking place (Bertrand Jones et al., 2016; Guthrie et al., 2017). As Chapters 1 and 2 stressed, it is important to highlight how many marginalized communities have been left out of

TABLE 3.1   Importance of This Environmental Context From a Socially Just Lens

Five Dimensions	Importance of This Environmental Context From a Socially Just Lens
Historical Legacy of Inclusion and Exclusion Dimension	Without acknowledgment of the legacy of inclusion (or exclusion) an institution holds first, it is hard to develop leadership initiatives that effectively speak to diversity and inclusion within a university/college second.
Compositional Diversity Dimension	Diversity is not only highlighting numerical representation of historically minoritized faculty, staff, and students represented on a campus, but also how that diversity influences the ideology and perspectives introduced within the campus environment.
Psychological Dimension	Asking educators to consider the tone and context of students' thoughts as they relate to values like diversity, differences, and productive conflict.
Behavioral Dimension	Contextualizing the interactions between students and paying particular attention to the quality of those exchanges is important for leadership educators when differentiating the espoused and actual values of diversity and inclusion.
Organizational and Structural Dimension	Leadership educators must not ignore but attend to the frameworks and processes in place that guide the day-to-day decision-making of institutions.

the leadership conversation in the past (Bertrand Jones et al., 2016; Guthrie & Chunoo, 2018; Guthrie & Chunoo, 2021; Dugan, 2017). For many learners, the word leadership is hard to identify with, and in some instances, comes as a title or position (Bordas, 2016; Dugan, 2017). In many ways, the authors of the CRLL model acknowledge oversights and gaps in centering context, identities, and backgrounds of leadership learners engaged in the leadership process (Bertrand Jones et al., 2016). Acknowledging the importance of context through a socially just lens with the five dimensions below (see Table 3.1) and defining leadership from relational and holistic perspectives, we hope leadership educators will start/continue to imagine how to operationalize the CRLL model in their own learning contexts (Bertrand Jones et al., 2016).

Breaking Down the Five Dimensions of Culturally Relevant Leadership Learning

Analyzing the diversity of a student leadership course roster is one measure of an inclusive leadership program, but other factors such as the history of the classroom building name where the course is taught, the psychological influence of the curriculum, authors in the course syllabus, and behavioral interaction of students outside of the class are just as important according to CRLL (Bertrand Jones et al., 2016). The multiple layers of campus context influence what and how students are learning leadership inside and outside of the college classroom. Environmental cues are often a result of a combination of historical, structural, behavioral, and psychological forces and are often clear messages to internal and external audiences of a university culture. For example, intentional structural and behavioral choices would lead to diversity with the ranks of top administrators sending a strong message that the institution values difference in roles of influence. As the structural number of transgendered students rises, psychological concerns may raise enough awareness that new bathrooms are installed on campus. This action signifies to students that the institution values student development and provides the necessary support for all students. These two seemingly separate actions are clear indicators of an inclusive campus context.

These five dimensions work in tandem as considerations for developing CRLL. Used as a framework, the domains can begin to transform student leadership programs and the larger university system as a whole (Bertrand Jones et al., 2016). Our contexts and differences influence knowledge of self, knowledge of others, knowledge of cultural systems, and ultimately students' knowledge and enactment of leadership. To this end, culturally relevant leadership development programs equip all students with the knowledge and skills to navigate more socially just settings and lead culturally diverse groups and teams (Bertrand Jones et al., 2016; Chunoo et al., 2019).

Summary

Not only does context matter, but context and environmental dimensions are key parts of the interrogation process for CRLL. Acknowledging campus climate and cultural experience by intentionally discussing the challenges and assets of various contexts, will only provide a more solid foundation for developing and delivering leadership programs from a CRLL framework. As you can see, context is critical for consideration in interrogating the when and where of leadership learning. Leadership educators who are aware of the context in which they are working, can better understand the stakeholders, including student learning, and therefore can better construct learning objectives that meet learners' needs (Guthrie & Jenkins, 2018).

As we interrogate and consider applications of the CRLL model, we must acknowledge how leadership education has roots in interdisciplinary, multidisciplinary, and transdisciplinary (see Chapter 2) thinking and the

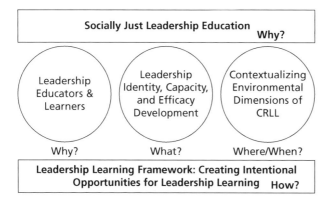

Figure 3.3 Interrogation of leadership education.

ways it is uniquely positioned to champion continued efforts to lead the charge in breaking down the silos that hinder student learning across the academy (Chunoo et al., 2019; Guthrie & Jenkins, 2018). However, leadership learning without the framing of being culturally relevant from a socially just lens, only perpetuates inequities and dominant narratives of leadership and leader. The framework of CRLL builds upon the ideas, highlighted in Chapter 2, of developing leader identity and leadership capacity of students who hold minoritized identities. CRLL and socially just leadership learning proposes infusing the leadership development process with an understanding of how systemic oppression influences educational contexts and with an engagement in and across cultural differences (Bertrand Jones et al., 2016). As leadership educators, we must be prepared to center context, specifically in relation to learners' identities and backgrounds, in our curriculum development and program initiatives to address the ongoing and evolving issues of the world.

4

Operationalizing Culturally Relevant Leadership Learning Through Personal Development

While leadership educators may share the goal of creating a better world with others, Chapters 1–3 provide insight of the language of leadership, context of leadership education, and the need for providing a space for centering socially just perspectives (Chunoo et al., 2019). Socially just leadership perspectives have goals of sharpening analytic perspectives, enhancing personal engagement, promoting the development of a critical consciousness, and centering social change (Bell & Adams, 2016). There is a difference between wanting to generally promote change in the world and acknowledging how difficult it can be to address deeply rooted issues of equity and justice (Chunoo et al., 2019). What makes a leadership educator a culturally relevant leadership educator is rooted in a commitment to understanding oppression as pervasive, restrictive, hierarchical, complex, and cross-cutting, internalized, context and manifested in a web of systems

Operationalizing Culturally Relevant Leadership Learning, pages 41–60
Copyright © 2021 by Information Age Publishing
All rights of reproduction in any form reserved.
41

known often as -isms (Bell & Adams, 2016; Bertrand Jones et al., 2016; Chunoo et al., 2019).

In agreement with Bell and Adams (2016) and Chunoo et al. (2019), we believe the goals of culturally relevant leadership learning (CRLL) are connected to socially just education and are rooted in understanding oppression and socialization, as well as working towards changing oppressive and marginalizing social systems. We suggest the most effective and efficient ways of meeting these demands is through leadership educators starting this work with centering themselves and their lived experiences with power, privilege, and oppression (Pierre et al., 2020). In this chapter we (a) explore the context of personal development, (b) demonstrate the need for cultural competence leadership education, and (d) conclude with narratives of educators who have made a commitment to personal development through CRLL strategies. Throughout the chapter, the narratives offer thoughts, feelings, and experiences as we attempt to make sense of how best to know, be, and do CRLL through our teaching, facilitation, research, and lived experiences.

Cultural Competence

Cultural competence requires leadership educators understand culture and its role in leadership education, they take responsibility for learning about their students' culture and community, and they interrogate their own identity, culture, biases, and privilege to critically assess and strengthen their instructional practice (Bertrand Jones et al., 2016; Ladson-Billings, 2006).

> When cultural competence is playing out as it should, the classroom can be described as full of mirrors and windows—students see themselves reflected in the classroom (mirrors) and have opportunities to learn more about and see into the lived experiences of others (windows). (Escudero, 2019, para. 10)

With this example, it highlights how the leadership educator must use their students' culture and identities as the basis for learning. Leadership educators should support students, while also recognizing and honoring their own cultural beliefs and practices (Bertrand Jones et al., 2016). In order for leadership educators to guide learners through this process, they must first interrogate their own cultural beliefs and practices. By leadership educators modeling their own mirrors and windows, they can personalize the process their students are embarking on through culturally relevant leadership education.

Self-Work and Personal Development

Self-work and personal development offer a way for leadership educators to free themselves from old programming and the status quo of engaging in leadership education and allow them space to explore what truly matters to them. Without leadership educators knowing their why, they are in danger of living unconsciously as educators continuing to perpetuate the status quo of centering dominant narratives in leadership education. As educators, our *why* in life is the compass to the ship. We strive to be, do, and have what we want in life, but the importance of figuring out where our passions are rooted gives us direction and purpose as leadership educators.

The narratives shared in this chapter provide rich illustrations of how the CRLL model is operationalized through leadership educators' personal journeys with becoming more culturally competent and relevant when facilitating leadership learning spaces. Jennifer Batchelder shares how she navigates understanding her own Chicana identity and leader identity. O'Juan Edwards shares his own process of mentoring Black and Latinx students interested in pursuing graduate education and the role representation plays in minoritized students developing their leader identity. Michael Cobden frames his narrative using the analogy of the baboon and the elephant and navigating multiple leadership roles. Juan C. Mendizabal provides applicable examples of how he feels comfortable in his "house of self" and how educators can support students to make meaning of difference and intersecting social identities. Sherrina Loften offers a narrative that centers the psychological dimension in her own CRLL journey. Dr. Leonard Taylor offers his process of reflection when centering his own identity, capacity, and efficacy as he prepares to teach from critical perspectives. Finally, Yang Li provides her experience as an international student from China navigating leadership from a U.S. perspective through her graduate program and highlights how international students learn and explore their leadership identity in a culturally relevant way.

LEADERSHIP THROUGH MY CHICANA IDENTITY
Jennifer M. Batchelder

I was inspired to learn about leadership education through a course in my master's program while studying higher education. After working 5 years in student affairs, I knew I wanted to continue my studies to learn more about leadership development in college students. It was in my early doctoral coursework that I read about CRLL and I was inspired! I found the model had given me a form of permission to explore my own understanding of leadership through my cultural lens. It felt strange I had not made this realization on my own; I had every right to, and yet, I never really had. With this in mind, I began exploring my study of generativity and leadership through my Chicana/Latina cultural perspective with the notions of identity, capacity, and efficacy in mind.

Considering the important relationship between the individual and leadership learning, I took on the call for reflection in my own identity in relation to leadership. As I spent time reflecting on who I am and where I came from as the foundation and influence on my practice of leadership, I saw it relate directly with Juana Bordas' work on Latino leadership (2013). She describes how Latinos prepare to practice leadership through *conciencia* (Spanish for consciousness or awareness) or "tapping into the intuition that allows one to be aware of her motivation, values, intention, and internal dynamics" (Bordas, 2013, pp. 67–68). As I spent time on the identity component with a focus on my Chicana culture in mind, I found myself reviewing and learning more about my family heritage, cultural history, and reflecting on what my culture had taught me. I thought about how my cultural values of family, respect, hard work, generosity, serving others, education, and persistence have granted me my own foundation of understanding and practicing leadership. There was even a moment where I thought, "Wow! Why have I not thought about leadership in this way before? It makes much more sense!" I recognize this as a moment when I was solidifying my leadership identity through my cultural lens.

While I felt confidence in the values passed down to me by my family, being only "half"-Chicana, White passing, and growing up not speaking Spanish led to community experiences which constantly had me questioning whether I was Chicana enough to claim my cultural identity. My cultural self-efficacy was constantly challenged. Further, when considering taking a Latin* cultural perspective on my dissertation research on leadership, I even remember questioning whether I was "enough" to speak about this cultural perspective. It was conversations with my community of fellow doctoral students of color who provided me with the encouragement to see myself as "enough" when speaking about my identity and cultural values. With their support and practice, I began to take an asset-based approach to understanding my culture which helped me develop my identity, efficacy, and deeply consider my cultural leadership capacity.

I recognized how my cultural experiences and values had taught me the leadership capacity to learn, share knowledge, and empower others in my community to work toward a positive purpose that will endure. While I already had a strong philosophy and practice of leadership before, exploring leadership from my cultural lens helped me to understand my intuitive practices that were based on my cultural values. Learning about these aspects helped me to shape my practice of leadership from a more natural approach that gave me more efficacy and confidence in how I worked with students, my peers, and with others in my community. I found myself less resistant to developing my leadership identity, capacity, and efficacy and I'm hoping that as we instill this value of self-reflection further into our leadership education practices, our students will also find a deeper connection within their practices of leadership too!

Jennifer's exploration of her own identity, capacity, and efficacy as a Chicana was grounded in her research on leadership identity development and generativity. Jennifer's narrative highlights how own cultural experiences, values, and understanding of experiences with others taught her about her own capacity to learn, share knowledge, and empower others in her community to engage in leadership for the purpose of working towards a positive purpose that will endure (generativity). Jennifer shares the process of understanding her intersecting identities as a White passing Chicana who does not speak Spanish and navigating the self-work and coming to the conclusion that she is "enough." Jennifer's narrative is an example of navigating the process of personal development and taking an asset-based approach to understanding your own culture when developing one's leadership identity and deeply considering one's cultural leadership capacity. Next, O'Juan offers his reflective narrative of being a mentor to Black and Latinx students and the role of representation in developing a leader identity.

A MENTOR TO BLACK AND LATINX STUDENTS
O'Juan D. Edwards

I am a Black, Gay, man, and doctoral student who serves as a mentor/teaching assistant to undergrad students in a program tailored explicitly to attend graduate school after earning their bachelor's degree. I do this because I love to serve. I do this because I am paying it forward. I believe to whom much is given, much is required, and I have a lot to pay forward. Therefore, the CRLL model reminds me to bring students along with me as I climb the ladder of success.

CRLL allows me to support my student's identity, capacity, and efficacy. For instance, I teach my students how to speak to professors they have never met before, so they feel comfortable when they visit their potential graduate programs' interview days. I also teach my students how to prepare for job interviews. Additionally, my identities are intersecting, and that is why I am relatable as a leader to minoritized students at a predominantly White institution (PWI). Students feel comfortable talking to me because I have a shared lived experience concerning what they are going through. For instance, one of my students needed to learn how to write a personal statement for a graduate program as a first-generation college student. There was a time when I did not know how to write a personal statement for a graduate program, so I gave them feedback and examples on some of the things that I did to help me succeed. I am grateful for the program at my institution that allows me to demystify the graduate school application process for Black and Latinx students. As Bordas (2016) described, "To be effective with changing demographics, leadership educators must design programs, processes, and courses that resonate with our growing mosaic society" (p. 61). Moreover, when students see someone who looks like them in graduate school, I think it makes a difference in their thought process concerning if pursuing a graduate degree is attainable for them to achieve for themselves.

To my way of thinking, access to higher learning institutions is essential for Black and Latinx students disproportionately affected by systemic racism. Bordas states, "Communities of color offer a rich foundation for building inclusive environments and respecting differences, which can take collaboration to a higher level by encouraging equal access and urging the involvement of all the diverse segments" (Bordas, 2016, p. 61). Diversity in the classroom is essential for the professor and the students in the collegiate community. I believe the university setting should mirror what the world looks like; the global society is diverse amongst ethnicities, gender, age, sexual orientations, and religious beliefs. Moreover, colleges and universities diversifying their application process fit the CRLL model precisely through students looking at themselves as leaders. "Leader identity is a student's own conceptualization of themselves as leaders, whereas leadership capacity is the learning and practice of leadership skills and behavior" (Guthrie et al., 2013, p. 30). Therefore, colleges and universities need to intentionally consider their application process to have diversity and representation amongst prospective students and students who matriculate into their programs. This will allow continuous knowledge sharing from different perspectives amongst lifelong learners who are present in the classroom.

I began to develop those thoughts and feelings on my own. As I began to look around the room and saw few individuals look like me, I began to question my intellectual capabilities concerning whether I had what it took to be successful in one of the nation's top graduate programs. The CRLL model mentions a similar idea. Guthrie et al. (2016) stated, "As a consequence, students from marginalized populations do not see themselves or representatives of their communities as leaders, nor do they read work written by or about their perspectives in the leadership canon" (p. 16). The imposter syndrome is something that I had to work through, and eventually, it went away in terms of graduate education. However, it is essential for the Black and Latinx students I serve to be aware of imposter syndrome. Before they step foot into a graduate program; that way, they will not be so nervous till the point that they drop out of the program without completing their degree.

O'Juan's narrative is an example of navigating imposter syndrome due to his minoritized identities in historically White spaces in higher education. His process of reflection and disrupting his imposter syndrome is another example of the asset-based approach to understanding your own culture when developing your leadership identity. O'Juan reiterates how representation for minoritized students can be a key aspect of them making meaning of their own leadership identity, capacity, and efficacy. Similarly, Michael Cobden shares in the next narrative his process of understanding his own leadership identity and capacity and how self-confidence and self-belief contribute to one's efficacy when engaging in the leadership process.

ARE YOU A BABOON OR AN ELEPHANT?
Michael Cobden

I'd like to start by sharing something I recently read about how there are two different types of leaders. The first type of leaders are baboons, who grab power for their own sake and for what they can gain personally. The second type of leaders are elephants, who lead for the benefit of the whole group. This really resonated with me while I was reflecting on the current world leaders such as Donald Trump, Boris Johnson, Vladimir Putin, Jair Bolsonaro and more, who share similar narcissistic personality traits and who hold some of the most powerful leadership roles in the world. I'd view my own personal leadership style as more of an elephant, but then again, who would want to admit that they are a baboon and potential narcissist?

In my current role as the head of Wellbeing at the University of West London (UWL), United Kingdom, I manage a multidisciplinary team of professional services staff. I am responsible for leading four separate services, counseling, disability, mental health, and faith, which all sit under our "Wellbeing Service" umbrella. UWL is a "widening participation" university recruiting lots of students from low socioeconomic backgrounds, many of whom are the first generation in their family to attend higher education where English could be their second, third, or fourth language. One of my biggest challenges in this role is to successfully support a team who are under increasingly heavy workloads every academic year. Promoting and maintaining positive mental health and well-being amongst my staff enables them to provide a high quality and innovative service to meet the increasingly complex needs of our student population.

As I reflect on my identity as a leader, I like to view myself as a calm, cool, and confident leader who makes each individual within the team feel valued, respected, supported, and heard. The idea of a hierarchy of importance makes me feel uncomfortable. Everyone is equal but we have different job roles and responsibilities that we perform, which contribute to the overall success of the team or organization. The term "boss" or "manager" does not sit well with me, as I think it reinforces an elevated level of importance between one individual and another. The term "leader" or "head" resonates with me more as it seems to have more supportive and democratic connotations, which is more in line with my personal values. I am very aware of the fact that I am a White privileged male, who is the head of a service in a female dominated profession, which is reflected in my team. In addition, I work in London, in a multiracial and multicultural city and university. I view it as my ethical and moral duty to use my privilege and position of leadership and power to break down institution and societal barriers to support social mobility, for not only the students we serve but also the staff that I/the university recruit and develop.

In terms of my capacity, I know that I am human and far from perfect. Reflecting on my strengths is important, but so too is feeling empowered to be vulnerable not to hide my weaknesses. I believe a successful leader will utilize the diverse skills and strengths of other team members, openly giving credit and praise to the individual, which increases confidence and commitment from individual team members. "Owning" your own limitations and asking for help from others in my opinion shows great strength and leadership. The ability to constantly be able to reflect on your own ability, attitudes, beliefs and behaviours is crucial to evolve and develop. Quite often you see people in leadership roles who have stagnated and not evolved, whose reputation becomes damaged and legacy tarnished.

Self-confidence and self-belief are crucial for efficacy as a leader, but are also situational specific. I know successful and unsuccessful leaders all experience imposter syndrome from time to time. Perhaps this speaks of their underlying lack of self-confidence or their situational specific confidence to successfully achieve an identified outcome, perhaps it is a combination of both? Interestingly, I believe I have developed high levels of self-efficacy through playing sports. As a child playing soccer, I quickly realized I was pretty good and better than the majority of my peers. This alone was extremely helpful in developing my sense of self. I was competitive and wanted to win and would step up to take control in high-pressured situations, evolving to become a leader in the team, despite my introverted personality. I had an uncanny ability to learn from previous failures without getting attached to the associated emotions, therefore limiting the damage to my confidence. Sport made me believe in myself, value my role, the role of others, communicate effectively, manage egos, recover from setbacks, enjoy successes, work hard, and be disciplined. I believe that the growth and development I have achieved through sport molded me into the leader that I am today. Being an active leader can be exhausting though and the idea of a quiet, less stressful life in the future does sound appealing. I will continue to be an elephant leading the pack until my time comes to step aside and let a new intelligent, energetic, and motivated leader take the lead.

Michael's narrative offers an analogy of two types of leadership; those who grab power for their own sake for what they can gain personally and those who lead for the benefit of the whole group. Through Michael's reflection, he stresses the importance of recognizing one's own limitations as a leader in order to continue to build a capacity and efficacy for leadership. Michael's sharing of his own "active leadership" are vivid examples of engaging in the leadership process and building one's own leader identity, capacity, and efficacy when willing to reflect, learn, and grow from those experiences. Next, Juan Cruz Mendizabal frames accountability through the process of self-work as a leadership educator by queering leadership.

ACCOUNTABILITY THROUGH SELF-WORK
Juan Cruz Mendizabal

When I choose to engage in self-work, it is a radical act of healing and growth. It is not the kind of work that appears on my CV, as my intention for self-work is not to increase my professional value; it is to develop the "me" that exists outside a professional identity. By acknowledging that I have inherent value outside my work, I am challenging my capitalistic socialization of using all my time for career advancement. I do not entertain thoughts of self-work being selfish. By caring for my human evolution through self-work, I am aligned with Audre Lorde's (1988) words, "Caring for myself is not self-indulgence. It is self-preservation, and that is an act of political warfare" (p. 205).

In this spirit, a foundational element of the CRLL model is grounding leader identity in personal identity. For me, this has meant cultivating a steady sense of peace: feeling comfortable in my "house of self" and not being afraid to enter any of its rooms. Earlier in my career, I was disproportionately investing in my professional identity development to the extent that I had lost my personal grounding. By engaging in self-work focused on personal/professional tensions, I have learned when healthy boundaries can help me distinguish role from self and when it is worthwhile for me to examine my personal and professional development as mutually influential. The latter has been empowering to affirm the importance of my lived experiences that led me to my work.

Growing up as an outsider with closeted queer and nonreligious identities within my family of origin, I cultivated invaluable insight and courage to learn how to be my authentic self while also blending in for survival—a dynamic that would eventually influence my choice to hold a leadership educator outsider status while still wanting to be connected to and accepted by mainstream leadership education. I connect my childhood lived experiences to my leadership educator identity with the two common threads of *challenging the process* and *queering* as a pedagogy. I feel powerful when I queer leader identity development through astrology, birth charts, oracle cards, labyrinths, and other tools perceived as unacademic, using vulnerability as a default expectation to teach one another through storytelling. I like that I challenge traditional conceptualizations of power and social justice education by utilizing veganism as an intersectional social justice framework. By engaging in interdisciplinary work that is uncommon in leadership education, I am reclaiming my outsider status by creating unique entry points for students' leadership journeys.

Self-work is not always freeing and gratifying; however, my efforts to decolonize leadership education may satisfy my commitment to social justice and align with my irreverence toward tradition, but genuine self-work challenges me to constantly examine whether my well-intended values are harmful in execution. In the process of creating lesson plans that critique capitalist, heteronormative, and White supremacist notions of leadership, it is tempting for me to believe that because I am challenging others' walls of whiteness (Brunsma et al., 2012), I am implicitly challenging my own. This is not true. As a White man, it is convenient for me to forget that I am always living inside walls of whiteness, protected and supported even when I choose to challenge systems of power. The CRLL model challenges me to notice when my progressive leadership lessons are overcompensating for my lack of personal anti-racist work, helping me interrogate whether I choose to do the work only when it is observable to others, involves others, and deflects attention off me. If I convince myself that it is "enough" to live my best critical leadership educator values only in professional contexts, then I am hiding behind my job to resist self-work, sustaining the performative nature of White liberalism in which folks want to be known for doing the work they aren't doing.

Whether creating break*throughs* or break*downs*, engaging in self-work has helped me first and foremost be honest. I have become comfortable with self-work's contradictions: I challenge myself while being gentle, I make goals for myself while being patient, and I forgive myself when I let myself down. Ultimately, the CRLL model holds me accountable for understanding the impact of my choices as a leadership educator in a motivational, rather than punitive, way. I am grateful for the reminder that my work is important and that my stories always matter.

Juan's narrative does a beautiful job of illuminating how self-work is not always self-gratifying. Juan stresses how his efforts to decolonize leadership education may satisfy his commitment to social justice and align with his discontent toward tradition and the status quo and how genuine self-work challenges him to constantly interrogate whether his well-intended values are harmful in action. Juan offers his process for creating lesson plans that critique capitalist, heteronormative, and White supremacist notions of leadership, and he acknowledges how it is tempting for him to believe that because he is challenging others' walls of Whiteness he is implicitly challenging his own. Juan concludes that his self-work process of acknowledging the contexts of his own power, privileges, and oppression help him to center honesty as a leadership educator. Next in Sherrina's narrative, she offers her own honesty through her narrative of understanding the five dimensions of the CRLL model, particularly the psychological dimension.

CHANGING MY WORLD TO CHANGE THE WORLD
Sherrina S. Lofton

As a Black woman, graduate student, and full-time employee, I recognize my ability to take on the role of leader while navigating the environment of a predominantly White institution can be quite exhausting. I have come to learn navigating this space requires a level of endurance that is well outside of my capacity, given Dugan's (2017) definition. However, it is my leader identity and efficacy that have allowed me to take more calculated steps in exercising my right to call to question the intent of those who are considered leaders in this environment. Thus, I have begun to assess how I can operate as a leader for myself and others while in this space and beyond this space. One model that has been helpful in the process is the CRLL model.

The CRLL model is designed with campus climates in mind, which allows individuals to self-assess and reflect on their position within the institutional community (Bertrand Jones et al., 2016). CRLL also provides five domains through which individuals can ascertain their respective positions in isolation or holistically through their complex, yet entangled relationship. Those domains include historical legacy of inclusion/exclusion, compositional diversity, behavioral dimensions, organizational/structural dimensions, and psychological dimensions (Bertrand Jones et al., 2016).

I have unfortunately encountered significant moments I consider to be of the psychological dimensions. "The psychological dimension emphasizes individual views of group relations, perceptions of discrimination or conflict, attitudes about difference, and institutional responses to diversity" (Bertrand Jones et al., 2016, p. 17). Although socially constructed, I understand that my identity both as Black and woman is grounded in historical, political, and cultural norms (Jones & Abes, 2013) and results from my navigation and meaning making of myself, context, and relationship within this society (Abes et al., 2007). As such, when situations arise that call to question the kind of leader I want to be, given my understanding of my identity, capacity, and efficacy, I have to act accordingly.

Recently, a situation resulted in me writing a letter to the leadership of the institution due to the way they handled an issue of diversity. Understanding most college campuses have diverse populations, regardless of breakdown, the responses to issues should be equally and equitably offered when issues of race, gender, religion, and so on occur. However, that was not the case. I recognized that in the climate of a second or possibly third wave of "Black Lives Matter," being cautious of your words was painfully important. However, the leadership disseminated responses that only added to the pain that Black faculty, staff, and students felt, myself included.

Before I decided to actually send the correspondence, I consulted a close friend/colleague to discuss my thoughts and intentions. True to form, she gave me both the culturally relevant and professional perspectives after interrogating me to ensure I had thought through my plan and actions. She understands the "brick wall" of diversity and social justice work that Ahmed (2012) describes. We both understood that *if* higher education was where I wanted to do my life's work, this electronic letter could very clearly put me in a certain position that could hinder my professional growth. We also understood the pent-up tension from being constantly disrespected, minimized, and undermined intellectually was overwhelming at that point. As a Black, woman, graduate student, and staff member, I have a responsibility to speak up when issues of social justice or discrimination are committed. As a result, I compiled a very intently worded letter addressing the president, dean, and two directors.

I explicitly stated their actions were further minimizing and silencing the voices of the Black population within the campus community. Using labels such as: minorities, Black *and* people of color, Brown people, and America in response to the slaying of *Black* men, women, and children at the hands of police was completely disrespectful. I recall other issues that impacted other demographic groups and the university leadership was very clear in stating who those messages were directed to and in support of. The institution may not have intended to create a conflict space, as Bertrand Jones et al. (2016) states. However, the responses, or lack thereof, from my letter indicated to me that the institution more so appeals "to those who do not come up against it, the wall does not appear—the institution is lived and experienced as being open, committed, and diverse" (Ahmed, 2012, p. 174).

Not that I was hoping for a result, because I also understand my position within the community, which is a psychological struggle in and of itself. As I mentioned, navigating these spaces can be quite exhausting but understanding who I am as a leader allows me to address them accordingly. I tell my students all the time why it is important to know their identity to guide how they operate in the world. If a professor graded them wrong, I tell them to schedule an appointment to discuss that grade. If they had personal matters going on, I tell them to reach out to inform their professors. However, I also recognize the same things I am telling my students to do, I must do myself. I recall my senior quote from high school:

"Before you can change the world, you must change
that part of your world first."
—Mr. Carter

I don't recall who Mr. Carter was, but that quote still resonates with me today, which is why I work at practicing what I preach. I also want my students who will decide to take on the leader role to also understand the importance of speaking up for what is right and holding "leaders" accountable to their duties. So as the quote says, I am changing parts of my world, so I can change parts of the larger world.

Sherrina's narrative shares how her understandings of both her Black and woman identity are grounded in historical, political, and cultural norms and how she navigates and makes meaning of her identities in context to her relationship to society. Sherrina highlights how different environmental contexts and situations can call into question the kind of leader she wants to be given her understanding of her own identity, capacity, and efficacy for leadership and she must adjust and proceed accordingly. Finally, Sherrina expressed how she models for her students the importance to decide when speaking up for what is right and just and holding those in power accountable to their role and duties should be expected as a leader engaged in the leadership process. In the next narrative, Leonard shares his process of navigating being a Black queer critical pedagogue and cultivating liberatory learning spaces as an educator.

PREPARING TO TEACH CRITICALLY
Leonard Taylor, Jr.

I am a Black queer critical pedagogue. I am committed to cultivating liberatory spaces for students in my courses and myself. I am committed to empowering students to consume, interrogate, critique, and change the worlds around them and within them. My ongoing journey to realize and enact these commitments are what brought me to CRLL as a pedagogical resource.

Through the lens of CRLL, educators support students in exploring and growing their *identity, capacity,* and *efficacy,* the domains of CRLL. Thus, I find it important to reflect on my own identity, capacity, and efficacy in the context of my role as a leadership educator. I have approached this task focused on three specific considerations. First, it is necessary I take inventory of my own social identities and the intersections therein, consider my social location as a Black queer cisgender man, and articulate my own leadership identity and how it has emerged and evolved over time. Second, as a critical pedagogue, I am regularly contemplating my institutional position/location as a pre-tenured faculty member, how my faculty role and social identities intersect, and the complex and sometimes contentious ways I am positioned as a broker/bridge between institutions and students. Lastly, in concert with the previous two considerations, I use CRLL and other critical pedagogical approaches to inform and complicate my curricular and pedagogical considerations and choices. Having operated as a leadership educator in various capacities, formal and informal, I like to believe these considerations have become habits of the mind that sometimes explicitly and other times subconsciously guide my day-to-day work. As romantic as this notion is, I also acknowledge that my engagement with these considerations is ever evolving, always incomplete. As thoughtful as I commit to being, I also am always learning my own shortcomings, oversights, biases, and learning new things about myself as I learn and grow.

Promoting CRLL requires a learning environment where students can explore and develop their identity, capacity, and efficacy (Bertrand Jones et al., 2016). I have worked to cultivate such spaces alongside students, with attention to three commitments.

First, recognizing the oppression and suppression students experience in classrooms often happens in subtle and discursive ways (Bertrand Jones et al., 2016), I am committed to empowering students by cultivating their voice (and other modes of expression). Not only do I invite students to express their thoughts and ideas, I invite students to think, speak, and express themselves with a degree of *epistemic authority*—the belief that their ways of knowing are legitimate and worthwhile. This is especially important for students who come from marginalized communities or hold minoritized identities, their ways of knowing and being are often questioned in classrooms, across campus, and in society.

Second, it is important to me that students can locate themselves and their interests in course syllabi. To this end, while designing or revising courses I try to think about: who is (or is not) represented in the content, who is best or least served by the scope and format of assignments, what are a range of applications for the knowledge/learning generated in the course, and who should review provide feedback of my syllabi and course materials. Also vital to this is creating space for students to provide feedback on their learning experiences, and actively seeking that feedback throughout the semester.

Third, to be intentional in supporting students with their identity, capacity, and efficacy, I work to be judicious in my pedagogical choices. To this end, I draw from intentional emergence (Werner et al., 2016), to challenge the rigidity of the *traditional* classroom, which we have been socialized to prioritize over the immediate learning/human needs of students and instructors. Similarly, I draw on Taylor and Brownell's (2017) critical approach to leadership to enrich my discussion of power and oppression on local and societal levels, regarding leadership.

Lastly, aligned with Guthrie et al. (2016) discussion of structural and systemic vestiges of oppression, my work outside of the classroom also involves advocating for changes in policies, hiring, evaluation, and training that align with my critical and culturally responsive aims. This is important for institutionalizing the CRLL commitments beyond the classroom (Taylor & Brownell, 2017).

Leonard explicitly names his identity as a Black queer critical pedagogue and outlines his three commitments to cultivate classroom learning environment that center his students' identity, capacity and efficacy. First Leonard notes, the importance of recognizing the oppression students' experience in the classroom often happens in subtle and discursive ways and it is equitable and just to allow space for students' voices in a safe and culturally relevant way. Next, he gives the example of students locating themselves within the course curriculum, and finally he discusses his personal process of his pedagogical choices that are equitable and just. Leonard offers these three steps as examples for leadership educators and those who consider themselves critical pedagogues engaged in leadership education. In the next narrative, Yang shares how being an international graduate student has contributed to how she will approach her research on international students learning leadership in a more culturally relevant way.

AN EVOKING MOMENT
Yang Li

I am a female, first-generation, nontraditional, and international graduate student in the United States. With genuine interests in student affairs theories and educational policies in higher education, I am also a graduate assistant, working at the international student office, facilitating international student services, and hearing dual voices from both student affairs professionals and international student communities. With a strong commitment to empowering international student communities, I pursue to become a qualified researcher and educator in the future.

Carrying these identities and reflecting on their intersecting influences on me, identity exploration of international students in the United States is what I am passionate, dedicated, and driven to support. Inspired by the Reconceptualized Model of Multiple Dimensions of Identity (RMMDI; Abes et al., 2007) and International Student Identity (ISI; Kim, 2012), I delve into the acculturation influence on international students' identity formation across different stages and how the path to achieving the self-authorship shape or is shaped by their identity development (Baxter Magolda, 2001). Nevertheless, leadership identity never struck me either in my own identity reflection nor my research exploration on international students. I was contemplating the reason until I was evoked by the CRLL. CRLL brought me a transforming lens to examine my own identity, reshape, and reconstruct my research scope of international students' identity.

Foreign students, or international students, are defined as sojourners who have tentative membership in the U.S. society (Church, 1982). They are deemed as "assets" to the U.S. institutions in both financial and cultural perspectives yet seeking for their belongingness, value affirmation, and fitted identity in this country. International students are experiencing structural and systematic exclusion from their institution (Collier & Rosch, 2016) and the society as a whole; they are vulnerable, marginalized, underrepresented, and oppressed and they are receiving conflicting experiences compared to their domestic counterparts. While acknowledging these vulnerabilities, I work for this community by unmasking barriers and struggles for more attention and to claim for their belongingness in this foreign land, yet, I often forget to reflect that these vulnerabilities are separated or hidden from me. The five domains discussed in the CRLL evoked me and dispersed the mist for me. Particularly, oppressions and conflicting experiences in the historical, organizational, and psychological domains erect a "brick wall" between me and my leadership identity. I am blocked to rouse leadership identity and consolidate it into my multiple layers of identities, which impedes my engagement in the leadership process (Owen, 2012), as well as the leadership identity exploration of my research of international students.

As I was diving more into the CRLL, the dynamic interaction between the individual and leadership process was also an awakening moment for me to review international students' leadership identity. International students are hampered in their leader and leadership identity development due to the environmental context. Admittedly, they struggle with adaptation to U.S. institutions, such as unwelcoming campus environment (Chapdelaine & Alexitch, 2004), discrimination (Greenblatt, 2005), and stereotyping (Poyrazli & Grahame, 2007). These marginalized experiences oppress their leader identity and push them to self-segregation (Rose-Redwood &

Rose-Redwood, 2013), which further diverts their intention from interpersonal growth and social capital construction in their leadership identity development (Day, 2011). CRLL sheds light on the dynamic interaction between individual and leadership by pointing out that identity in leadership development "is a building block that creates meaning and organizes new leadership knowledge," which further interferes with their leadership capacity and efficacy (Bertrand Jones et al., 2016, p. 13). Lee and Rice's (2007) findings reinforce this statement. In their study, international students claimed they "lack confidence" being a leader in an unwelcoming environment with discriminations and language barriers.

Through the lens of CRLL, I see a different scope of international students' identity, as well as my own. It is a transforming experience for me identifying as an international student, and a future researcher and educator. I am evoked, empowered, and enacted by my commitments to creating social change for this marginalized group as Bertrand Jones et al. (2016) indicated in the CRLL. It enlightens my future research direction to underscore the significance of campus climate and social context on international students' identity exploration, as well as their leadership engagement (Bertrand Jones et al., 2016). Also, it enlightens how to clear the fog for international students and how to present them the "right" environmental and social context (Bertrand Jones et al., 2016). Finally, it shows how to evoke their leader and leadership identity and stir up the dynamic interaction between the individual and the leadership process which are the transforming and critical commitments of me to reach the depth and breadth of international students' identity exploration, through the lens of CRLL.

Yang offers a different perspective as an international student when developing a leader identity in a U.S. context. Yang also stresses her role as a researcher to underscore the significance of campus climate and social context on international students' identity exploration, as well as their leadership engagement. Yang offers how CRLL can be applied when thinking about one's own self-work and professional development when working with international students engaged in the leadership process.

The narratives in this chapter demonstrate how CRLL can influence personal development but can also be applied in various contexts of the professional lives of leadership educators. Although, Batchelder, Edwards, Cruz Mendizabal, Lofton, Taylor, and Li are examples of the process of reflecting on one's own identities in various contexts, CRLL can provide the necessary framework and support in centering one's identity in relationship to building capacity and efficacy as an educator facilitating more CRLL opportunities. Cobden offers his meaning making reflection of his leader identity in the context of his role and environmental contexts. In conclusion, we offer questions, in Table 4.1, for your consideration and reflection when working to operationalize CRLL in your own self-work and personal development contexts. These questions focus on identity, capacity, efficacy, and the five environmental dimensions that can provide first steps in self-work and personal development as a leadership educator.

TABLE 4.1 Culturally Relevant Leadership Learning Considerations: Process of Personal Development

Culturally Relevant Leadership Learning Constructs	Questions for Consideration
Identity	• How do your past experiences with leadership contribute to your current approach to understanding students' leadership identity? • What role do you feel your social identities play in how you have conversations on culture and leadership? • What does cultural competence mean to you?
Capacity	• How would you define your capacity for leadership? • Who, what, and when contributed to building your leadership capacity? • How can you continue to grow your capacity for cultural competence and culturally relevant leadership?
Efficacy	• What resistance to social justice issues and frameworks have you experienced teaching and facilitating leadership education? • How is resistance contributed to your own confidence when leading topics on diversity and social justice? • How did you navigate the resistance? What would you have done differently?
Historical Legacy of Inclusion and Exclusion	• What culture(s) do you consider yourself a member of? • What is the history of your culture(s)' legacy of inclusion/exclusion in society? In higher education? In leadership? • In what ways have you perpetuated historical legacies of inclusion and exclusion personally and professionally?
Compositional Diversity	• What is your process in understanding your own social identities?—In what spaces do you hold minoritized identities? • How are individuals who hold minoritized identities centered in your pedagogy or work as a leadership educator? • How do your identities align with institutional, local, state, national, global demographics?

(continued)

TABLE 4.1   Culturally Relevant Leadership Learning Considerations: Process of Personal Development (continued)

Culturally Relevant Leadership Learning Constructs	Questions for Consideration
Psychological Dimension	• What language is used in your syllabi or program materials you design and what messages do these send? • How do you incorporate diverse perspectives in your own work? • How do your internal and external beliefs show up in your work as a leadership educator?
Behavioral Dimension	• How do you model leadership learning as a self-work and personal development process for leadership learners? • In what ways can you model for learners to engage across difference in culturally relevant ways? • How can you engage in critical reflection to unlearn and relearn culturally relevant approaches to leadership learning?
Organizational and Structural Dimension	• How will you interrogate your own complicity within organizations and structures that perpetuate inequities for some groups? • In what ways can you continuously interrogate your role in the leadership identity, capacity, and efficacy for learners? • What role will you play in generative practices centered on socially just outcomes for organizational structures in leadership education?

5

Operationalizing Culturally Relevant Leadership Learning in Professional Development

Education expands our understanding of ourselves, the worlds in which we live, and the possibilities of what we can become. Developing a culturally relevant leadership learning (CRLL) environment starts with leadership educators. Leadership educators must be willing to embark on the journey of continuing education and professional development to grow and expand their own knowledge of being culturally relevant (Beatty, Irwin et al., 2020). Leadership educators can build their cultural knowledge base through professional development. Leadership educators can also model the importance of CRLL by facilitating professional development opportunities that center interrogating one's own pedagogy and practice (Chunoo et al., 2019; Guthrie & Jenkins, 2018; Beatty & Manning-Ouellette, 2018). When examining the use of CRLL in the process of professional development and professional identity development, leadership educators create space for their own ongoing learning and unlearning.

Operationalizing Culturally Relevant Leadership Learning, pages 61–84
Copyright © 2021 by Information Age Publishing
All rights of reproduction in any form reserved.

Leadership Educator Professional Identity Development

Seemiller and Priest (2015) addressed how leadership educators are not neutral facilitators of learning; they are instead the "hidden who," whose professional identities influence and dictate the learning environment. Owen (2012) defined leadership educator professional identity as encompassing the identities of leader, educator, and leadership educator at the same time and is shaped by both self-perception and validation from others (Sutherland et al., 2010). Priest and Jenkins (2019) acknowledge professional identity is not static and name how becoming and being a leadership educator are elements of a complex and fluid developmental process.

Priest and Jenkins (2019) outlined four key areas of leadership educator professional practice: (a) foundational knowledge, (b) scholarship and creative works, (c) teaching and learning, and (d) identity (Priest & Jenkins, 2019). A group of leadership educators from across the country authored the National Leadership Educators Research Agenda (NLERA) for 2020–2025 (Pierre et al., 2020), in which they called for research intended to advance the preparation of leadership educators through graduate and professional programs. Additionally, they called for professional development opportunities delivered through professional associations and organizations, including empirical exploration and/or evaluation in each of the four key areas outlined by Priest and Jenkins (2019).

While the NLERA (Pierre et al., 2020) called for researchers to explore empirical studies that center the professional preparation of leadership educators, we also suggest that leadership educators constantly explore their own professional leadership educator identity through the four key areas of leadership educator professional practice. Not only those preparing to be leadership educators, but also those of us who identify as leadership educators must engage in ongoing professional development opportunities that explore and identify the responsibilities and expectations of professional leadership educator roles (Pierre et al., 2020). As Chapter 4 noted, a continuous self-exploration between the influences of self-work and professional development are important to understand in order to realize how our own professional development impacts the preparation, development, recruitment, and retention of leadership programs and curriculum (Pierre et al., 2020).

The narratives shared in this chapter provide practitioner and educator examples of how the CRLL model is operationalized in the implementation of various professional development opportunities. Adrian Bitton offers her narrative of designing and implementing professional development opportunities for a decentralized campus offering leadership programs across campus through a more culturally relevant leadership framework. Specific approaches on operationalizing CRLL are shared by Lisa Bardill Moscaritolo, who shares her narrative of navigating a completely different country and culture in the UAE. Lisa offers her experience of actually engaging in leading a student affairs division abroad and how she implemented CRLL opportunities for her student affairs team. Carlos Ordonez offers his narrative as he focused on implementing curriculum for the global leadership development program Up With People (UWP), that focused on the psychological and behavioral dimensions. Marissa Mainwood shares how through her role advising the student leadership council, she implemented a leadership learning framework so students could develop their own identity and share with them how to use that to strengthen their leader development. Linnette Lopez Werner offers how she makes meaning and operationalizes CRLL through intentional emergence (IE), which applies what emerges to connect theory with practice, but in addition takes into consideration the importance of identity and its influence on teaching along with the developmental needs of emerging adults for compassion, authenticity, and a balance of challenge with support. The final two narratives explain how leadership educators can apply the aspects of the CRLL model when framing anti-racist professional development opportunities. Destiny Caldwell reflects on how she suggests a consolidated version of CRLL to colleagues and allies interested in doing anti-racist work. Finally, Mac Benavides, Tess Hobson, and Kerry Priest outline how they developed a storytelling workshop for the Kansas State University Leadership Studies team grounded in CRLL and antiracism.

EDUCATING LEADERSHIP EDUCATORS: DESIGNING A STAFF LEADERSHIP COHORT
Adrian L. Bitton

The brilliance of the CRLL model is in the multiple ways it can be operationalized. At Northwestern University, CRLL has been an invaluable resource for the development and implementation of Northwestern's Leadership Framework. This work began in 2015 when the office of Leadership Development and Community Engagement (LDCE) was created with the explicit goal of developing a leadership framework for student affairs that would guide the division's leadership development efforts. As a newly established office, we were mindful of the organizational dimension. Northwestern operates as a decentralized campus. We sought to disrupt the mindset that LDCE were the "owners" of leadership development on campus and instead positioned our office as the backbone support so that leadership development was embedded within all functional areas of student affairs. Over the last 5 years, LDCE has facilitated communities of practice, developed a centralized assessment strategy, and built resources for staff and students.

In addition to the division of student affairs, multiple other units on campus have also integrated the leadership framework to support the leadership development of the students they engage within the scope of their work. In order to fit the needs, capacity, and relevancy of our colleagues, we created multiple opportunities and levels for engagement. For our most engaged colleagues, I piloted a staff leadership cohort using CRLL as a framework to build their capacity, efficacy, and identity as leadership educators. I invited six staff members from various offices and departments including Hillel, Residence Life, Social Justice Education, Multicultural Student Affairs, Fraternity and Sorority Life, and the Medill School of Journalism. These colleagues were already brought into the concept and tenants of the leadership framework and wanted more concrete strategies for implementation.

During our first meeting, I facilitated train-the-trainer leadership-oriented icebreakers so the group could get to know one another while also thinking about how they could take back what they learned and use it with students. We also spent a good portion of time co-constructing the curriculum so they could identify topics of interest and areas for growth. This ensured that we focused our time and energy on the subjects that would be beneficial for their growth as leadership educators. Each colleague was also asked to identify a particular leadership project they wanted to work on that was related to their jobs. The projects ranged in size and scope. The only criteria were that it had to support students' leadership development and it had to address a need related to their work responsibilities. This gave participants a chance to reflect on the effectiveness of past leadership initiatives or programs and address issues of inclusion/exclusion within their departments. For example, one chose to rewrite and update curriculum for an upcoming leadership retreat and another chose to design and sequence their student leader-trainings using the northwestern leadership framework.

For the format of the remaining meetings, we would spend the first half of our time together discussing different aspects related to facilitating leadership learning including pedagogical approaches, program design, developmental sequencing, and assessment. During the second half, the participants would have dedicated time to work in the space applying the new concepts to their projects. Participants really enjoyed this format because it allowed them to make progress on their projects before returning back to their offices. Participants really appreciated having this built-in time for applied learning. It enabled them to translate theory into practice in manageable amounts to make meaning of theories and apply them to their functional areas, which further developed their capacity as leadership educators. It also allowed them to work at their own pace with the added benefit of having peer support for brainstorming or instant feedback. This cohort model and shared experience supported their identity development as leadership educators.

Participants began to think of themselves beyond their functional area of "I'm a residence life person" or "I work with the fraternity and sorority life community" as they learned new strategies to facilitate leadership learning with their students. They often asked me to send them electronic copies of activities we did during our meetings so that they could share them with their colleagues and students. This prompted me to create an online shared folder they could access with facilitation guides, leadership articles, and assessment tools. Centralizing resources and providing additional opportunities for self-directed learning also contributed to their growth in capacity and efficacy as leadership educators.

CRLL is a great framework for the design of the staff leadership cohort. Their projects allowed them to translate theory into practice by customizing leadership learning to fit the needs and leadership culture within their functional area. Although we all worked in different functional areas and had different backgrounds related to leadership education, bringing together a dynamic group of individuals committed to supporting the leadership development of students was beneficial with all participants reporting gains in their capacity, efficacy, and identity as leadership educators.

Adrian shares a practical and accessible example of engaging staff and centering the CRLL model in the curriculum for professional leadership development. Adrian's example offers suggestions of going beyond one office or certain functional area in order to have conversations on CRLL. At Northwestern, the program Adrian designed incorporated professional development for different functional areas with different backgrounds related to leadership education. This allows space for bringing together an intentional group of professionals committed to supporting the leadership development of students. Through the professional development program professionals were able to acknowledge their own gains in their capacity, efficacy, and identity as leadership educators. In the next narrative, Lisa offers an international perspective of understanding and honoring culture in the leadership and professional development process.

LEADING AMONG TWO CONTEXTS
Lisa Bardill Moscaritolo

With 25 years of experience in the United States as a student affairs leader, I embarked on a new opportunity to use my experience, skills, and interest and passion for college students in a new culture—the United Arab Emirates (UAE). Using elements of the CRLL model, I will share a bit of my journey, a year into my position as Vice Provost for Student Life at the American University of Sharjah (AUS). AUS is a not-for-profit institution based on the American style of higher education and is part of the Arab World. In 2018, the *Times Higher Education* ranked AUS as the #1 institution in the World for diversity. Our students represent 90 different nationalities and 50 different nationalities in our faculty and staff.

As a leader for a department of 80, my identities as female, United States of America passport holder, upper middle-class status is salient. I am part of a senior leadership team with four academic deans and two other vice provosts and the provost. We are very diverse from different backgrounds and gender, yet, a common denominator is our passion for a liberal arts core.

As part of this team, I never feel uncomfortable, and my perspective is encouraged. With regards to my efficacy and capacity, it is high at this time of my life, maybe because of the many years of experience or the openness and encouragement I have from the senior leadership team and my direct reports at AUS. There are many female leaders I can emulate here at AUS. Perhaps, I am in a bubble as I have never felt uncomfortable as a woman in the UAE; however, this does not mean there is no gender discrimination, but possibly my social class, along with the level of education and the privilege I have, I am more protected.

Nationality, tied to social class, is the main factor impeding students and staff here in the AUS. Some staff cannot travel to conferences because of their passport status. It is not unusual for students to share their nationality as they are proud they are at AUS. Being a U.S. citizen, I carry certain privileges others on my staff do not have based on their passport status, thus, understanding my identity, efficacy, and competence is important as I support my staff and university in meeting its mission and objectives.

The CRLL house sketch on page 2 in Guthrie et al. (2017) calls us to acknowledge the organizational climate as we lead. AUS historically values inclusion, diversity, student access, and the liberal arts philosophy and I operate with these principles in mind. As I build a legacy for 3 years which may be extended, I want to ensure I leave my temporary home in good shape and that my staff who will stay longer are empowered.

Together with my staff and students, we are creating new organizational structures, that is, the walls of the living-learning house, that will improve student success and the student experience. One main focus from senior leadership is to decrease housing costs and better the student residential life experience. For various reasons for the last several years, students are choosing to live off-campus.

The main function of the staff who rotate between three shifts when housing was founded was to serve as supervisors and ensure students were following curfew and other local rules set by His Highness Sultan bin Muhammad Al-Qasimi, Ruler of the Emirate, and AUS President. There have been past attempts to offer more residential life as in the United States, but it was hard to get traction, mainly because of the inexperience of past leadership. Together, the recently hired director, who is local and was born in the UAE, and I visited different universities to evaluate the various staffing structures. From our evaluation including conversations with students, we agreed a change was necessary, but we needed to en-sure we had a 24-hour staff presence in each hall, as security and safety is a large part of the culture.

We started by redesigning job descriptions and titles from a "dormitory supervisor" to "residence hall coordinator" in order to help change the mindsets of the staff in how they interact with their residents. Yet, this was halted because of COVID-19. We had to eliminate many positions as it was not sustainable financially for the university to keep staff who did not have a specific role or could not be moved to another position. This was not an easy decision as most would lose their visa, as well as their job, and would return home where it may be harder to find work.

As we rebuild the student residential life department (SRLD), my team helps me understand the UAE way of life. In return, I have shared my years of experience and other professional development opportunities, especially for the director for SRLD who has no experience in residential education. The new staffing model in SRLD will improve the student experience, in-crease student interest to move on campus, reduce staffing expenses, while keeping the Emirate context in mind. The plan allows for us to grow local talent from AUS student leaders, who after graduation can take on a full-time role in housing. Presently, 17% of our students are local so we hope in a few years the staffing in SRLD will better represent the student body.

As the senior team for student life, we continually balance the needs of the students living on campus and the laws of Sharjah. The students are amazingly bright and understand we may be an American University, but we are deeply rooted in the local society, as most of them appreciate the value of the UAE, the laws that provide for safety and political stability, the excellent academic experience at AUS, and agree to live by the standards. Small changes to their living environment and overall student experience are appreciated so we are moving in the right direction.

Lisa highlights the importance of context through her narrative of leading a Student Life division in the United Arab Emirates during the COVID-19 pandemic and implementing a new staffing model. Not only was the environment important, but also the time and context these changes were being implemented. Through Lisa's narrative, she highlighted the complexities of being a professional leader and making decisions that impact the livelihood of your team. Lisa addressed not only how the new staffing model could be more culturally relevant, but also how the plan allows for the Division of Student Life to grow local talent from AUS student leaders, who after graduation can take on a full-time role in housing. In the next narrative, Carlos Ordonez offers his experience working with a nonprofit organization that brings people together from different countries and different cultures in order to engage with leadership.

UP WITH PEOPLE PROFESSIONAL EXPERIENCES
Carlos Ordonez

Throughout my life, I have been fortunate enough to participate in different types of organizations, working alongside brilliant people from and in various countries. All my life I have been curious about people and cultures, therefore, I have looked for those types of experiences and learning opportunities. Today, I am proud to be a Mexican-Canadian. Analyzing my experiences through the lenses of the CRLL model has helped me to identify how the model's different elements interact with one another. Here I share some of those experiences.

Some of you might be familiar with a nonprofit organization based in the United States of America called Up with People (UWP). For over 55 years UWP's multicultural leadership program has attracted more than 20,000 students ages 17–29 from many different countries. The program has three main components: performing arts, community service, and international traveling and staying with host families. As someone who has personally experienced the program, as a cast and staff member, I can see the interaction of the four components of leadership learning identified by

Guthrie and Osteen (as cited in Bertrand Jones et al., 2016): education, training, development, and engagement.

As part of the curriculum, we held education workshops co-facilitated by staff and students; every community service activity had a student in the role of "service crew leader"; we had an internship program where students had the opportunity to learn about different aspects involving the operation of the cast such as finance, education, logistics, and marketing, among others. Besides, there were internships related to show production: dance, lighting, vocals, band, and sound. Every single cast member was engaged in the show, the community service, and lived with host families. We also had an internal code of conduct. The organization has no religious or political affiliations; therefore, everybody is welcome.

Before the tour started, we worked on the behavioral and psychological dimensions, allowing every person to learn and grow was essential for group dynamics. During the year, we had frequent discussions about cultural aspects, values, and belief systems of the countries we were going to visit, and the ones cast members represented. We usually refer to certain things as being "common sense," however, when you spend 24/7 with people from different cultures and extend this for a year, making common sense common is important. My first cast was composed of 170 people from 24 countries. English was our common language. We intentionally used the word "leadership" to promote the program in Canada, Mexico, and the United States of America. However, when we went over to Europe, where Germany was our first country to tour in, we were instructed to avoid using the words "leadership" or "leader" to describe the program since the connotation of these words in that country were not associated with something positive. This was in the late 1990s. Without a doubt, my time in UWP helped me to learn about my own identity, increased my capacity and efficacy as a person, and the more I learned, the more I wanted to continue, so after my student year, I became a staff member. I served on the road, and later on, at the UWP headquarters. This experience impacted me in such a way that I talk about my life before and after UWP.

To understand Tec de Monterrey's philosophy on leadership we must talk about Don Eugenio Garza Sada who, after graduating from the Massachusetts Institute of Technology (MIT), led a group of entrepreneurs and founded the Instituto Tecnológico y de Estudios Superiores de Monterrey (known as Tec de Monterrey) in 1943. At the time the world was at war, Don Eugenio saw the perfect opportunity and time to invest in the education of the new generations. Today, Tec de Monterrey has more than 30 high schools and 26 university campuses in 20 Mexican cities serving more than 87,000 students from high school to graduate school. The companies led by Don Eugenio were the first ones in Mexico to have access to free medical services as part of their benefits, even before the Federal government introduced the Instituto Mexicano del Seguro Social (IMSS) to provide social security to the country. Don Eugenio's legacy continues to lead Tec de Monterrey's approach to social leadership. Every year FEMSA, one of the companies led by Don Eugenio, and Tec de Monterrey recognize the impact of social leaders with the "Eugenio Garza Sada Award" (Treviño, 2020). In its 2020 edition, the awards went to one person and two organizations whose efforts are directed to improving the well-being of others.

Talking about inclusion, in the 1970s Tec de Monterrey became the first university in Mexico to use feminine grammar forms on their degrees to recognize that the recipient was a woman (Villanueva, 2018). In 2014, the Institution started "Leaders of Tomorrow" as a scholarship to recognize and support outstanding students with social projects whose socioeconomic status requires 100% support in tuition fees to study an undergraduate at Tec. According to Tec de Monterrey's (2020) diversity and inclusion report (p. 47), the 7th generation of leaders of tomorrow welcomed 185 students in August 2020, 52% women and 48% men who now are part of the 1,345 students benefited so far. In 2017, after a thorough review and an international benchmark, the Student Affairs Department at Tec was transformed into Leadership and Student Development, or simply LiFE (by its acronym in Spanish), which became an integral part of Tec's new educational model Tec21 where students must take different weeks (Semanas Tec) designed and facilitated by LiFE staff to complete their degree requirements. We are designing a new student leadership program, hopefully, one that can give us more Don Eugenios, and the CRLL will be a very useful framework to consider.

Carlos has a unique experience with UWP, and through his narrative he offers an example of critically thinking through the behavioral and psychological dimensions. Carlos shares how through the leadership development curriculum he wanted to allow every person to learn and grow when considering difference and diversity when working with people from around the globe and bringing different cultures together to learn and grow from one another. In the next narrative, Marissa offers her journal of advising the Student Leadership Council for the College of Business at Florida State University (FSU).

GUIDING FUTURE BUSINESS LEADERS
Marissa P. Mainwood

One of the duties I assumed when stepping into my current role was advising the college's student leadership council. Within the first few months of advising, I noticed the group was primarily comprised of groups of friends who all had a similar major and profile. In addition to not having a very diverse representation of students, many members did not seem to have much interest in being actively involved in the programs and activities the council supported. From my observation of the group, it appeared that instead of the students positioning themselves as leaders, they were simply doing what they had always done and were told to do by college administration. There was a lack of both leadership development within the group and individual leader development (Day, 2001). I knew the current model needed to change and, in order to do so, the students would need to feel more empowered in their roles to move the organization forward. My goal was—and still is—to return the council to the widely recognized and admired status it used to have among students and college administration.

When I started advising the group, I was not familiar with the CRLL model. The model includes five domains (Bertrand Jones et al., 2016, p. 15) with a focus on "students' capacity for leadership, individual identity development, and efficacy, or their belief in their own ability to enact leadership in a variety of settings" (Bertrand Jones et al., 2016, p. 12). Without intending to do so, I slowly began helping the students foster an environment that supported development of each of the three learning processes in the model.

Many of the students had a good sense of their personal identity as a leader, but they seemed uncertain of how their role as a leader fit in with the overall leadership development of the group. One of the first actions I encouraged within the group was having students assist with reorganizing the structure of council officers to allow for additional positions of leadership and roles students could step into to feel empowered and confident in their role as a leader. The students determined what roles each of the positions would play in the council to lead the group and ensure it was operating within the mission of the group to support the college. This organizational restructure and role definition activity directly related to students' leadership capacity and their tying in what they knew of typical business organizational structures, other student organization operations, and the vision of moving the group forward in a more collaborative manner that encouraged participation from all members. Furthermore, the activity impacted the students' efficacy in that encouragement from myself and other staff, as well as the approval and acceptance of the structure by all members of the organization, gave the students a sense of accomplishment and increased self confidence in their leadership abilities among their peers. The students created a group they wanted to be involved with and felt more connected to. Together, we continued to transform the council by rewriting outdated bylaws for the group that were decided upon by the students, with guidance from me as to college and university policies. Additionally, meetings were restructured to include a professional development activity at the start of each meeting to provide leadership training in a variety of areas relevant to individual student leader development, such as public speaking and working as a team. Each semester, council members hold a community service project to enhance their awareness of issues others may face and give back their time and talent to campus and local communities. Another development project that enhances their overall leadership experience is working on college-specific initiatives provided by the dean where they are asked to give their recommendations for activities and processes on a variety of activities such as creating a diversity in leadership week, leading college fundraising campaigns to benefit student initiatives, and enhancing the public areas for students. By encouraging the students to make these few changes to the council structure, members have continued to grow and are now more enthusiastic about participating and sharing ideas. They are stepping into leadership roles that challenge them to continue to grow and recognize the impact they can have at the college and in future positions in the business world.

Now that I am familiar with the CRLL framework, I believe more than ever that it is important as an educator to encourage students to develop their personal learning style in this method. We must encourage all students to recognize and find their own identity and share with them how to use that to strengthen their leader development. In addition to the learning processes, educators need to be aware of each of the five domains of the model and how they fit with the overall climate of not only the campus, but the college as well. Business college educators in general need to ensure they are very aware of the domains focused on the historical legacy of inclusion/exclusion and compositional diversity (Bertrand Jones et al., 2016, pp. 16–17). For me, as an advisor, this means encouraging a broader group of students to apply for the opportunity to participate on the council and have their voice heard, as well as continuing to guide current members to understand the importance of inclusion and the benefit of having a diverse council membership.

Marissa's example shares her process of slowly supporting students and fostering an environment that supported development of each of the three learning processes (identity, capacity, and efficacy) in the CRLL model. Marissa also does a good job of addressing the learning processes leadership educators must be aware of when considering the environmental context of how students fit with the overall climate of not only the campus, but the academic college they are engaged with. Marissa shares how she encourages minoritized students and not just students with dominant identities to engage with leadership programs and opportunities in the College of Business. A key foundation of culturally relevant pedagogy is centering students of color and minoritized identities in the leadership learning process (Bertrand Jones et al., 2016; Ladson-Billings, 1995). In the next narrative, Linnette offers leadership educators an emergence framing for operationalizing CRLL.

EMBRACING EMERGENCE
Linnette R. Lopez Werner

When I first started teaching leadership in the Fall of 2001, I had not yet heard of CRLL—in fact, I had barely heard about leadership studies. I would say that as a newly minted PhD, I placed emphasis on protecting my competencies, maintaining control, and teaching students how to properly cite their work using APA. Moving into a practice of culturally relevant pedagogy (Ladson-Billings, 2017), and even more specifically, CRLL (Bertrand Jones et al., 2016), took time, many mistakes, and many gracious supporters (most of them my students). Now, nearly 20 years after teaching my first leadership course, bringing CRLL into the classroom is still a practice, but more of an art form than a wandering in the dark and begins with the pedagogy I choose.

Freire (1973), hooks (1994), Ladson-Billings (1994), Miles (1997), and other scholars have asserted the pedagogy we employ reflects our belief in the equality of others. When I first started teaching leadership, my students sat in rows and faced the front of the classroom. When someone asked a question for which I had not planned, my unconscious desire was to regain control of the classroom and to protect my identity as a competent professor. Although I was using small-group work, simulations, case studies, and other student-centered approaches, at the foundational level of my teaching I was enacting what Freire (1973) calls the "banking model" of education. I believed my students were empty vessels and my role was to make knowledge deposits. Luckily, one of my students intervened and asked me to read Freire and hooks.

In 2007, along with my colleague David Hellstrom, I began to explore a leadership pedagogy based on the work of Ron Heifetz at Harvard through case-in-point teaching at the graduate level (Parks, 2005). Heifetz was using what emerged in the classroom as a way to bridge theory with practice. With the help of Sharon Daloz-Parks and others, we created a pedagogy inspired by case-in-point called intentional emergence (IE, Werner et al., 2016). Like case-in-point, IE uses what emerges to connect theory with practice, but in addition takes into consideration the importance of identity and its influence on teaching along with the developmental needs of emerging adults for compassion, authenticity, and a balance of challenge with support.

Within the IE pedagogy, there are four main components along with a container/context that work together to develop teachable moments: instructor identity, student identity, instructor intention, and emergence (all within a teaching context that values compassion and authenticity while balancing challenge with support; see Figure 5.1). As Ladson-Billings (2017) suggests, in a culturally responsive classroom, we first start with an understanding of our own identities as well as the identities of our students. We then intentionally create/bring assignments, readings, activities, lectures, and other planned materials to the classroom that honor and

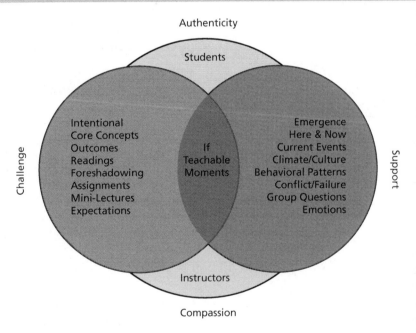

Figure 5.1 Intentional emergence pedagogy: Student/instructor identities interact with instructor intention, and emergence to generate teachable moments within a container.

support diverse and marginalized perspectives.

Within IE pedagogy, there is an added layer that tempers the intention (control) of the instructor through the wisdom of what is organically emerging. According to Guthrie et al. (2017), emergence is an important part of the CRLL process and they suggest "emergence is the collective, dynamic reformulation of a system that produces something fundamentally different from its previous form" (p. 63). For example, in my experience of teaching with the IE pedagogy, allowing emergence to play out creates a more equitable community-based learning environment because emergence itself embraces the needs, actions, and feedback of all who are involved in the learning space.

By starting with a pedagogy that supports the development of community and minimizes the control of the authority figure, I am now able to set a foundation of responsiveness (versus command). I teach from a circle instead of rows. I look forward to the unanticipated questions and other emerging events I would have seen as undermining my plan for the day in the past. Most importantly, I can implement CRLL at deeper levels than before.

From an instructor's perspective, the work may start with their own identities ("What are their privileges and power in these and how will they be perceived?") and their intentions/expectations for the class such as readings and assignments. They may see their students' identities as the next layer within this process and carefully consider how to honor and represent their students' identities with their readings, assignments, and materials. Once they step into the classroom container/context, they may work hard to establish a foundation of compassion and strive to engage authentically with students while offering a balance of challenge with support. At the same time, things outside of their control such as current events, lived experiences of students, and emotions emerge naturally as part of the leadership class. What emerges is seen as supportive, guiding, golden opportunities to tie the theory of leadership with real moments and students are co-creators of the curriculum and the experience.

Linnette offers a framework for IE pedagogy, with the four main components of instructor identity, student identity, instructor intention, and emergence. Linnette stated all of these main points are within a teaching context that values compassion and authenticity while balancing challenge with support. When considering CRLL, leadership educators can implement main components of intentional pedagogy by not only centering students' identity, capacity, and efficacy, but also considering the learning environment and context leadership learners are navigating. With an emergence approach to leadership education grounded in CRLL, leadership educators can then intentionally implement assignments, readings, activities, lectures, and other planned out materials to the classroom that honor and support minoritized perspectives. In the next narrative, Destiny offers her personal narrative of implementing anti-racism professional development by framing the current times of navigating COVID-19 and addressing racial justice.

USING CRLL AS A TOOL TOWARDS ANTI-RACISM
Destiny Caldwell

2020 was the year of accountability. From a Western perspective, quarantine brought on by the COVID-19 pandemic forced folks globally to stop and reflect on the world around them. Reflections that centered on how to stop the spread of COVID-19, or whether or not to attend a wedding or Thanksgiving dinner, were just a few of the challenging decisions individuals living in the United States had to acknowledge. However, the conversation of racial injustice in the United States has been one of the most nuanced discussion pieces to flow throughout social circles. In May 2020, individuals quarantined at home had no choice but to witness the unspoken truth of racial injustice through an 8-minute, 46 second video of the murder of George Floyd.

With the video going viral across media platforms, the actualization of the question—"Have I been doing enough?"—came to the forefront of many personal, professional, and academic conversations. June 2020 saw the emergence of reading lists, solidarity statements, curriculum reform, and policy amendments curated to proclaim allyship. For weeks, the United States experienced an influx of inquiries about how to do more as an ally. Professionals ranging from activists to scholars and community organizers tirelessly worked to spread their work to educate the masses. For once, marginalized groups and those that work closely with them felt a semblance of hope that meaningful change would actually be happening.

As the year 2020 ended, the world turned its focus away from racial injustice. Many of the curated reading lists had been forgotten about, and higher administration was failing to reach the needs proposed by anti-racist committees. Corporations, organizations, and influencers had taken the phrase "Black Lives Matter" out of their email signatures or Instagram biographies. Meaningful conversations and social media posts had slowed down. Social justice trainings that were supposed to be enforced to all employees were now just strongly recommended sessions to attend. The hope towards liberation for marginalized communities feels less likely as time passes. With this understanding in mind, I ask you, "How do you continue doing the work when no one is watching?"

The CRLL model was introduced to me in my first year as a master's student in a higher education program. I felt an immense connection to CRLL, as I felt that the model was a great guide for someone who is new to social justice work. This connection in particular was salient for me, as my foci in anti-racist work is rooted in the belief of making information accessible for all. My aim is to express a consolidated version of CRLL to allies interested in doing anti-racist work.

To first explain CRLL, I think it's imperative to acknowledge how I define "anti-racist." In *How to be an Anti-Racist*, Ibram X. Kendi (2019) describes anti-racist as an individual who is "expressing the idea that racial groups are equal and none need developing" and "is supportive of policy that reduces racial inequity" (p. 24). By this definition, I understand anti-racism to be a system, rather than an individual, of undoing racial injustice. CRLL can be used as a tool towards anti-racism in two capacities: lifelong learning and empowerment.

I understand CRLL to be a framework which centers the experiences of marginalized communities and their pathway toward leadership identity development. To understand CRLL, it is vital to understand the historical and social foundations which surround marginalized communities. To support one's development, you first have to understand who they are and how their identities are impacted based on societal norms. I believe lifelong learning to be a process which one commits themselves to a forever understanding that knowledge is infinite. To be a lifelong learner is to acknowledge information is malleable and changes as more voices and ways of thinking become visible. Understanding that nothing is concrete allows one to develop a stronger sense of critical thinking. Anti-racist work is centered around the lifelong experiences of minoritized identities; regardless of background, it is imperative to continue educating yourself (through listening to marginalized groups, participating in trainings, doing readings, attending seminars and conferences, following scholars on social media, and so on) to best support others.

Guthrie et al. (2016) center CRLL around three domains: identity, efficacy, and capacity. Each domain contributes to the overall development of not only an individual, but informs their leadership process (Guthrie et al., 2016). I believe to enact the domains of the CRLL model is to encourage empowerment. I understand empowerment to be acts of displaying fervent support that is both visible (i.e., verbal affirmation) and "invisible" (i.e., mentoring, advising, etc.) to followers and constituents. For example, a practitioner working with diverse student leaders can empower their student's needs by affirming their feelings, challenging their assumptions and supporting their identity development (through mentoring, referring to resources, etc.). Finally, empowerment can also be dependent on privilege; those with privileged identities can and should use their privilege to support those with oppressed identities.

Finally, as we think about using CRLL for anti-racist work, the primary focus should be rooted in honesty. Being an anti-racist agent means approaching your feelings, biases, and assumptions with honest and critical reflection. This work is rooted in not always knowing the answer, being wrong at times, and inevitably, complete failure. Being a change agent is an everyday process, meaning that all work you do is rooted in anti-racism. While this doesn't have to show up as joining a diversity committee or spearheading a training session, this should be evident in your daily discourse. How you choose to show up as a leadership educator matters; your words, your actions, and your decisions reflect your beliefs. Now more than ever, the call for prominent allyship is dependent on how one shows up in all spaces. Only true passion, determination and "putting in the work" can see us towards liberation.

Destiny offers important context when considering CRLL in the United States during a global pandemic and as citizens of the United States fighting for racial justice. Destiny shares how she frames CRLL for the purpose of anti-racist work in leadership education. Destiny's narrative frames how the CRLL model can be empowering to not only learners, but also leadership educators. Destiny acknowledges doing socially just work with the goal of anti-racism is not rooted in always knowing the answer, but acknowledging leadership education is ongoing learning and putting in the work. The final narrative offered by Mac, Tess, and Kerry operationalizes the CRLL model through a professional development activity of storytelling.

PROFESSIONAL DEVELOPMENT THROUGH STORYTELLING: DEVELOPING LEADERSHIP EDUCATORS' CAPACITY FOR ANTI-RACISM
Mac Benavides, Tess Hobson, and Kerry L. Priest

The Fall 2020 semester presented several challenges for higher education in the United States. In addition to a global health crisis significantly altering the learning experience for students and educators, there was renewed attention around systemic racism and the disproportionate impact of police brutality on Black communities and other communities of color. In preparation for this unprecedented fall semester, faculty, staff, and graduate students of the Staley School of Leadership Studies at Kansas State University recognized the need for self-work—as well as collective sense-making—around our beliefs, values, and teaching and programmatic practices. We (authors) developed a storytelling workshop for our team grounded in CRLL and antiracism. The goals of the workshop were to challenge ourselves to (a) uncover patterns in the stories we tell about our school and about ourselves, (b) to seek to understand those patterns in new ways, and (c) to identify next wise actions for transformation and possibility.

Drawing from Bell's (2010) model of storytelling for social justice, we focused our facilitation around three primary story types: stock stories, concealed stories, and transformative stories. We also used Kendi's (2019) work on antiracism to situate our workshop as an interrogation of the structural and organizational manifestations of racism in our school, the university, and the field of leadership studies at large. The antiracism model requires that we acknowledge racism exists, unpack how whiteness is normalized, critically examine our processes and structures, and actively move from colorblindness to antiracism. The storytelling and antiracism frameworks served as outstanding overlay for operationalizing CRLL.

Stock stories are those told by the dominant group, passed on through history, celebrations, public rituals, law, the arts, education, and media to name a few (Bell, 2010). Stock stories illustrate what a society considers important and meaningful, and thus, provide a foundation for analyzing racism. Our team worked in small groups to identify stock stories about race and racism that operate in our school and on our campus to justify and perpetuate an unequal status quo.

Concealed stories are often told by people on the margins and largely invisible in mainstream culture (Bell, 2010). These include stories of and by communities of color about their struggles and survival in the United States, as well as stories that reveal privileges that White people receive. Concealed stories show the underside of racism, but are often not represented in mainstream stories. As a predominantly White team, it was challenging to think of concealed stories about race and racism without tokenizing the few people of color in the room. Therefore, we focused our conversations on questioning why we do not hear these stories and how we could actively seek them out.

By examining stock and concealed stories, members of the Staley School explored the CRLL domains of historical legacy of inclusion/exclusion and the organizational/structural dimension. While these domains are embedded in the curriculum of the leadership studies minor, there are still gaps in our ability to readily recognize when we operate from a place of normalized Whiteness. The foundation of antiracism in this workshop created space for our team to reflect intentionally on how we approach leadership learning. We were also able to have meaningful discussions about the challenges of achieving compositional diversity at a predominantly White institution. Despite our efforts to present concealed stories of leadership across cultures and contexts, students rarely hear these stories from faculty and staff of color.

The final story type from Bell's (2010) model is the transformative story. Transformative stories are new stories that challenge stock stories, build on concealed stories, and offer ways to interrupt the status quo to work for change. They enact continuing critique to stock stories, deconstruct taken-for-granted racial patterns, and ask us to imagine new possibilities for inclusive human community. In other words, through transformative stories, we can imagine alternative scenarios of racial equity and develop strategies to work toward those changes. To construct transformative stories, we asked our team to consider what we can draw from any known concealed stories to create new stories about what ought to be. Given the compositional make-up of our team, we also engaged in discussion on how we can co-construct transformative stories with people of color without tokenizing or burdening them. Critically thinking through transformative stories served as an opportunity for our team to engage in the psychological and behavioral domains of CRLL.

We ended this session with the question, "Now What?" Our team considered and committed to next steps as individuals, teaching and program teams, and for our school as a system. This may be the most difficult question of all, prompting a *movement* from talking *about* the issue to taking action that leads to change. We did not leave with solutions; the issues did not resolve. However, the challenge—and our purpose—was clearer. Self-work is integral to leadership educator development and practice, it is an ongoing process of inquiry, action, and reflection.

Mac, Tess, and Kerry offer an activity for a professional development workshop with the goals to challenge participants to: (a) uncover patterns in the stories we tell about our school and about ourselves, (b) to seek to understand those patterns in new ways, and (c) to identify next wise actions for transformation and possibility. They outline how a professional development workshop for anti-racism can be grounded in the CRLL model. Mac, Tess, and Kerry's narrative offers an example for leadership educators creating professional development opportunities in a context of addressing anti-racism through self-work and professional identity. For leadership educators to engage in professional development work that critically deconstructs stock stories, criticize taken-for-granted racial patterns, and reimagine new possibilities for inclusive leadership learning, they are then working toward more inclusive leadership learning communities.

A CALL TO ACTION: EXPLORING THE CRLL MODEL IN A PROFESSIONAL ASSOCIATION BOOK CLUB
Avani Rana, Christine Hernandez, and John Egan

NASPA—Student Affairs Administrators in Higher Education is an international organization focused on administrators of colleges and universities. NASPA Knowledge Communities (KC) address the varied subareas of student affairs administration and are targeted toward affiliation groups and content areas. The Student Leadership Programs Knowledge Community (SLPKC) focuses on leadership education. Soon after the racial injustices of summer of 2020 came to light, the SLPKC leadership team met and developed a plan of action to focus on anti-racism as part of its mission for the upcoming year. An email sent by the leadership team to the community best describes the collective call to action:

> In our leadership programs, we need to reject colorblindness and acknowledge the foundation of leadership theory and education is centered on whiteness and the oppression of marginalized voices. We need to challenge and critically examine our leadership programs, theories, and models.

Prior to the racial unrest of 2020 the SLPKC leadership team spoke about topics or areas to focus on that would expand the knowledge base of all members and retain individuals of color in the profession. The racial injustices of 2020 highlighted the relevance and timeliness of the topic to the staff working with these topics.

Recognizing that discussion is not enough, the SLPKC adopted the Culturally Relevant Leadership Learning model (CRLL) to engage members. We developed a four-part series in a book club format that concluded with a call to action for participants. The book club format provided space for practitioners to reflect on areas of improvement for their own programs. Individuals then identified to personal action they would commit to as a response to their identified areas of improvement, wrote them down, and shared them with the group as added levels of accountability. As a result of this series, one person shared they would open the conversation on diversity and inclusion in student leadership spaces. Another person shared that they would build more space for students to engage in identity development learning. Another participant committed to seeing themselves as a leadership educator in other aspects of their life.

Participants discussed the challenges and barriers in successfully practicing the CRLL model. In order to do the work, practitioners must invest time in self-reflection, be vulnerable, admit to mistakes, and strengthen facilitation skills. Practitioners must also spend time creating spaces for students to be in community with each other. As trust is built, students and practitioners engage in more honest dialogue. Practitioners also discussed the need to embrace conflict as a part of the process.

One of the challenges of leadership education in this context is that it often seems limited to students and colleges. Students are given the tools to lead in their communities, but the work led by student affairs practitioners remains primarily on campus. A participant asked, "How can we expand leadership education outside of higher education?" In order to create a more socially just world, culturally relevant leadership learning must reach beyond academia. In the closing session, at least two participants committed to sharing the concepts of the model outside of higher education and into their other community spaces.

In conclusion, the book club gave the members an opportunity to explore their personal *identities*. Authors with diverse identities introduced diverse perspectives that challenged participants to look outside of Eurocentric perspectives of leadership. The goal of the book club was to build knowledge and capacity through sharing individual ideas, hearing about different perspectives, sharing best practice resources, and creating safe spaces to have conversations. These efforts lead to building participants' *efficacy*. While sharing ideas, capacity, and knowledge lead to building confidence in the participants, they enable participants to have these conversations with their students and their colleagues.

Raina, Herenandez, and Egan offer a common professional activity of a book club, except they highlight the benefits of facilitating the club at the national association level. Through engagement with the book club, leadership educators were able to explore and continue to make meaning of their own social identities as leadership educators. Additionally, the book club professional development opportunity allowed participants to discuss the challenges and barriers in successfully practicing, implementing and assessing the CRLL model for their respective leadership education contexts. Raina et al. highlight how practitioners must invest time in self-reflection, being vulnerable, admitting mistakes, and strengthen facilitation skills. The

NASPA SLPKC Book Club provided leadership educators a space to spend time creating community with each other.

The strategies shared by the narratives in this chapter that highlights specific contexts for professional development for leadership educators are great examples of the ongoing work CRLL employs all of us to embark on. Just as Bitton, Caldwell, Benavides, Hobson, and Priest shared how CRLL is supportive in implementing leadership educator professional development, specifically for social and racial justice outcomes. Ordonez, Mainwood, Bardill Moscaritolo, and Werner offered the professional development needed to engage and advise students and how with appropriate framing, professional development for faculty and staff can be intentional and more culturally relevant. Finally, in conclusion, we offer questions for consideration in Table 5.1. These questions are framed for you to consider how your own professional development can be designed and implemented in a more culturally relevant way.

TABLE 5.1 Culturally Relevant Leadership Learning Considerations: Process of Professional Development for Leadership Educators

Culturally Relevant Leadership Learning Constructs	Questions for Consideration
Identity	• In what ways do you consider your social identities with your professional leadership educator identity? • How will you use tools, like intentional emergence pedagogy, in instructional and assessment strategies? • How will identity be integrated throughout a professional development opportunity for the purpose of reflection and self-work?
Capacity	• What reflection and professional development strategies will be used for you and other leadership educators you work with to practice considering CRLL and anti-racism frameworks? • How will professional development outcomes center your own capacity development for engaging with diverse students? • How will you develop an ongoing process to assess your evolving capacity to facilitate and engage in culturally relevant leadership learning?
Efficacy	• How can professional development opportunities center more diverse voices and experiences? • How can professional development redefine who you and other leadership educators consider can be leaders and what leadership is with a socially just lens? • What assessment strategies will be used to assess your own professional development ongoing growth?

(continued)

TABLE 5.1   Culturally Relevant Leadership Learning Considerations: Process of Professional Development for Leadership Educators (continued)

Culturally Relevant Leadership Learning Constructs	Questions for Consideration
Historical Legacy of Inclusion and Exclusion	• What histories need to be acknowledged in order to center an anti-racist framework for leadership education? • How can leadership educator professional development be redesigned and not center historically white learning environments? • How will historical narratives of minoritized leadership educators be used in leadership educator professional development opportunities?
Compositional Diversity	• Have you done an audit of identities represented as leadership educators in your professional context? If so, what can you determine from who is represented as leadership educators? • How will who is included or excluded from being identified as a leadership educator be addressed? • How will race, class, gender, and sexuality be acknowledged and honored in the professional development space and contribute to the ongoing learning of leadership educators?
Psychological Dimension	• How will space be created for you and other leadership educators to reflect on your own journey in leadership education? • What opportunities will you create for yourself and your colleagues to confront differing worldviews from both content and cultural perspectives? • In what will you and other leadership educators be challenged to consider and confront the cultural realities that resist necessary change?
Behavioral Dimension	• In what ways will behaviors of being a leadership educator be redefined to include and center more minoritized leadership educators? • How will observations of the behavior of current leadership educators be discussed through professional development? • How will critical reflection be used both as a professional development strategy as a self-work strategy?
Organizational and Structural Dimension	• How will anti-racist pedagogy and intentional emergence pedagogy be integrated throughout professional development curriculum to challenge dominate ways of being a leadership educator? • In what ways will relevant depictions of leadership educator across social identities, social locations, and organizations be integrated into all aspects of professional development? • What opportunities will be created for discussion regarding current societal contexts?

6

Cocurricular Program Development Using Culturally Relevant Leadership Learning

Intentional development of opportunities for leadership learning in a cocurricular context is essential for holistic growth of students. Developing programs is a competency necessary for educators, especially in cocurricular spaces (Aiken-Wisniewski et al., 2020). As leadership educators, we must acknowledge students and what they bring in the shape of their own knowledge, skills, and lived experiences (Ladson-Billings, 1995). In cocurricular contexts, these individual student contributions can be used to empower and encourage leader identity, capacity, and efficacy (Guthrie & Rodriguez, 2018).

Strategies for Cocurricular Leadership Learning Opportunities

Leadership educators who develop programs must focus on the development of all students and validate their lived experiences as strengths rather

Operationalizing Culturally Relevant Leadership Learning, pages 85–103
Copyright © 2021 by Information Age Publishing
All rights of reproduction in any form reserved.   **85**

than weaknesses. Guthrie and Rodriguez (2018) offer strategies for educators to create leadership learning opportunities in cocurricular contexts, including establishment of a strong programmatic foundation, guarantee of programmatic diversity, representation of diverse voices, and intentional use of language at all points in development.

Establishing a Strong Programmatic Foundation

A strong programmatic foundation of leadership learning is one of the most important concepts to develop. The six aspects of leadership learning, including knowledge, development, training, observation, engagement, and metacognition (Guthrie & Jenkins, 2018), should center learning in all programs. Advisors need to provide a foundation of leadership knowledge that ensures a shared comprehension resulting in having a socially constructed understanding of leadership. In cocurricular contexts, leadership training typically focuses on skill development within specific moments of time such as workshops, retreats, or positional role training. As educators and cocurricular advisors, we need to inspire students to consider how their perspectives, lived experiences, and truths about those with differing identities allow for a greater understanding of leadership.

Leadership development requires facilitation from educators and advisors to reinforce how knowledge gained from educational experiences and skills obtained from training are strengthened through reflection. Reflection is an essential component of leadership learning (Volpe White et al., 2019; White, 2012). The introspection component to reflection prompts student leaders to develop meaning around their experiences. Furthermore, during reflective exercises, students gain clarity on their own identities, and their identity as a leader, which makes them better equipped to create inclusive environments. These are the first steps in creating a strong programmatic foundation to program development.

Programmatic Diversity

Diversity in programming is essential for cocurricular program development. With culturally relevant leadership learning (CRLL) in mind, we must look at events being planned both by the students and for the students. We must evaluate whether cocurricular programs being developed and offered are not only representative of the student body but provide a welcoming environment for all identities to thrive. Assessing student identities at events is an indicator of whether programs are connecting with diverse student populations or not. Advisors and educators can create environments where cocurricular CRLL opportunities can occur, often when other opportunities are not available. Cultivating such environments leads to increased student engagement.

Representation of Diverse Voices

Representation of different identities in every capacity is critical for creating environments for CRLL to occur. This should appear in the form of educators, administrators, advisors, faculty, and other higher education professional positions, as well as students. The importance of having a diverse staff is often underestimated. However, it is important for students to see individuals with similar identities as them in leadership positions, as it reduces imposter syndrome and increases their self-efficacy (Bertrand Jones et al., 2016).

Having educators from diverse identities models diverse students seeing themselves as leaders. Once students self-identify as leaders, they can engage and thrive in the leadership process. For this to be accomplished, language and imagery of diverse individuals used in student-facing materials is essential, which is part of the need for intentional use of language in cocurricular program development.

Intentional Use of Language

Designing inclusive and CRLL spaces, especially in cocurricular contexts, start with the language educators use. As Guthrie and Rodriguez (2018) discuss, language influences how learning spaces are created and how others see that space. Educators role model inclusive environments by the language used. Language is essential for creating inclusive environments and influence how students perceive themselves. Culturally relevant leadership educators need to be mindful of what is said in every environment, as all language demonstrates how significant it is to be respectful in spaces where leadership learning happens.

As language changes and evolves, it is important to stay in touch with these changes. Being informed and willing to adapt not only role models how important staying culturally relevant is, but how creating culturally relevant learning spaces takes constant work. In listening to the language students use, educators should use that information to influence how students perceive themselves as leaders.

The examples shared in this chapter provide rich narratives of how the CRLL model is operationalized in cocurricular program development. AdriAnne Yvette Archie Sternberg shares how CRLL aided in the centralization of leadership development as being defined beyond positions and included everyone, at Belmont University. CRLL supporting a student organization transformation is shared by Adrian L. Bitton. Darren E. Pierre reflects on how an exercise he facilitated with a team of student affairs educators examined each domain of CRLL and juxtapose it to their cocurricular programs. Alan Acosta shares how CRLL was operationalized in student conduct spaces, which shows the expansiveness of the model. Considering graduate students, Onyedikachi Ekwerike and Kerry L. Priest share how CRLL is used in Kansas State University's graduate student leadership development program (GSLDP). Finally, Adam Kuhn explains considerations for the use of CRLL in leadership educator curriculum development from his own experience.

FOUNDATION FOR BOLD—
BELMONT OFFICE OF LEADERSHIP DEVELOPMENT
AdriAnne Yvette Archie Sternberg

In 2015, Belmont University began discussing ways to increase student leadership development on its campus. The Student Leadership Development task force, consisting of stakeholders from a variety of academic colleges and Belmont offices, was one of many teams formed to ultimately create the Vision 2020 plan to guide the institution for the next 5 years. The task force proposed leadership development be centralized across campus and strategic changes be made in the campus-wide culture, climate, and view of student leadership from administrators to students. Belmont viewed students with formal positions as leaders.

I was hired in 2017 to design a framework for leadership development and operationalize plans for all students to engage in the leadership process. After 6 months of continued research, benchmarking, and interviews with 145 Belmont stakeholders, I understood CRLL would be the foundation needed for Belmont students to successfully learn, engage in, and demonstrate leadership. Dugan et al. (2013), explained that students' self-efficacy is empowered or constrained based on messages from our social context and normative assumptions about what a leader should look like or act. The task force's research showed Belmont was sending unclear messages about who could and could not be a leader. The new information gathered revealed that if the campus worked to create and highlight accessible leadership development opportunities, students' belief in themselves would be heightened provided they are given a chance to practice, make mistakes, and learn leadership with or without a formal position. Bertrand Jones, Guthrie, and Osteen (2016) emphasized that the old paradigms of leadership and learning needed to be challenged in order to present new ways to educate students and develop leaders who challenge inequity and help bring about social change. CRLL would serve the overarching desires of the student leadership task force and Belmont as a whole.

The Belmont Office of Leadership Development (BOLD) framework was established to create experiences for students to enhance their capacity to lead and serve ethically. I mapped and aligned the domains of the Council for the Advancement of Standards (CAS Standards) with the leadership theories and models emphasized at Belmont. These theories and models were then aligned with the university mission, vision, values, task force recommendations, university academic curriculum, learning outcomes and goals, and general education framework. Once each part of the framework was aligned the BOLD mission, vision, values, engagement levels and competencies were formed. This theoretical and philosophical framework is an accessible and accessible leadership framework with learning objectives and outcomes which allow administrators to implement programs that help students increase their capacity to lead and serve ethically.

At Belmont, leadership is now defined as a values-driven process of individuals from diverse backgrounds working together to boldly and ethically engage and transform the world. The values of BOLD are service, experience, and ethics. Each value of BOLD is aligned with one of four levels of engagement. These levels form a 4-tier competency-based program with seamlessly aligned curricular and cocurricular leadership development experiences seamlessly integrated and aligned in and outside of the classroom. The value of ethics is aligned with the belonging—aspiring leader level and believing—emergent leader level; experience is aligned with the becoming—engaged leader level; and service is aligned with the being—transformative servant leader level. Each level focuses on one or more of the six BOLD competencies: ethics, resilience, collaboration, inclusivity, and communication, and service. Programs like Bruin Lead, the Pulse Leadership Advance were created for each level of engagement and emphasize BOLD competencies. Academic courses, campus-wide leadership experiences and service-learning are highlighted for students to make meaning of their leadership process.

BOLD begins with self-identity and leads to transformation, increased capacity, and efficacy over time. Each level of engagement builds off of the previous level allowing the students to gain additional leadership practice while collaborating with other students and reflecting on their progress along the way. BOLD allows students to make sense of who they are through the strategically designed programs and experiences. Students return to the classroom, internships, community, and campus community more prepared and confident to lead. BOLD has positively contributed to Belmont's campus climate, which the five dimensions of CRLL encompass, and as Guthrie et al. (2013) explains, directly affect student growth, development, and learning (p. 15).

At Belmont University, CRLL helped provide one of the foundational underpinnings of the BOLD framework. As Sternberg shares, this redesign of leadership development at a campus level created an opportunity to focus beyond leadership as a position and create learning opportunities for students to enhance their capacity to lead and serve ethically. In tandem with other frameworks, CRLL provided focus on the student development of identity, capacity, and efficacy while considering context. BOLD offers an example of how a strategically designed program, with intention experiences to scaffold learning can positively contribute to a campus climate and directly influence student growth and development as current and future leaders. Another important context for student learning are student organizations; Bitton shares her experience with a redesign of an organizational structure inspired by CRLL.

TRANSFORMING A STUDENT ORGANIZATION
Adrian L. Bitton

As college campuses, student populations, and the leadership landscape continue to evolve, the CRLL model allows leadership educators to effectively customize leadership programs for a variety of student organizations by/while centering the needs and experiences of students with minoritized identities. At Northwestern University (NU), Student Enrichment Services (SES) and Leadership Development and Community Engagement (LDCE) collaborated to create a series of targeted leadership learning experiences for the executive board of Quest+ (formerly Quest Scholars Network). Using CRLL as a framework, we considered the broader campus climate and context to build students' identity, capacity, and efficacy as leaders.

SES is an office dedicated to supporting first-generation, lower-income, and/or undocumented undergraduate students. Founded in 2013, SES is the result of Quest Scholar students' advocacy and leadership in collaboration with administrators to garner additional support for first-generation and/or low-income (FGLI) students. In 2016, the president announced a university-wide priority to admit 20% Pell-eligible students by Fall 2020. This goal was achieved 2 years early in 2018 and Quest+ and SES have worked closely together to create a welcoming campus community for low-income students. The change in name from Quest Scholars Network to Quest+ which reflects the students' commitment to inclusivity and desire to lessen the distinction between Quest Scholars and the broader FGLI population.

With the name change and expanded mission, the Quest+ executive board and SES staff took the opportunity to reexamine their organizational and leadership structure. Quest+ tended to rebuild itself every year with each new executive board, rather than building on previous boards' initiatives. This new board wanted to create stability and generativity for future student leaders of the organization. Additionally, since Quest+ predated SES, they had not taken the time to establish what their relationship meant. I worked with the board and advisors to develop and facilitate a series of leadership retreats that would address these needs. Considering the quarter system, we committed to quarterly retreats that included the entire Quest+ executive board, SES advisors, and me. In between the retreats, I also met regularly with the smaller leadership team, which consisted of the SES advisors and the Quest+ co-presidents and vice president so that they could build trust and establish clear expectations for their working relationship. During these meetings, we also assessed the board's group development, discussed the transition progress, and brainstormed solutions to emerging challenges. Their own individual efficacy, capacity, and identities as leaders grew as we worked together to plan, facilitate, and debrief each retreat.

The executive board was eager to establish a new organizational structure with roles that enabled them to work more efficiently and effectively. However, the leadership team recognized the value of taking the time to build the leadership identity, capacity, and efficacy of the board members on both an individual and group level. This became the main focus of the leadership retreats before creating structure and roles. We wanted to foster their leadership identity to complement their strong identification and pride in their FGLI identity. Therefore, we facilitated activities that helped them reflect, explore, and share their motivations for taking on a leadership position within Quest+.

Additionally, the board was composed of mostly younger members with only a few returner students. This, in combination with the lack of clarity in their roles, led many to express lower levels of leadership efficacy. In order to build their efficacy, we worked to shift mindsets from a deficit perspective to one that recognized their cultural capital and life experiences as opportunities where they developed critical leadership skills and engaged in leadership development. We also used assessments, such as StrengthsQuest, to help them recognize their natural talents as leadership strengths and provide them with a common leadership language. They were prompted to examine the ways that each of them contributed to the leadership of the board by utilizing the Team Talent Map and establishing their collective identity as a board. We engaged in meaningful group development activities such as creating a mission statement, identifying core values, and integrating them into their decision-making. This, in turn, allowed them to restructure the board in alignment with their values. The new organizational structure provided greater role clarity and eliminated redundancy, which led to more successful implementation of programs and positive feedback in the changes to weekly board meetings.

These gains were palpable in the morale of the board as they learned to work together, hold each other accountable, and empower themselves by taking ownership of their new organization. Throughout these quarterly leadership retreats, individual board members and the board as a collective progressed in building their leadership identity, capacity, and efficacy, and the entire NU FGLI community has benefitted as a result.

As Rosch (2017) explores in *The Role of Student Organizations in Developing Leadership*, student organizations offer powerful spaces and places for students to engage in their development of leader identity, capacity, and efficacy. In her narrative, Bitton shares how at Northwestern University, she was involved in the restructuring of a student organization. As this restructuring was occurring, her team considered what leadership learning experiences the executive board and members needed for the greatest learning outcome. They used CRLL to consider campus environment and how students' identity, capacity, and efficacy as leaders could be best developed through clarifying roles, shifting diverse students' mindsets from deficit to empowerment through lived experiences. This powerful redesign provided intentional learning opportunities for diverse students to engage in an entirely different way. In addition to student organizations, Pierre offers insight into how his student engagement team examined practices in how they were offering programs using CRLL.

LEADERSHIP AND STUDENT ENGAGEMENT
Darren E. Pierre

Historically, leadership has been seen through a privileged lens. Meaning, leadership has historically cast a net on those who identify as White, cisgender, Christian, and male (Dugan, 2017). This net is problematic, it becomes an incubator of who is and who is not part of the leadership conversation (Stock & Özbeck-Pothoff, 2014). While leadership theories have evolved over the years and have become more inclusive overtime, there is still work to be done to acknowledge the historical exclusionary underpinnings of what informs modern day leadership education.

The beginnings of leadership education date back to "The Great Man" theory (Northouse, 2019). The great man theory was inherent with notions of trait-based leadership, patriarchal in nature, and values derived from a Western vantage point (Dugan, 2017). While one can argue these early beginnings are not where the current state of leadership within cocurricular programs, it does explain why a number of people, including communities of color, do not see themselves in the prototype of what it means to be a "leader" (Arminio et al., 2000). As educators whose work takes place in cocurricular spaces, we have a responsibility to dismantle some of the hegemonic traditions that have been part of the dominant narrative of not only leadership development, but also student engagement.

I believe CRLL responds to the gaps laid open by the historical legacy of leadership theories. CRLL and its five domains: Historical legacy of inclusion/exclusion, psychological dimension, compositional diversity, behavioral dimension, and organizations structural dimension each offer space for a counter perspective to leadership and leadership development (Guthrie et al., 2016). It was from this place, I worked to build a more inclusive framework for student leadership engagement in cocurricular programs.

Working with a team of dedicated student affairs educators, we examined each domain of the CRLL and juxtaposed it to the topography of our cocurricular programs. We troubled the historical legacy of our department, our division, and our university surrounding values of diversity and inclusion. We looked at the compositional diversity of our cocurricular programs, paying close attention to who was and more importantly, who was not represented. Using empirical and anecdotal data, we asked hard questions about the perceptions of how our office valued diversity and inclusion. As an office, we interrogated how we were authentically supporting students to engage across differences (enacting the behavioral dimension of CRLL). Finally, we paid attention to the structures and processes that informed our day-to-day work. From this work, we learned a great deal about how our practices celebrated and impeded diversity within our cocurricular programs.

To facilitate this exercise, each of the staff read the *New Directions Series for Student Leadership: Developing Culturally Relevant Leadership Learning* (Guthrie et al., 2016). With a full-day blocked off on calendars, markers and flip-chart in-hand, we plotted out each of the five domains of CRLL in concert with relevant leadership theories. For example, when thinking about "compositional diversity," we questioned how we went about considering speakers, panelists, and facilitators. In this analysis of past programs, we realized some hard truths. We spent more energy and attention looking at availability and price of speakers than we did race, gender, ability, sexual orientation, and a host of other socially constructed identities. In a move toward efficiency, we were prognosticating the same exclusionary practices we were trying to dismantle.

As a team, we critically analyzed our day-to-day practices, and troubled policies. For example, why were we asking for the president of an organization's information, rather than allowing student groups to choose a primary contact of their own design. Again, connecting CRLL to the literature, we know not all communities subscribe to "traditional" forms of hierarchical leadership (Dugan et al., 2008; Meriwether, 2018; Ostick & Wall, 2011; Spencer, 2019). In turn, we had a responsibility to make a change. From considering who is represented as panelist and speakers, to changing the terminology of registration forms, these are two examples of how we used CRLL to help shape more inclusive and culturally relevant cocurricular engagement experiences.

The exercise we engaged in as an office allowed us to unlearn and relearn our ways of being and engaging as leadership educators and ambassadors for diverse and inclusive student engagement initiatives. Dugan (2017) calls it a deconstruction that leads to reconstruction; however, you label it, practitioners have a responsibility to reeducate themselves on how leadership theories are activated, how student experiences in cocurricular programs are cultivated, and how values of diversity and inclusion are propagated within campus activities and leadership education.

Pierre powerfully states in his narrative that leadership educators have an obligation to dismantle the dominant narratives that have plagued not only cocurricular spaces, but higher education. The example of how his team deconstructed every aspect of their cocurricular program offerings and processes using the five dimensions of CRLL in relation to relevant leadership theoretical frameworks. This daylong retreat led to constant work in deconstructing and reformulating day-to-day practices and policies that were unknowingly contributing to the oppression of diverse students. Student engagement and activities offices are often spaces, like student organizations, for strong messages about a university's climate in cocurricular contexts. However, offices of student conduct are another space where viewing cultural relevance is critical of overall campus climate and student learning. Acosta provides insight into how training of conduct boards using CRLL not only develop students involved on the boards, but shape campus climate on how the adjudication process is presented.

STUDENT CONDUCT
Alan Acosta

The field of student conduct has recently placed a greater emphasis on the importance and necessity of infusing diversity, equity, and inclusion into its contemporary standards of practice, particularly in its resolution processes (Hudson et al., 2018; Schrage & Giacomini, 2009). One resolution method on many campuses is recruiting and training students to serve on hearing panels, often referred to as conduct boards. Many positive advantages of using conduct boards as a resolution method exist, including having peers hold each other to the community's standards, and in providing students with an opportunity to practice and grow their leadership skills. As practitioners look for more ways to incorporate inclusion into student conduct work and enhance the training conduct boards receive, board trainings are one aspect of practice ideally situated to benefit from the CRLL model.

Much of the focus with the training of conduct boards centers on the logistics of the adjudication process. This is understandable, as the maintenance of students' due process is paramount in the student conduct process (Lancaster & Waryold, 2008; Waryold & Lancaster, 2013). Beyond the logistics of adjudicating a conduct case, student conduct professionals need to train conduct boards on how to be aware of how the cultural background of each student, as well as the campus culture may show up in a hearing setting.

There are several dynamics related to the CRLL on which student conduct professionals can train conduct boards. Student conduct professionals must facilitate learning about how the social identities of a historically marginalized or underrepresented group may influence their perception of the conduct process. Many students from historically marginalized populations, based on the history of systemic mistreatment of members of their group, may have a general mistrust of the perceived fairness of the process or authority figures in general, conduct boards included. It is also helpful to facilitate learning for conduct boards to be aware of any potential expectations of behavior and consequences that students going through the process may have from their families, as well as any cultural expectations students going through the process may receive from their peers (i.e., not "snitching").

There are numerous other issues related to diversity and inclusion issues student conduct professionals can train their students on that will increase their use of CRLL with their students. Some additional issues worth training conduct boards on include language barriers for students from other countries; participation barriers for students who have a disability; or the connection between current social issues and the conduct process.

Student conduct professionals should integrate diversity and inclusion activities into the training process. Professionals can also remind conduct board members that they themselves may relate to the feeling of mistreatment based on their identity or membership in a particular group and can draw on that experience to relate to or ease the concerns of students alleged to have violated policy during the hearing. Utilizing CRLL and nurturing conduct boards on diversity, equity, and inclusion issues to find ways to incorporate these practices into hearings can increase conduct board members' leadership capacity and provide a more holistic experience for students navigating the conduct process.

Oftentimes student conduct is not considered in respect to leadership development. However, not only do educators in student conduct roles have an incredible opportunity to provide leadership learning to students on conduct boards, but also to students navigating the conduct process. Currently, most of the training of conduct boards centers on the logistics of the adjudication process. Although this is understandable due to the complexity and legality of some cases, Acosta highlights how important awareness of cultural identities is important to interactions in hearing. By considering CRLL, not only can conduct boards be cultivated on diversity, equity, and inclusion issues, these practices can be incorporated into hearings. Conduct board members' capacity can be increased, as well as more developmental experiences for students navigating the conduct process. Just as student conduct is often a place overlooked in leadership development, graduate students are often overlooked as well. Ekwerike and Priest offer insight to a GSLDP they have created using CRLL.

GRADUATE STUDENT LEADERSHIP DEVELOPMENT PROGRAM
Onyedikachi Ekwerike and Kerry L. Priest

As a land-grant institution, Kansas State University was founded on the values of providing access to relevant, practical education to all, and improving quality of life through education, research, and outreach. Yet, we also acknowledge that our institutional systems have not always lived up to these espoused values of inclusion, equity, and relevance. As leadership educators, we play a direct role in preparing students to be global citizens who are ready to engage their careers and communities in order to make progress on the world's toughest challenges. The values and processes necessary to engage and live out this mission reflect socially responsible leadership. While our institution has a 20+ year history of undergraduate leadership education and development, only recently have we turned our attention to intentional graduate-level leadership development.

After a pilot year in 2015, the GSLDP was developed in 2016 with the purpose of increasing access and opportunity for leadership learning and development of graduate students. As the GSLDP has evolved, the CRLL framework has helped us to become more intentional, recognizing and responding to the role we can play in creating and supporting a campus climate of inclusion, belonging, and well-being through program design and delivery.

The GSLDP is a one-semester cocurricular leadership program, with a cohort of 35–40 students per session. We recruit students who have interest and potential in exercising leadership in their spaces of work and study. We are intentional that this program is open to all graduate students, not only those holding leadership roles or positions with student organizations. In the application and selection process, we are conscious of compositional diversity as represented by programs of study as well as gender. Our participants' racial and ethnic diversity (including both international and domestic students) sets the foundation for an intercultural learning experience.

The program is designed around concepts and skills of authentic leadership development, socially responsible leadership philosophy, and adaptive leadership practice. The objectives are for participants to (a) build a learning community, (b) explore perspectives and practices to exercise leadership for change, and (c) develop tangible strategies to engage others and mobilize change with your own teams, organizations, and communities. Students engage through a combination of large-group workshops, as well as a peer coaching team (5–6 people). We will describe culturally relevant considerations that support students' development of leadership identity, efficacy, and capacity.

As Bertrand Jones et al. (2016) point out, students from underrepresented populations seldom see themselves as leaders due to lack of representation of such individuals in positions of leadership, leadership literature, and leadership development programs. We utilize a life story approach to help all participants see themselves *already* in the work of leadership. Through the development of a journey map, participants reflect on and share stories of significant life moments or events that have shaped their perspectives and trajectory into their current work or role. Through reflection, participants begin to see themselves as leaders and capable of leadership. Additionally, the very practice of storytelling is supported by CRLL as an activity familiar to all cultural groups. As Carter-Black (2007) asserts, a storytelling pedagogy can be perceived as less threatening to all social groups due to its cultural familiarity. An increased sense of safety allows students to deeply interrogate complex subjects, such as their own leadership journey.

The GSLDP utilizes sociocultural conversations with peers as a high impact experience that helps students develop leadership capacity (Bertrand Jones et al., 2016). During the peer coaching process, participants have the opportunity to discuss leadership challenges they face in their current work, which are grounded in differing cultural contexts. This cross-cultural dialogue helps students to see how their leadership identity is connected to their social identities, which in turn builds their capacity for intercultural leadership. To illustrate, during one peer coaching session a participant from a country in the middle east, who identifies as a woman, shared her challenge with leading her department in a context in which women are perceived as incapable of leadership. Through the coaching experience, this student responded to questions and received suggestions and ideas on how to make progress on her challenge from her teammates. It was important for them to acknowledge that their suggestions were grounded in their own cultural contexts and may not translate to hers. Nonetheless, she left the session with a few new ideas with which to experiment. Through this experience all participants in the group gained a deeper understanding of leadership challenges in a different cultural context and an increased consciousness of the ways in which their social identities impact their leadership.

As highlighted by Bertrand Jones et al. (2016), students from underrepresented populations may often lack leadership efficacy due to dominant narratives that only certain people are capable of effectively engaging in leadership. The GSLDP attends to this by drawing on two assumptions: (a) leadership is an activity and (b) anyone can lead at any time and anywhere (KLC). These principles were emphasized all through the program to reinforce in the hearts of participants the truth that they are capable of successfully enacting leadership. Taking into cognizance the importance of modeling in building efficacy (Bandura, 1997), Onyedikachi who is an African, was a co-facilitator in the program and shared about the leadership work he does in Nigeria to support women struggling with postpartum depression. We drew on his work as a case study to teach participants how to distinguish between technical and adaptive challenges. Having a facilitator from an underrepresented background who has successfully led change efforts in his country not only contributes to students' efficacy, but also helps to build their capacity and leadership identity.

In giving feedback, participants report that their learning experience is meaningful and relevant. Participants gain relationships across campus, new perspectives and understandings of self and of leadership, and courage to speak and act even when the outcome is uncertain. As these graduate students continue their study and work on our campus and in future academic or professional spaces, they will advance CRLL.

As Ekwerike and Priest state, the GSLDP at Kansas State University is a recently new program. It was developed to increase access for leadership learning opportunities for graduate students. Although this program was always focused on supporting students' development of leadership identity, efficacy, and capacity, more recently creating a climate of inclusion was included as a focus of this program. Ekweike and Priest offered that CRLL assisted in their recognition and response to creating and supporting a campus climate of belonging through how the program was designed and ultimately delivered. As we acknowledge this work to be culturally relevant to provide socially just learning spaces is ongoing, Kuhn offers how he is working towards this with the student life staff he leads.

DEVELOPING CULTURALLY RESPONSIVE STUDENT AFFAIRS EDUCATORS
Adam Kuhn

If we are interested in animating CRLL in our programs and services on our campuses, we must commit to contending with historical and sociocultural contexts in which our higher education institutions are situated. Before we can engage strategies for enhancing student leadership learning, we must first consider our own capacity to do so.

For me, as a settler (Truth and Reconciliation Commission of Canada, 2015) who leads a department comprised primarily of settlers and guests, this commitment includes creating ways for our student life staff to explore the historical legacy of colonial violence and cultural genocide enacted on Indigenous people and the ways in which postsecondary institutions have been and continue to be complicit in these legacies. This type of work cannot be accomplished in a 1-day workshop or by simply striving to check "Indigenous learning" off a competency checklist. To me, developing a capacity for CRLL means working to resist the checklist and embracing an ongoing, habitual, career-wide, and lifelong commitment to learning and action. Colonialism in Canada is ongoing, violent, concerns the land, and requires a specific structure of ideology to continue (Cote-Meek, 2014). With this in mind, the commitment to advance CRLL requires that we as student life staff explore our identities in relationship to our shared colonial context and strive to develop our own capacity and sense of efficacy to start and sustain anti-colonial work.

The work of the Truth and Reconciliation Committee of Canada (TRC) guides our department's work, which was formed to document and analyze the lasting impacts of the Canadian residential school system on Indigenous people. The TRC released a summary report of its findings alongside 94 "Calls to Action" in June 2015. At an entrustment ceremony at the University of Toronto on January 13, 2017, elder Andrew Wesley presented our institution's president and provost with a detailed response to the TRC's call, offering 34 recommendations specific to the University of Toronto.

Entitled *Wecheehetowin* (a Cree word, meaning "working together"), the report specifies short- and long-term goals to implement the TRC's calls to action on our campus in areas including research ethics, hiring practices, curriculum, and campus space. The introduction of the report identifies that for far too long, postsecondary institutions have viewed Indigenous learners with a deficit lens and assumed low rates of Indigenous student enrolment, persistence, and graduation was due to students' unpreparedness. In contrast, the Steering Committee that produced Wecheehetowin approached their work from the perspective that the University of Toronto "needs to do more to be deserving of Indigenous students, and to be in right relationship with Indigenous people" (University of Toronto, 2017, p. 2).

With this powerful statement in mind, it was clear for student life staff that in order to take on the important work of advancing the report's recommendations, we needed to critically reflect on how we can contribute to a campus community that is truly deserving of Indigenous students and in right relationship with Indigenous people.

As a student affairs and services team, we evaluated our programs and services to consider ways to act on *Wecheehetowin's* recommendations. We realized quite quickly that before we could responsibly step into this work, we would first need to assess our own capacity. Indigenous leaders on our campus have said repeatedly that before we can move towards reconciliation, we must first come to know the truth. Accordingly, our team would need to seek out research, stories, narratives, and histories that were actively excluded from our own formal educations. To develop our own capacity in this area, we would need to devote time, energy, and resources towards learning about the historical context of exclusion and violence toward Indigenous people in the land we now call Canada.

As a way to enhance our own collective capacity in this area, our team committed to ongoing learning strategies including training, group learning and informal individual professional development activities such as listening to podcasts, viewing films, and reading fiction and nonfiction. We participated in experiential activities such as tours of our campus led by a local nonprofit organization whose goal is to invite participants "to explore Toronto's history as told from the perspective of Indigenous communities" ("First Story Toronto App and Bus Tour," n.d). In the Summer of 2018, our team read *Colonized Classrooms* by esteemed scholar and administrator Dr. Sheila Cote-Meek. Each week team members (including full-time staff and student interns) collaborated to facilitate discussions and activities to help process what we were learning and make connections to our work in cocurricular spaces. As another example, part of our ongoing reflective practice is to collectively consider the politics of land acknowledgements and how settler and guest staff can responsibly engage in the practice in a meaningful way to demonstrate a commitment to right relationships, rather than an impersonal rote procedural requirement. This has involved dialogue and discussions with campus partners, Elders, and institutional leaders to ensure that this learning is taking into account the rich pluralism that exists within local Indigenous communities.

These are just a few examples of how our staff have committed to the continuous process of learning (and unlearning) necessary to advance the work of *Wecheehetown*. We must continue to develop an awareness of the historical legacies and sociocultural contexts we are working within, which means devoting the necessary time and resources to continually enhance our abilities to responsibly step into this work.

At the University of Toronto, Kuhn has dedicated himself to having the hard, ongoing conversations about the historical and sociocultural contexts in which higher education institutions are situated. He acknowledges that embracing a commitment to learning and action is beyond a checklist, but is an ongoing and lifelong commitment to engaging in the hard work. In doing so, Kuhn believes that educators can then develop a capacity to offer CRLL to students. In designing cocurricular programs, it is critical to provide these spaces for educators to learn and unlearn dominant ways of providing leadership learning opportunities.

Though Kuhn focused on educator development for those who facilitate development of cocurricular programs, these points of stepping into the hard work is applicable for all learners. Various contexts and levels in a higher education institutional environment, CRLL can provide the necessary framework and support in moving towards cultural relevance in leadership learning. Whether it is redesigning an office, as Sternberg offered, or a student organizational structure, as Bitton offered, or how day-to-day practices of a student engagement office, as Pierre offered, these structural reformulations have great influence on campus climate. Often overlooked places and populations can also provide great opportunity for CRLL to influence intentional leadership learning. Just as Acosta highlighted opportunities in student conduct offices, Ekwerike and Priest also did this for graduate student learning opportunities. These examples beautifully share how CRLL can influence cocurricular program development but can also be applied in various contexts. In conclusion, we offer questions, in Table 6.1, for consideration when working to operationalize CRLL in cocurricular program development. These questions focus on identity, capacity, efficacy, and the five environmental dimensions that can provide first steps in development of a culturally relevant program.

TABLE 6.1 Culturally Relevant Leadership Learning Considerations: Co-Curricular Program Development

Culturally Relevant Leadership Learning Constructs	Questions for Consideration
Identity	• How will you incorporate identity development as a learning outcome for all co-curricular programming? • What reflective strategies will be used to support students' answers to "Who am I?" • How can you incorporate a life story approach to help all learners see themselves already in the work of leadership?
Capacity	• In what ways will individual leadership learning plans be incorporated for capacity development of student leaders? • For semester long programs, how can you intentionally scaffold learning for maximum capacity development? • How will engaging across differences be integrated in all programs?
Efficacy	• How do you redefine leaders beyond only holding positions? • During student leader trainings, in what ways will you deconstruct and examine internalized subordination and dominance? • In what ways will you create opportunities for students to reflect on what they believe they can do to enact positive change?

(continued)

TABLE 6.1   Culturally Relevant Leadership Learning Considerations: Co-Curricular Program Development (continued)

Culturally Relevant Leadership Learning Constructs	Questions for Consideration
Historical Legacy of Inclusion and Exclusion	• From examining the historical legacy of your program, department, division, and university surrounding values of diversity and inclusion, how do you need to redesign your programming? • How is the history of your institution examined in your leadership learning programs? Do you acknowledge the land you use? Why are buildings named after specific people? • What historical leaders do you present as archetypes in your programs? Do they hold diverse identities?
Compositional Diversity	• What is your process in considering speakers, panelists, and facilitators? Are diverse identities represented? • How are diverse individuals represented (or not represented) in student government and other student organizational leadership positions? • Do student affairs staff demographics align with institutional, local, state, national, global demographics?
Psychological Dimension	• What language is used in your marketing materials and what messages do these send? • Are diverse students included in decision making process for co-curricular programming? • How will participants be invited into the program by both internal and external beliefs?
Behavioral Dimension	• How do you model leadership learning as a liberatory process throughout your programs? • In what ways can you authentically support students to engage across difference? • How do we engage in critical reflection to unlearn and relearn ways to dominate ways of knowing, being, and doing?
Organizational and Structural Dimension	• How will you interrogate student organizational positions and how those positions are selected? • In what ways will development of identity, capacity, and efficacy be integrated into organizational leader trainings? • How will generative practices be intentional in student organizational structures?

7

Implementation of Cocurricular Programs Using Culturally Relevant Leadership Learning

Opportunities for leadership learning in cocurricular contexts continues to be a crucial component of the undergraduate experience (Morgan Acosta, 2018). These opportunities vary from gaining leadership knowledge through speakers, workshops focusing on skill development, training for organizational leader positions, and many other formats. Times vary from short hourly opportunities to longer semester, yearly, or even multiyear programs. Just as higher education mission statements focus on leadership development (Chunoo & Osteen, 2016), the expansion of student opportunities to participate in leadership development in more inclusive and socially just ways are critical for the future of our world (Guthrie & Chunoo, 2018).

Operationalizing Culturally Relevant Leadership Learning, pages 105–122
Copyright © 2021 by Information Age Publishing
All rights of reproduction in any form reserved.

Delivery Strategies for Cocurricluar Programs

Leadership educators serve in various positions across higher education, especially in student affairs roles focused in cocurricular settings. These professionals need to work intentionally to create culturally relevant and socially just learning spaces (Guthrie & Rodriguez, 2018) for all students to feel welcome. In addition to considering the dimensions of the historical legacy of inclusion/exclusion, compositional diversity, psychological, behavioral, and organizational and structural (Bertrand Jones et al., 2016), educators must be intentional about creating culturally relevant cocurricular spaces.

Since leadership is socially constructed (Guthrie et al., 2013; Dugan, 2017), the spaces students inhabit are critical to their view and understanding of leadership. These settings include what is discussed, interaction with others, and what is learned. As Rosch and Collins (2017) state, "Students can learn from their peers, incorporate new perspectives, and practice new behaviors" (p. 10). Co-curricular contexts, such as student organizations and programs, "serve as environments where students learn how to lead, either through the experiences that they encounter or through their interactions with others in these situations" (Sessa et al., 2017, p. 24).

Culturally relevant and socially just learning spaces provide opportunities for personal narratives to be shared and interaction with others who may have different identities, resulting in diverse perspectives. Engaging in conversations from differing perspectives can be challenging but rewarding if supported appropriately by not only program structure, but implementation of programs by educators. Providing opportunities for students to learn from others and experience dissonance from their own perspectives being challenged leads to growth (Guthrie & Rodriguez, 2018).

Language has a profound influence on how space is developed and the comfort of others in that space. It is critical to consider how language is constantly evolving and educator's willingness to learn and adapt demonstrates commitment to strive towards culturally relevant environments. What language educators include in every interaction, such as inclusion of pronouns or identity descriptors in email signatures, are simple but powerful examples in how educators can use language in productively creating culturally relevant and socially just spaces.

Through intentional implementation of cocurricular leadership learning opportunities, diverse students can begin to identify as leaders, develop stronger senses of self, and gain confidence in their abilities. As students get involved in cocurricular student organization and programs appropriately implemented, they "experience threefold levels of growth—as their skills improve, their leadership self-efficacy grows as well, given the real-world impact they see . . . their motivation to lead increases as well" (Rosch & Collins, 2017, p. 17). When we introduce diverse students, especially marginalized leaders, to these culturally relevant learning environments, the effect can be powerful and invite other diverse students into the learning community as well.

The narratives shared in this chapter provide rich illustrations of how the culturally relevant leadership learning model (CRLL) is operationalized in the implementation of various leadership learning opportunities in a co-curricular context. Trisha Teig and Lauren Contreras share how their work with the Colorado Women's College (CWC) leadership scholars program at the University of Denver (DU) has used CRLL to enhance such an affinity-cohort model. Next, lessons learned by offering an intercultural leadership program (ILP) at the University of Nebraska–Lincoln (UNL) are shared by Mac Benavides and Sayrar Chansomebath. Sharrell Hassell-Goodman provides applicable examples of how educators can support students to make meaning of differences in social identities. Organizational change for the Hugh O'Brian Youth Leadership (HOBY) organization, which facilitates leadership development programs for high school students in the United States, is shared by Juan Cruz Mendizabal. Finally, Bailey P. Albrecht and Erin Sylvester Philpot provide how Florida State University (FSU) has based an extended orientation program for first time in college (FTIC) students on CRLL, where students learn about identity, capacity, and efficacy while examining the dimensions.

AFFINITY-COHORT LEADERSHIP LEARNING
Trisha Teig and Lauren Contreras

The CWC Leadership Scholars Program was established in 2016 on the DU campus. DU is a mid-sized, private, predominantly White institution (PWI). In 2018, 25% of DU students identified as persons of color, and only 18.7% were first-generation college students. In recent years, DU has grappled with racial and ethnic discrimination as well as gender violence. For example, in Fall 2018 an e-mail with racist, homophobic, and sexist language targeting a DU administrator was sent campus-wide (Carson, 2018). Research indicates that when students of color face microaggressions, their academics, sense of belonging and well-being are adversely affected (Solorzano et al., 2000; Yosso et al., 2009). When considered through the lens of intersectionality (Crenshaw, 1991), interlocking layers of discrimination compound these issues. Higher education scholars emphasize the need to consider intersectionality, or the "processes through which multiple social identities converge and ultimately shape individual and group experiences" in all programs (Museus & Griffin, 2011, p. 7). It is necessary to build leadership programs that recognize and combat the intersectional oppressions faced by students (Jones, 2016) *and* highlight the strength, possibilities, and collective power of claiming and utilizing intersecting identities of gender, race/ethnicity, and sexuality as part of leadership growth and development.

The CWC Leadership Scholars Program was created to provide academic, financial, and emotional support for undergraduate women who identify as first-generation college students and/or students with underrepresented identities at DU. The program creates a unique ecosystem for participants to create strong, lasting relationships, articulate experiences with others who share similar identities, and imbue leadership learning to empower and enrich participants' personal and professional lives.

The CRLL model outlines five dimensions of the campus climate that impact student leadership development, and this narrative accounts for the psychological dimension, which "focuses on individual views of group relations, perceptions of discrimination, attitudes about difference, students' cognitive and personal growth, and institutional responses to diversity" (Osteen et al., 2016, p. 100). As DU is a PWI, the CWC Leadership Scholars are in an environment where they encounter both racialized and gendered discrimination. The intersectionality of these oppressions (Crenshaw, 1991) compounds the nuanced labyrinth students must navigate in their leadership development (Jones, 2016). Within this challenging context, the scholars are attempting to better understand their leadership identities. Bertrand Jones et al. (2016) call on leadership educators to "assess the learning environment for marginalized students and create opportunities that foster acceptance of differing opinions and experiences while encouraging trust" (p. 18). We strive to create a space in the classroom environment and in cocurricular activities for scholars to better understand how they can engage in learning about leadership as women-identified first generation, and racially underrepresented students in the context of a PWI.

The CRLL model emphasizes the importance of carving out brave and safe spaces for students (Guthrie et al., 2016). In the learning environment, we utilize critical feminist pedagogy, which breaks down hierarchies between the faculty member and students and values the lived experiences of all in the classroom (Danowitz & Tuitt, 2011; hooks, 1994). Initially, this type of pedagogy can create dissonance for scholars. However, this pedagogy allows for scholars to develop a trusting relationship with the faculty as well as their peers. Bertand Jones et al. (2016) explain that students may experience pain as they are unlearning and developing their identities as leaders. As such, the instructor must be patient, understanding, and vulnerable as she assists students in their leadership development.

Our cocurricular programming reinforces classroom learning by strengthening the CWC scholars community and building trust. Twice during the academic year, scholars are required to attend off-campus retreats, where they engage in activities that allow them to develop relationships with each other. Scholars have written "I Am Poems," where they reflect on who they are and where they are from within an asset-based framework. We ask scholars to be vulnerable with one another in order to better understand each other and build trust. The scholars represent a myriad of backgrounds and we understand not all women of color and first-generation women will share the same experiences. Through these activities, the women are able to see how they relate to one another as well as learn about each other's differences. Scholars often remark that they find a home at DU within the CWC scholars program because it is a place where they can be themselves. They report feeling supported and accepted when they may not in other spaces on campus.

The CWC scholars program enhances students' development as leaders. In consideration of two of the three elements of leader development in the CRLL model (Guthrie et al., 2016), the program administrators have incorporated key factors for student growth. We create these opportunities based on best practices identified in the model and through observation and communication with students about their leader development needs.

Conversations with students in the classroom and in cocurricular programming about leader identity development expands through the program curriculum in identifying their own definitions and philosophies of both leaders and leadership through an intersectional lens. Students expand their leader identity development from the first to the second year, particularly as students are presented with opportunities to consider distinctions between leaders and leadership, as well as how leader identity is influenced by their own social identities.

We encourage students' leader identity growth through supporting them in navigating their campus leadership roles. The 2018 email incident placed several scholars in the difficult position of responding as leaders of their organizations. At a rally organized by diversity-oriented clubs, Maria (name changed), a Latina and vice president of the Latinx club, spoke to the crowd emphasizing the need for change on campus. She expressed this was a moment of growth for her in realizing her leader identity as an influencer on campus. However, Maria also expressed frustration with the lack of response from university administration and the burden placed on students of color. This moment clarified for Maria her role as leader, but she also came to recognize the existence of leaders in a hierarchical organization does not equate to the successful accomplishment of leadership processes, particularly for marginalized voices.

Leader efficacy examines the degree to which a person believes they can be a leader or do the work of leadership (Guthrie et al., 2016). Our program focuses on enhancing participants' leader efficacy through the work of two required mentoring programs. Mentoring has been proven as a significant factor in successful progression for college student leadership development (Campbell et al., 2012). The scholars are required to identify postgraduate mentors who encourage their growth. In their first year, students are trained on identifying a mentor, then build a mentor/mentee relationship with goals for each quarter and long-term goals for the year. In their second year, students must maintain their previous mentor and/or identify a new mentor. These structured expectations allow for a firm progression of leader efficacy. The external support from a mentor allows for students to envision their own goals and success by seeing how a role model has accomplished her dreams.

In addition, we incorporate peer mentoring. First year scholars are placed with volunteer upper-class student mentors, which has increased upper-class students' leader efficacy. The women recall challenges in learning to navigate a PWI as a woman of color and/or first- generation college student. They express empathy and hope for how their learning could be useful to first-year scholars. The dedication of the women mentors to ensuring new scholars feel loved and supported is a clear indicator of growing leader efficacy.

Utilizing the CRLL model in the context of a cohort-based affinity group structure allows for a deep application of theoretical foundations. Students' leadership learning cannot be enhanced unless it is contextualized through a critical, intersectional lens. The success of a leadership development program must consider how students' social locations, the intersectionality of participants' identities, the history of exclusion and inclusion at the institution, and the environment students experience within and outside of the program influence their development in leader identity, capacity, and efficacy. For the CWC Leadership Scholars, we recognize and intentionally respond through the frame of the CRLL model to the needs of first-generation women of color to be supported and heard in a unique, brave, and powerful space for leadership learning.

At DU, the CWC) Leadership Scholars Program demonstrates how not only intentionally developing a program with cultural relevance in mind, but so is the implementation. Teig and Contreras share how CRLL is operationalized through the psychological dimension and brings to light how important environment and context is to leadership learning. Since the CWC was created to support undergraduate women who identify as first-generation college students and/or students with underrepresented identities, the intersectionality of these oppressions (Crenshaw, 1991) compounds the nuanced navigation of leadership development. Teig and Contreras offer strategies in how critical considering of social locations, intersectionality of identities, history of institutional exclusion and inclusion, among others influence student development in leader identity, capacity, and efficacy. This affinity-cohort based model provides insight into environments, as does Benavides and Chansomebath's example of delivering an ILP.

INTERCULTURAL LEADERSHIP PROGRAM
Mac Benavides and Sayrar Chansomebath

The Office of Academic Success and Intercultural Services at the UNL offers an 11-week ILP designed to develop students' capacity to foster an inclusive community on campus and beyond. The curriculum of the ILP is grounded in a blend of the CRLL, intercultural development, and strengths-based leadership. Learning objectives include exploring connections between cultural identity and leadership, increasing leadership capacity through developing an understanding of strengths and culture, and improving one's efficacy to engage in the intercultural leadership practice of bridging cultural gaps.

To understand the connection between identity and leadership, ILP sessions were designed with several domains of the CRLL in mind, specifically the historical legacy of inclusion/exclusion, compositional diversity, and the organizational/structural dimension. By engaging in in-depth explorations of individual and structural power and privilege, students were given space to consider how they fit into oppressive and exclusive spaces. To that end, we created an illustrative activity in which students used words, phrases, or images to represent their role in building and/or sustaining an inclusive community. We provided students the last 10 minutes of each session to work on this activity and reflect on how the topics covered that day influenced how they perceived and understood their cultural and leadership identity. The program concluded with a poster presentation in which students articulated their intercultural leadership stories, as well as how they plan to create change moving forward.

Due to limited time, we created additional opportunities for students to engage in rich dialogue around cultural differences. Students were assigned intercultural leadership accountability partners, typically in groups of three. Recognizing the challenges inherent in intercultural learning groups (Turner, 2009), we assigned students based on a number of factors including their identity (race, gender, and geographic origin) and their results on the Intercultural Development Inventory (IDI; Hammer, 2012). Partners met at least three times to discuss their experiences with inclusion/exclusion, how they were or could have been using the content covered in class, and how they could support each other. In this way, students gained more profound understandings of the diverse experiences of their peers and the concept of multiple truths. Each student had their own way of interpreting the world, their place within U.S. society, and their interactions with others. This was a key concept for students to confront, especially for those from dominant identities.

We utilized developmental assessments as one means of increasing students' leadership efficacy. The IDI allowed students to recognize any potential dissonance between perception and reality regarding their capacity to effectively navigate intercultural interactions. By connecting this to the concept of intent versus impact, students made appropriate developmental goals to improve their intercultural competence. Additionally, we provided several coaching sessions to shift students' perspective from a narrative of deficit to one of strengths (Lopez & Louis, 2009). Throughout the ILP, students reflected on how their strengths related to intercultural leadership tools and strategies. Another efficacy-related activity was the active rejection of narratives of normalcy. Assuming the belief that everything is cultural, students questioned how "normal" is determined, and who is subsequently excluded due to socially constructed norms. We addressed deeply embedded biases that negate minoritized ways of being and knowing. By validating these "othered" experiences, we taught minoritized students to reject obvious and hidden messages that tell them they cannot engage in leadership. Students from both nondominant and dominant identities were exposed to ways in which they could foster an inclusive community by breaking down barriers that impede minoritized groups.

In its 2 years of operation, the ILP has positively impacted dozens of students at UNL. However, we must continue to improve the curriculum and the student learning experience. For example, we need to more intentionally dive deeper into difficult conversations around the historical legacy of inclusion and exclusion. Surface-level dialogue, while more comfortable, does not yield deep understanding of minoritized experiences. Educators must create a learning experience that embraces discomfort. Without this, students' ability to build bridges will likely fall flat. Additionally, students reported they would benefit from more role-playing or case-study activities in which they apply their learning in more realistic scenarios. This would enhance students' capacity and efficacy to engage in leadership activity.

The above activities and approaches outline how the ILP was designed to align with CRLL. Framing the curriculum within the model of CRLL created a powerful learning experience for students that has led to real change on campus. Implementing what they learned in the ILP, we have had alumni of the program advocate for more inclusive application review processes in the student governing association, create intercultural learning initiatives within student organizations, take on leadership and mentorship roles with the multicultural community, and more.

Benavides and Chansomebath share powerful examples about implementing the ILP at the UNL. CRLL is operationalized in several ways, including focusing on identity and capacity development, as well as considering historical legacy of inclusion/exclusion, compositional diversity, and organizational/structural dimension. Throughout this 11-week cocurricular program, consideration of power and privilege and reflection on oppressive spaces and how students potentially fit into these oppressive spaces are influential in their leader development. Using visuals to illustrate students' roles in an inclusive community allows for diverse voices to be represented in new ways. This activity is an example of using art as not only an instructional strategy, but also as a learning assessment strategy for facilitators to see if the program is meeting the learning outcomes. As we know, providing multiple, unique opportunities for reflection on identity and space for leader identity development is critical to maximize student learning. Hassell-Goodman provides another example of how she has focused on identity development in leadership in cocurricular spaces.

IDENTITY DEVELOPMENT AND LEADERSHIP
Sharrell Hassell-Goodman

Leadership programs often offer curriculum to address differences in race, gender, and sexual orientation, but educators often fall short in prompting students to make meaning of these differences. In fact, despite employing leadership frameworks, I have created a series of leadership programs as a student affairs professional that neglected equal consideration of students' developmental needs with students' diverse social identities. Though I was intentional in creating environments to engage students in conversations on privilege and oppression, it was challenging to establish an inclusive learning environment when students possessed various developmental readiness for those conversations. Moreover, complications arose when students were triggered by peers whose understanding around issues of diversity and social justice were mismatched. Thus, I have searched for a framework that acknowledges the historical legacy of exclusion and ways leadership can be synonymous with oppression. The CRLL model provides a framework for how leadership educators can honor students' individual identities while also creating capacity and efficacy within the context of their own leadership learning (Bertrand et al., 2016). CRLL increases students' cultural competency by making meaning of the social construction of identities, in relation to systems of oppression, as a foundation to the leadership learning process.

Leadership experiences that mismatch participants' levels can destabilize the identity journey. For example, when considering Black and White students' identity development, Cross (1991) and Helms' (1984) models address the progress through which students' developmental levels differ. Both demonstrate how students are initially unaware of their racial identity and then move towards an internalized understanding; however, in the identity development process students often experience dissonance when their current developmental level is mismatched with that of their peers. Helms' (1984) research is clear that minoritized identity development occurs at a faster pace than those with more privileged identities.

Therefore, leadership programs must consider an array of student identity development models to create experiences that are developmentally appropriate and foster environments that are prepared to support students with conflicting developmental needs. For instance, I have facilitated leadership programs in which students from underrepresented populations chose not to participate, not because they were incapable or uninterested, but rather because they *chose* to retreat from oppressive social structures. Instead, they were searching for community. In many of my leadership programs, Black students have expressed frustration when asked to talk about their experiences with racism on campus and may be resistant to finding commonalities with White students. Perhaps they have experienced a racist incident on campus recently or a series of microaggressions. This can be challenging for those White students who want to learn how to be antiracist by spending time with Black students.

Though I have been focusing on race, students possess multiple identities (Jones & McEwen, 2000), which create circumstances for marginalizing experiences in relation to their race, gender, ethnicity, sexuality, nationality, class, and ability, and so on. In fact, many students' identity development and saliency are connected to systems of oppression (Abes & Kasch, 2007; Jones & Abes, 2013; Reynolds & Pope, 1991). The reconceptualized model of multiple dimensions of identity (Abes et al., 2007) incorporates meaning-making capacity and shows how students perceive their social identities as they navigate contextual influences such as peers' stereotypes. While student identity development frameworks may help in understanding students' experiences, these models can marginalize oppressed students (Abes et al., 2019) and create monolithic expectations around students' experiences, so they must be considered in relation to power and systems of oppression. For example, women of color must navigate leadership hierarchies differently than White males, as they must establish credibility in ways that their White male counterparts do not. Furthermore, an Asian cisgender woman's expectation around credibility may look completely differently than that of a Black trans woman, particularly in varying contexts such as residence halls or academic classrooms. Therein, leadership educators must consider students' identity development, especially as students learn to navigate university settings.

The key to social justice is addressing power inequalities across communities. Power dynamics occur in leadership programs when students with multiple oppressed intersectional identities are expected to teach their peers about oppression and inclusion whilst experiencing microaggressions. Some may believe these students are being given opportunities to lead by sharing their experiences, but this is based on oppressive styles of leadership. Further, leadership itself is a historically elitist construct, so leadership programs should address power dynamics by providing thoughtful attention to student development theory while being careful not to create a monolithic story of students.

For instance, I now begin every leadership education experience by asking students and facilitators to discuss moments in which they have been marginalized and have participated in acts that have marginalized others. This sets the tone that while some have experienced more oppression and privilege than others, we are all continuing to learn and grow. This allows the group to create common language around what it means to be triggered and how to make meaning of these moments. We work through examples and potential fears participants have about this leadership experience and create community expectations, including honoring but not expecting participants to be vulnerable, while also respecting students who need to retreat from the conversation for self-care or opting out of the challenge. I also make sure to recruit facilitators with identities that represent national and institutional demographics, moving beyond one token facilitator of color. Also, when trying the new curriculum, I try to engage in mini pilot leadership sessions with students of varying identities in other venues (i.e., service learning, student activities) to solicit feedback and avoid negatively impacting marginalized identities. I acknowledge I will make mistakes along the way and feedback is part of the refinement process. Leadership education work is never completed.

The above strategies align with the purpose of the CRLL model to increase students' leadership capacity and efficacy by being intentional about integrating students' unique and intersectional identity development with leadership pedagogy and curriculum. As students continue engaging in leadership education framed by this model, they become more culturally competent and engaged in leadership learning.

Hassell-Goodman highlights how CRLL provides a framework for how educators can respect students' individual identities while developing capacity and efficacy within the context of their own learning. However, she expresses how as educators we need to be aware of how students will have different developmental readiness to have such conversations about identity, oppression, power, and privilege. This is a powerful reminder, especially in cocurricular spaces, in developing leadership learning opportunities where everyone can participate. As Hassell-Goodman suggests, considering a multiple student identity development model to create experiences and foster supportive environments can help students engage with conflicting developmental needs. This is true for all students (undergraduate or graduate), contexts (cocurricular or academic), as well as other educators as they continually develop. Hassell-Goodman provides tangible examples that help remind us that while we all come to leadership learning with different lived experiences, especially regarding identity, power, and oppression, we all continue to learn and grow. In the spirit of learning and growing, Mendizabal shares how organizational change to be more culturally relevant can be challenging, but necessary and rewarding.

CRITICAL PERSPECTIVES IN ORGANIZATIONAL CHANGE
Juan Cruz Mendizabal

The HOBY organization is an international nonprofit that facilitates leadership development programs for high school students in the United States and around the world. HOBY hosts an annual World Leadership Congress (WLC) for 400 attendees, approximately one-third of which are international. Given HOBY's status as a premiere youth leadership development program that strives to be culturally relevant, recent WLC volunteer teams have created a sense of urgency about the extent to which the WLC culture and program curriculum do not reflect the organization's intercultural values. This operationalization example focuses on adaptive changes the HOBY WLC leadership team created for its 2019 Congress to begin a long-term organizational culture shift prioritizing inclusive and critically reflective practices. The CRLL model served as a compass for this team's work.

When diagnosing the WLC's curriculum, presenters, and volunteer staff culture, the leadership team determined that the changes needed to address cultural exclusion were beyond a series of tweaks. In response, the WLC volunteer chairperson created a global relations team dedicated to building relationships with HOBY's international affiliates as well as an inclusive wellness team dedicated to leading the identity-based organizational culture shift. The inclusive wellness team—intersecting mental health, physical health, and identity development—would be a team of medics, mental health counselors, and diversity educators who use a collaborative approach to frame the lack of cultural relevance at HOBY as a health issue with very real physical and mental consequences for marginalized attendees.

As the appointed positional leader for inclusive wellness, I led the WLC leadership team in naming and discussing the impact of HOBY's exclusive legacy. While the leadership team believed these conversations were vital and overdue, our struggle was finding the time to list the seemingly endless ways our default volunteer management and program development behaviors were financially inaccessible, White-centric, and U.S.-centric. It was ultimately the unexamined subtleties of our organization—our traditions, norms, and unwritten policies—that fueled our legacy of exclusion, not a strategic desire to be inaccessible. Every meeting we had included more structural and policy changes as proof of our repeated awakenings.

Communicating these changes with volunteers took a considerable amount of effort that often left us exhausted. Nevertheless, the leadership team was accessible for webinars, live chats, and individual phone calls intended to share our new vision of dismantling dominant narratives in WLC spaces. We specifically encouraged volunteers with high capacity and low efficacy to apply for roles with more positional power, as having a vision-aligned volunteer team was more important than selecting volunteers who felt they deserved roles because they "waited their turn" the longest—a norm representative of "old HOBY" volunteer selection.

We noticed how our messaging rocked the psychological foundation of many White volunteers who experienced anger because whiteness was no longer centered in our culture.

Programmatically, conversations about identity helped raise the temperature at WLC through an inclusive wellness-facilitated session called Identity Dinners. While students and volunteers with marginalized identities were able to discuss their lived experiences over dinner, the remaining students and volunteers learned how to talk about identity and allyship without relying on their marginalized peers to be educators. I will never forget the experience of seeing three volunteers of color embrace each other in tears after facilitating their identity group's discussion, grateful to temporarily feel reprieved from conforming to the dominant WLC culture of whiteness. Though other sessions explored intersectionality and identity in an integrated way, creating space that centered marginalized populations during Identity Dinners was described as generative and healing.

It is impossible to repair, in 1 year, the impact of decades-long exclusive leadership development programming. While I am proud of the WLC leadership team and inclusive wellness team's work to deconstruct and dismantle our ways of being, which include the examples offered here and a plethora of others, I understand that an organizational change process like ours will only work if enough people are willing to make unpopular choices to center marginalized voices in years to come. This change is personally and professionally risky as well as time-consuming, energy-depleting, and, at times, morally defeating. However, speaking truth to power and weathering the organizational storm seems to be an adequate beginning for the WLC, and I have hope for our ever-evolving process of realignment.

The HOBY organization strives for culturally relevant programming for high school students, but as Mendizabal discusses, there was room for positive change in the annual WLC. CRLL functioned as a compass for the revision of program curriculum to better align with the organization's intercultural values. One example shared was diverse students and volunteers were invited to discuss their lived experiences, while others learned how to speak about allyship without depending on others to be responsible for their learning. Mendizabal reminds us that engaging this work is not easy nor is it possible to completely deconstruct and reconstruct in a short time, but we must be committed for the long term in mending decades of oppressive programming by being exclusive. Albrecht and Sylvester Philpot share insights from an extended orientation program that engages in the long-term commitment in making positive sustainable change.

FIRST TIME IN COLLEGE STUDENT PROGRAMMING
Bailey P. Albrecht and Erin Sylvester Philpot

The Service Leadership Seminar (SLS) is a program for first time in college (FTIC) students that occurs before the fall academic term at Florida State University (FSU). This leadership program is rooted in connecting participants to their social identities and the ways in which they can create sustainable change through service. Founded in 2002, SLS has evolved from an extended orientation program to a program that helps students explore who they are, develop their capacity for leadership, and reconsider the impact of their service. In 2008, SLS began using the social change model of leadership development (Higher Education Research Institute [HERI], 1996; Komives et al., 2017), as a curricular framework. As the needs and aptitude of students evolved, and with an aim of adding content to the curriculum that addressed culture, socialization, and the intersectionality of identities, the program shifted to the use of the CRLL model as the conceptual framework for the seminar.

To ensure that student facilitators had the ability to deconstruct CRLL in a small group curricular model, weekly meetings were spent diving deeper into the model by starting with reading *New Directions for Student Leadership, No. 152* (Guthrie et al., 2016). Subsequent trainings focused on various aspects of the model in alignment with the mission and learning outcomes of SLS. Pairs of facilitators practiced helping students make meaning of CRLL by identifying personal and campus examples of each of the five frames.

In an effort to make CRLL easier to digest for FTIC students, CRLL content was delivered in three separate sections.

Establishing a common definition of leadership as a process, non-positional, values based, exploring social identities, and guiding participants in exploring their own identity, capacity, and efficacy specific to personal examples.

Introducing participants to the five dimensions of CRLL using examples from society and situating each frame in an FSU context served to ensure that as first-year students, participants had both a common frame of reference and orienting knowledge about the FSU campus culture, resources, and community norms.

Finally, guiding participants in putting it all together by connecting participants' understanding of self and their social identities with a capacity for leadership, students were asked to identify examples of ways in which they had the efficacy to create social change.

Student response to CRLL was overall positive. Entering with varying levels of self-awareness, students experienced moments of self-discovery and awareness of the ways in which they had been socialized to repress their identities or undervalue the identities of others, while others struggled to overcome their social privileges. One student shared that while he valued the transparency and candor with which we revealed examples of the five frames on our campus, he now also experienced fear around if he would be accepted and safe on campus because of his marginalized identities.

A strength of CRLL lies in the invitation to a larger conversation. In asking students to explore their identities, and then consider the five frames constantly at play in our daily lives, we invited dialogue around power, privilege, marginalization, and oppression. The courage to talk about challenging topics, the understanding of systems that created inequality, and the appreciation for the unique identities of others is critically important for students in their leadership practice.

However, when using CRLL with FTIC students, two major shortcomings were experienced. First, staff perceived a robbing of innocence taking place for some of the participants. Staff experienced dissonance between wanting to adequately prepare students to understand themselves as leaders and be equipped to create social change, and the awareness that the moments of celebrating the milestone of attending a college at a major research one institution were taken from them. Secondly, being able to view their campus through a critical lens was not necessarily reciprocated by their campus peers as participants navigated their first semester. A number of participants shared that following their SLS experience they felt empowered to create change, but have struggled to find peers, faculty, or student affairs staff who are prepared and comfortable engaging with them around difficult topics.

CRLL provides a critical approach to the individual and collective experiences of students engaging in leadership. However, the complexities of the model and the candor required to adequately address oppression and systemic bias may be better utilized in a theoretical framework, or with more mature student populations than this FTIC audience. Despite inviting critical conversations, CRLL lacks the "and so now what" piece that so many student leaders seek. Equipped with knowledge from the five dimensions, student leaders are left wrestling with the question of how to do something about the social injustices they could now clearly identify on campus.

The SLS at FSU committed to using CRLL as the conceptual framework for this extended orientation program. CRLL emerges through the implementation of the curricular content in both the student leader training and the student participant content delivery. As Albrecht and Sylvester Philpot share, they intentionally developed content to make aspects of CRLL digestible for first-year students. Although this created some culture shock for some students, by establishing a leadership definition based on social construction, framing the five dimensions CRLL in the institutional context, and supporting students' application to their understanding of self through identity, capacity, and efficacy. Although CRLL was created for educators to frame leadership learning, this program demonstrates how undergraduate students in a cocurricular context can learn about the model and situate themselves in it, which enhances their own CRLL, but also peers as they engage in the university culture.

The use of CRLL in the implementation of cocurricular leadership learning opportunities span various populations and specific contexts. Longer formats, such as Teig and Contreras example on an affinity-cohort model, or Benavides and Chansomebath narrative about an 11-week program, provide guidance to using CRLL as foundational to implementing programs. Hassell-Goodman motivates us to consider students' readiness to engage in tough conversations and engage appropriately. Mendizabal reminds us that organizational change is difficult but rewarding and Albrecht and Sylvester Philpot discuss how not only using CRLL as a framework, but in content delivery as an opportunity for leadership learning. The narratives in this chapter focus on the implementation of various programs in a cocurricular context, but are applicable across contexts, formats, and populations. We conclude this chapter with Table 7.1 where questions for consideration are offered as tools to integrate CRLL constructs into the delivery of cocurricular programs. Our hope is that these questions will offer a starting point in cocurricular programs being more culturally relevant.

TABLE 7.1 Culturally Relevant Leadership Learning Considerations: Implementation of Co-Curricular Programs

Culturally Relevant Leadership Learning Constructs	Questions for Consideration
Identity	• In what ways will you support students in acknowledging, reflecting, and honoring their salient identities? • How will you incorporate leadership identity development in student leader trainings? • How is identity foundational to co-curricular leadership learning opportunities you design?
Capacity	• What activities, role playing, simulations, case studies, or games will be used for students to practice deconstructing complex problems? • How will students be supported when engaging across differences? • How will diverse students be represented in capacity development in your programs?

(continued)

TABLE 7.1   Culturally Relevant Leadership Learning Considerations: Implementation of Co-Curricular Programs (continued)

Culturally Relevant Leadership Learning Constructs	Questions for Consideration
Efficacy	• How are diverse voices and experiences represented and modeled intentionally? • What reflective aspects of a program will support students' belief in their ability to be a leader? • How will your program redefine leadership to being socially just?
Historical Legacy of Inclusion and Exclusion	• How will you include land acknowledgement statements in your programs? • How will historical narratives of diverse leaders and followers be used in the learning of leadership? • In what ways will your program challenge dominant ways of leading (and being)?
Compositional Diversity	• From an audit of identities represented in your programs, what can you determine from who is participating? • How will individuals with diverse race, class, gender, and sexuality be acknowledged, honored, and invited to contribute to the program? • In what ways are your programs interrogating diversity beyond simple numbers of people?
Psychological Dimension	• How will space be created for participants to reflect on their leadership learning? • How will students be supported in confronting differing worldviews from both content and process perspectives? • In what ways will students be challenged to consider and confront the cultural realities that resist necessary change?
Behavioral Dimension	• How are your programs including diverse leaders' ways of being? • In what ways is reflection being modeled as a critical strategy for all leadership learning? • How are your programs interrogating current leader's behaviors?
Organizational and Structural Dimension	• What tools will be utilized, such as critical feminist pedagogy (hooks, 1994), to break down hierarchies between facilitator and students, in the program structure? • How will students be encouraged to use criticality in their own student organizational structures? • How will space be integrated into programs for tough conversations about oppressive structures?

8

Development of Academic Programs Using Culturally Relevant Leadership Learning

As collegiate leadership development programs have increased, growth has occurred in both cocurricular and academic contexts (Guthrie & Jenkins, 2018), as well as in various disciplinary and interdisciplinary frameworks. In research of academic leadership programs in the United States, Guthrie and team (2018) examined 1,558 programs, which represent a diverse group of degree types, including associates ($n = 13$), certificates ($n = 241$), bachelor's (majors and minors; $n = 324$), master's ($n = 651$), and doctoral ($n = 329$). Majors ($n = 206$) were offered almost twice as much as minors ($n = 118$) within bachelor's degrees. The dataset used by Guthrie and team (2018) contained 59 undergraduate leadership certificates, 170 graduate leadership certificate programs, and 12 were unidentifiable according to level. The most frequent graduate level degrees include: Master of Arts ($n = 216$), Master of Sciences ($n = 190$), Doctor of Education ($n = 167$), and Doctor of Philosophy ($n = 125$; Guthrie et al., 2018).

Operationalizing Culturally Relevant Leadership Learning, pages 123–138
Copyright © 2021 by Information Age Publishing
All rights of reproduction in any form reserved.

As Hartz (1998) shared, the first documented teaching in higher education was over 2,300 years ago at Plato's academy. Although focused on philosophy, Plato's teaching was interdisciplinary and multidisciplinary in nature. Aristotle, Plato's most famous student, discussed the importance of educating future leaders (Burkhardt & Zimmerman-Oster, 1999). Aristotle's dedication to teaching future leaders can be seen in his mentoring of Alexander the Great. Looking at the early philosophers provides a foundational framework for the interdisciplinary and multidisciplinary nature of leadership as a discipline. This is especially important for situating academic leadership programs in higher education with cultural relevance at the heart.

Interdisciplinary and Multidisciplinary Concepts

Riggio et al. (2003) state that leadership learning benefits from multiple perspectives, the use of various constructs, and diverse contexts. They make the case that if learning is to be increased, leadership learning opportunities should be multidisciplinary. Students' understandings of various leadership approaches can be enhanced by studying leadership from historical, linguistic, psychological, political, cultural, and sociological viewpoints (Harvey & Riggio, 2011). Wren (1994) discussed examining leadership, as a process, from these multiple perspectives is critical to the foundation of leadership education programs. As Guthrie and Jenkins (2018) state, "Structuring leadership education as an interdisciplinary and multidisciplinary process opens the door to integrate skills and knowledge learned in various contexts" (p. 6).

Considering the various contexts interdisciplinary and multidisciplinary processes provide, using the culturally relevant leadership learning (CRLL) model in academic program development is a natural connection. Focusing on cultural relevance supports interdisciplinary and multidisciplinary frameworks in leadership learning and vice versa. These constructs considered together allow for a more complex, needed foundation for leadership learning to meet the needs of learners to be the future leaders we need in this world.

The narratives shared in this chapter provide rich examples of how the CRLL model is operationalized in the development of leadership development programs in an academic context. Jessica Chung shares her perspective as a curriculum writer and how CRLL has helped her also consider her personal life as well. Jesse R. Ford provides how he creates a culturally relevant syllabus and John Weng discusses how he focuses practicality in creating academic leadership learning opportunities. Finally, Vivechkanand S.

Chunoo discusses how he uses CRLL in an undergraduate course, collaborative leadership, and Audrey Cooper and Julie B. LeBlanc share their perspectives of how CRLL is operationalized in an experientially based undergraduate course. These illustrations of how various aspects of CRLL have been put into practice illuminates a path towards development of more inclusive and socially just academic leadership programs.

CULTURALLY RELEVANT LEADERSHIP LEARNING AS A MIRROR AND A LENS FOR PRACTICE
Jessica Chung

As many would agree, making movement on social justice issues on a personal and organizational level feels daunting. The CRLL (Guthrie et al., 2016, 2017) framework helped me break down the work in ways that felt manageable and more balanced, not only in my curriculum writing role but in my personal life as well.

As a curriculum writer for an academic leadership education and development minor, we very intentionally scaffold different skills and approaches to the lesson plans in our four courses; for example, we build from the individual, to community, to the field, to global, based on the social change model ([SCM]; HERI, 1996; Wagner, 2007). Similarly, we also wanted to scaffold knowledge and approaches to socially just leadership across our program. The CRLL model helps me see how each individual course highlights particular dimensions, and then encourages balance if needed. In our introductory class, the course is very focused on the behavioral and psychological dimensions, with a lot of discussions about individual beliefs and values, with a strong emphasis on group dynamics. Over the years, we've recognized the need for added discussion about the organizational dimension as well, so we incorporated readings and activities around this. Whereas in our global capstone course, there is quite a bit of focus on the organizational/structure dimension as students analyze the power structures of larger systems and their ability to practice leadership within them.

The interesting thing for us is balancing these dimensions within the course level as well as across the program. We realized that we didn't need to rely on the introductory course to do all the focus on structural analysis, but that we could lay the groundwork over time throughout the minor by beginning with focusing more on the individual behavioral and psychological dimensions first.

We as a program were focused a lot on attaining a higher compositional diversity, wanting to be a developmental space for students of color as well as for our predominantly White students. And yet, we would hear anecdotes from students of color who still felt out of place in our program. It was the classic conundrum of recruiting diverse bodies without also making sure it was a supportive space for diverse thoughts, expression, histories, and ways of being. We should have instead been focusing on robustly building on all the other dimensions to make that diversity possible.

So, the CRLL helped me develop our curriculum writing by focusing more of our readings and discussions on the voices that have been excluded in our topics by inviting critique about what may be missing and deconstructing how our structures (like our syllabus) are built for inclusion or exclusion by perpetuating values of whiteness. This hasn't been easy, and we have a lot more to do, but these dimensions helped me give a concrete name to the next steps in the program's evolution.

In similar ways to curriculum writing, the CRLL helps me make sense of and guide my personal development as well. As a middle class Chinese-American woman, it was overwhelming as I grappled with the psychological and behavioral dimensions of my cultural socialization and engagement with difference. I took for granted my own story until I could see how my own leadership journey revealed connections to the CRLL. For example, historically, I have learned more specifically over the years about the inclusion and exclusion of Asian Americans in not only U.S. history, but in organizational leadership roles (called the bamboo ceiling). Structurally, I realized how very few people there were in upper-level positions in my university that looked like me. And I realized how much all of these things influenced the extent to which I identified myself as a leader or felt like I could be successful at leading.

It became clear to me that our society easily identified a certain set of characteristics and strengths as "leader" while overlooking so many others. I finally connected the dots between my socialization as a "docile" Asian woman and how much I overlooked myself in comparison to other prototypical "leaders." It took me years to reshape the story I told myself about my skills—realizing finally that I am not a pushover, but in fact a deep listener and connector. That I wasn't only a follower, but someone who leads from the side via individual relationships. That I wasn't necessarily indecisive, but rather incredibly collaborative with the whole group. Thanks to amazing relationships, I have been able to push my leader identity and confidence in my capacity and efficacy. Seeing how much I discounted my own gifts became a fuel for my own teaching focus: students would know they were capable, that they have gifts to contribute, and that we simply needed to expand the way we see the gifts of others.

Since the burst of energy around racial justice education since George Floyd's murder in May 2020, a lot of jokes have been made about White folks finding their second Black friend in order to feel like a good ally. As an Asian-American woman that grew up in a very White town, this hit home for me. I inadvertently had found myself trying to make up for my homogeneous upbringing by diversifying my present-day friend group. But I had it all wrong. Austin Channing Brown, a Black femme author, talks about how she doesn't want her friendship to be the goal—instead, we should be doing the inner work overtime to make it so Black, Indigenous, people of color feel like a relationship can be built with you.

In some ways, CRLL is a map and in other ways, it is like a lens. Being able to identify the pieces that needed more emphasis helped guide my next steps. Just as helpful, it was a way to help me look at a new situation, a story, an organization, and break it down to questions I could ask, or processes to appreciate. It has been important to me to see CRLL as a process and not just an outcome. After a few years, I know that if we focus on laying a solid foundation in the behavioral, organizational, psychological, and historical dimensions in our spaces, genuine compositional diversity (with all its richness) will simply be inevitable.

In reflection on her role as a curriculum writer for an academic program, Chung says how important it is for her to view CRLL as a process and not just an outcome to try and achieve. This is a powerful observation as it helps to situate CRLL as a tool for ongoing work. It helps the goal of culturally relevant and socially just leadership education as a journey that is more manageable instead of something that at times, can feel unobtainable. Chung used the metaphor of CRLL being both a map and a lens, which is helpful in not only academic program development, but in various contexts, personal development, and scholarship as well. In the next narrative, Ford provides strategies to creating a syllabus that is culturally relevant, which sets the tone for program development and then ultimate implementation.

CULTURALLY RELEVANT SYLLABUS DEVELOPMENT
Jesse R. Ford

As a professor in a school of education, there are many new norms to make meaning of a first-time faculty member's socialization process. A new environment comes with a host of new challenges, faces, buildings, and a knapsack of feelings around developing identity, capacity, and efficacy, three vital components of CRLL (Bertrand Jones et al., 2016; Guthrie et al., 2017). These three areas are interconnected and are used to help students engage in the leadership process. However, these same three areas are critical to understanding my new role as a leader in the classroom. Students enroll in my courses with a host of identities, beliefs, and ideologies around the class, topic, and vicarious assumptions, which anchor their preconceived notions of the classroom and me as an instructor. My role as an instructor in this new environment leaves me to facilitate and create a learning environment. There are several different considerations around establishing a positive rapport, first day icebreakers, and classroom expectations. This environment starts with the construction of my syllabus.

My syllabus has critical components such as office hours, assignments, contact information, and a host of content, generally included in teaching syllabi. However, my syllabus is rooted in creating a culturally responsive and socially just engaging experience in addition to the essential elements. This document includes a land acknowledgment (which is a statement recognizing the traditional territory of the Indigenous people who called the land home before the arrival of settlers), a message on my values around social justice, equity and inclusion, and a snapshot of the CRLL model. It is positioned on my syllabus for two distinct reasons: (a) I inform students that we are cocreating a leadership learning environment where we must knowledge the influence of the five domains (Guthrie et al., 2017) and (b) I believe that all students can learn to be successful and succeed academically, through leadership education. However, based on my own identities and learning process, I know all students do not learn the same way and learning is not a 1-day process. As a result, I operationalize CRLL as a critical component of my process as an educator.

In addition to CRLL being a critical component of my syllabus construction, it is also a major element of class instruction. In my role, I teach a graduate level course called *Leadership in Higher Education*. As we develop leadership educator identities, we unpack the knapsacks of feelings around developing identity, capacity, and efficacy in the classroom. This discharging of feelings acknowledges the power and privilege as we constructed leadership educator identities in conjunction with social identities. As a Black assistant professor, this work is necessary for me in the classroom. For my students and me, the intersections of multiple social identities are critical for building community (Bordas, 2012). Knowing and understanding the context of the ever-changing identity-based learning models is vital as a Black scholar. I am also often working to understand my shifting identities as a leadership educator and a faculty member. This is critical for me as I work toward disarming students (Bloom et al., 2012) and creating a safe space where all voices are heard and valued (Bordas, 2012). While this could be perceived as a small act, in a classroom environment, Guthrie et al. (2017) position "the intricacies of culture and identity on college campuses speak to the need for campus personnel who contribute to creating more inclusive campus environments" (p. 64). As a faculty member teaching leadership in a higher education department, creating an inclusive classroom pushes the agenda forward for strengthening higher education professionals as culturally relevant leadership educators. As a result, my classroom has become a vehicle for creating a space designed to facilitate students' leadership learning, developing identity, capacity, and efficacy in their daily lives.

Ford's narrative points out how the development of a course syllabus is critical to not only establishing the content that will be delivered in an academic course, but also provides the doorway for culturally relevant and socially just leadership learning. Remembering that as leadership educators, we construct others' leadership identities in conjunction with social identities. Intentionally being conscientious of practicality in what and how things are taught emphasizes that learning is not a one-time opportunity or a 1-day process, but constantly evolves. This evolution especially occurs as students' learning is focused on developing their identity, capacity, and efficacy as leaders. In continuing the conversation on the importance of student learning in a culturally relevant way, Weng shares his approach to program development.

A SCHOLAR-PRACTITIONER CASE STUDY
John Weng

The leadership studies minor at the University of San Diego has traditionally utilized the SCM of leadership development (HERI, 1996; Komives & Wagner, 2012) as the predominant leadership model in its curriculum. Designed to be an opportunity for emerging scholars who are currently doctoral students and undergraduate students to collaborate and co-instruct, the leadership minor has traditionally operated with a fairly well-developed curriculum with outcomes aligned to the overall minor. And while teaching to a set and standardized curriculum is not something every instructor will need to work through, the reality of having to work within institutional parameters that align with accreditation and federal requirements around contact hours is likely not unfamiliar.

Using theory as a way to inform practice has been at the core of how I choose to navigate my professional life as a student affairs practitioner. At the same time, I am conscientious of how crucial practicality is when I consider how and what I teach in the classroom. The incorporation of the CRLL model (Bertrand Jones et al., 2016; Guthrie et al., 2017) then becomes particularly enticing and appropriate in the first-year emerging leaders course I've taught in the past. The CRLL model has been a key framework in how I engaged our students in understanding the 7 C's of the SCM. And while the SCM describes a way for students to lead through creating positive social change, I have experienced it as the desired state rather than an active process. The CRLL model is useful as a framework for me to understand how to create learning conditions for the classroom and its co-instructors to explore leadership and develop their identity, capacity, and efficacy as emerging leaders.

In many ways, learning leadership is also to learn about oneself. Indeed, literature exists on ways to utilize the "self-as-instrument" as a leader and consultant to understand others (Cheung-Judge, 2001). Hall (2004) has described the importance of understanding oneself as a way to understand others. Yet, creating a space for first-year undergraduate students to explore their identity involves undoing what they know, how they have learned, and trusting that the classroom can be a space to explore their various identities. Rooted in the Model of Multiple Dimensions of Identity (Abes et al., 2007), the emerging leader's curriculum invites first-year students to begin by understanding power, privilege, and oppression. Through the CRLL lens, this meant first incorporating these concepts in tangible ways they might understand through recent or current events. Then, the students are invited to enter in an exploration of their identity by simply getting in touch with how salient an identity is, framed as "how often they think about their identity." And while the frequency of thought is an oversimplification of saliency, it serves as an entry point in developing an awareness of their identity and brings the capacity training to explore their identities.

While capacity development revolves around what students know, do, and value, in many ways, it also starts with our students' exploration of their identity and developing a capacity to do identity work. In particular, it is creating conditions in a classroom where students can unlearn the didactic forms of education prevalent in primary and secondary education (Griffin, 2006) and transitioning to a modality of learning that is facilitative instead (Hellman, 2014). Then, through lower-risk activities and facilitating to explore theory and models, facilitation is used to explore identity within themselves and amongst their peers. Of course, other skills such as design-thinking (dschool, n.d.) are incorporated. These skills then form the toolbelt for which students can draw upon throughout their undergraduate careers and the rest of their lives.

Lastly, the skills the emerging leaders course emphasizes are introduced and revolve around the resolution of a social issue they identify. Core to the course is an attempt to rapidly prototype and attempt to resolve issues affecting them on the campus or local community. Drawing upon their identities and the capacity developed, efficacy is also developed as they see how they can use their own positionality to address issues directly affecting them or the areas around them. This is then presented to their peers and shared out as a way of helping them develop their sense of being able to enact change.

The CRLL model affords the opportunity for instructors and practitioners to incorporate the concepts of power, privilege, and oppression while centering each students' individual identities. In many ways, it has allowed me to provide my students with an exploration of self and the identities they hold, all while helping them explore their identities as leaders. Further, as instructors we are often burdened with the pressures to align with course outcomes, meet contact hours, and consider things like accreditation. The CRLL model offers an easy and straightforward opportunity to infuse important issues relating to identity and the intersections of power, privilege, and oppression that burden said identities in a tangible manner. Further, it allows the implications of these dynamics to be operationalized and made accessible for students who may be exploring them for the first time.

As a scholar–practitioner, Weng provided an example of how he operationalizes CRLL in the development of an academic program, a leadership studies minor at the University of San Diego. As highlighted, the SCM of leadership development (HERI, 1996; Komives & Wagner, 2012) is the theoretical underpinning of this academic program. However, Weng highlights the use of CRLL as a key component of engaging learners. Integrating leader identity, capacity, and efficacy development work in relation towards enacting social change provides an action orientation to this work. Making discussions of power, privilege, and oppression for diverse identities accessible and developmental, students will not only be exposed to such topics, but will be able to learn and continue to do the work beyond participation in an academic program. As we acknowledge, culturally relevant and socially just leadership learning is an ongoing process, helping students to develop a solid foundation in a brave space is a critical component of continued learning. In continuing the conversation of using CRLL in the development of academically based programs, Chunoo offers insights into a course he instructs at the University of Illinois at Urbana-Champaign.

COLLABORATIVE LEADERSHIP UNDERGRADUATE COURSE
Vivechkanand S. Chunoo

At the University of Illinois at Urbana–Champaign, I teach a course in collaborative leadership (LEAD 480). LEAD 480 is the capstone course for the undergraduate leadership studies minor; a semi-sequenced 17–18 credit program of study. The course is grounded in a collaborative leadership framework (Chrislip, 2002), with supplemental cases drawn from Sawyer's (2017) *Group Genius: The Creative Power of Collaboration*. Over the span of the semester, students work in self-assigned groups to solve self-identified problems across a variety of contexts while leveraging the support of local, state, and national collaborative partners. The goal of the course is to create a positive and sustainable change initiative that addresses each group's focal issue(s) while building new partnerships among relevant stakeholder groups. As a leadership educator who is attempting to leverage various parts of the CRLL model into my work, I actively seek out opportunities to develop my students into culturally relevant collaborative leaders.

In Collaborative Leadership, students have already taken extensive coursework in leadership and most are either holding, or have held, prominent leadership positions in clubs, organizations, and community agencies. However, collaboration in leadership requires students to not only be in touch with their own leader identities, but to understand how others construct their leader identities as well. Furthermore, students in this class work toward a collaborative project that requires them to reconsider their leader identities with respect to the communities they are working with and/or the social issues they seek to change.

Additionally, we use Chrislip's (2002) *The Collaborative Leadership Fieldbook* to guide the process of leading. Although we discuss how identity and other social dynamics impact these processes at every stage, the focus on leadership as a process is unmistakable. As part of the capstone experience, students regularly reflect on their authentic approaches to leading; incorporating the material from this course, as well as what they have learned from their prior coursework, training, and leadership developmental experiences. The course addresses the five dimensions in CRLL: historical legacy of exclusion and inclusion, compositional diversity, behavioral dimension, psychological dimension, and organizational and structural dimension.

The university provides a variety of statements to be included in course syllabi. Separately, a university-approved land acknowledgement exists for use at major activities and events. I include the land acknowledgement statement as a part of my syllabus to honor the historical legacy of the institution and the land upon which it sits as well as to begin to confront the legacy of inclusion and exclusion in higher education (and leadership).

I am the only male faculty member of color in my program, and one of just a few in my department across genders. I have no illusions that my social identities, especially around race and ethnicity, motivate some students to take courses in our area (or my courses specifically) because they see a faculty member "who looks like them." Increasingly, I have seen more students from underrepresented backgrounds in my classroom, leading me to believe that my embodied identities are contributing to a shift in the classroom (if not program) composition.

In Collaborative Leadership, students self-aggregate into groups around specific social issues. Shortly after group formation, we talk about who is in each group and why. I layer a critical social lens onto this discussion to get students thinking about cross-cultural communications. At least once a semester, we do an activity where group members travel into other groups to share their progress and listen to others. The goal of the "team ambassador" activity is to get students interacting and learning from one other outside of their siloed working teams.

Students contend with cognitive dissonance in at least two ways in my class: with respect to their topics and in regard to one other. Topical cognitive dissonance arises when students (and their groups) organize around a social issue they think they know well, and upon further inspection (which is required by the course), come to learn how limited their initial perspectives were. Additionally, interpersonal cognitive dissonance occurs when students realize that other people care about similar social issues, but perhaps for very different reasons (e.g., a student who cares about the health of the natural environment for agricultural purposes and one who cares about the environment to make money from natural resources). Both types of dissonance drive student leadership learning along the psychological dimension.

One of the more challenging parts of Collaborative Leadership is related to the volume of work that must be done outside of class. Students with jobs, those who participate in university athletics, or are taking additional rigorous courses often struggle to keep up with the workload. I actively and continually seek formal and informal feedback and change assignments and course policies and expectations to help students meet their goals. We regularly work together to get students access to the resources (university, department, program, etc.) to help them overcome obstacles and achieve a reasonable measure of success.

Using the CRLL lens to see my own classes helps clarify my values around teaching. Building experiences to be relevant to collaborative leadership in content and honor culturally relevant processes of leadership learning requires a bit of creativity, but yields considerable gains for the investment of time and energy. No course will ever be perfectly culturally relevant, but a deeper understanding of the cultural levers I have access to as an instructor means I can exercise greater flexibility and adaptability to my students' needs. While advanced students may benefit more from entire academic programs rooted in culturally responsive leadership learning, it is far better to have them encounter these ideas as they are wrapping up their college years than never considering them at all.

Chunoo reflects on how building experiences to be culturally relevant in a Collaborative Leadership course helps him clarify his own values in teaching. His goal to develop students into culturally relevant collaborative leaders, emerges in both content and processes of the course. He acknowledges that no course will ever be perfectly culturally relevant but exercising flexibility and adaptability to students' needs is critical in moving towards a culturally relevant and socially just program. The considerations Chunoo offers provides additional insight to the experience Cooper and LeBlanc share in a course, where one author was the instructor, and the coauthor was a student.

FOUNDATION FOR EXPERIENTIAL LEADERSHIP LEARNING
Audrey Cooper and Julie B. LeBlanc

The Leadership Experience course is part of the Undergraduate Certificate in Leadership Studies at Florida State University. In this course, students develop a 120-hour, semester-long experience that can be research, service, or internship focused at a site of their choosing. Over the semester-long course, online meetings supplement student experiences through the development of blog posts, completion of reflection exercises, and support amongst the community of peers in the course.

Julie serves as the instructor of Leadership Experience and Audrey was a student in the course in fulfillment of the certificate program. CRLL is a pedagogical approach that allows students to understand how leadership learning manifests in sites and experiences outside of the classroom. Specifically, in the context of the Leadership Experience course, Audrey and her peers applied and synthesized CRLL as a leadership framework in action. CRLL is a valuable teaching tool that encourages students to build their self-awareness as culturally relevant leaders and explore leadership as a culturally relevant process.

Audrey's Student Perspective

I became exposed to CRLL during my Leadership Experience opportunity, where I interned with an integrated marketing communications agency that served clients across nonprofit, real estate, and government sectors. I was immediately drawn to the culture at my site, which fostered learning, inclusion, and inciting positive change on behalf of its clients and employees. As an aspiring communications professional, it is important to me that I dedicate my time to tasks that challenge me intellectually and make an impact on others. Retrospectively, these characteristics that initially attracted me to the agency were early signs of CRLL in action.

For CRLL to emerge, it is first crucial to recognize the influence which identity, capacity, and efficacy have on the presence and strength of each domain within and across organizations. At the root of a client–agency relationship, the client's identity development shapes their interpretation of the partnership and their responsiveness to the agency's exchanges. This in turn affects their capacity for understanding the benefits of the relationship as well as their self-efficacy, or belief in the likelihood of success. In my experience, I most frequently observed the influence of these within the domain of compositional diversity. The compositional makeup of each of the clients we served vastly differed from each other, as well as from that of our own agency. Therefore, it was crucial that the necessary effort be taken to consider how this affects identity, capacity, and efficacy in order to represent them not only properly, but well. Often, our clients would provide their own internal communications professionals to help bridge this gap, resulting in some of the most progressive exchanges we produced. If not, measures were taken to meet extensively with clients to foster an open, collaborative partnership in preparation for encountering and overcoming obstacles that might emerge due to compositional diversity.

In addition to the agency's mission of building its clients' efficacy, it also prioritized building self-efficacy among its employees. Although my major coursework equipped me with the technical skills required of a successful communications professional, the concept of creating work for client use was foreign and intimidating. Fortunately, the agency leaders seized every moment as an opportunity to help us grow more comfortable and confident in ourselves professionally. Their dedication to helping us improve during such a formative period of life further reiterated my desire to guide others towards awareness of and consideration for CRLL, now that I am able to practice it myself.

With a new understanding of culturally relevant leadership and how to implement it effectively in order to accomplish goals and purposes, I have an increased awareness of how to assess whether or not an organization encompasses these qualities while I prepare to search for postgraduation employment. Ultimately, a true understanding of and desire to implement CRLL in any given group or organization allows for all members to feel valued for what they bring to the table regardless of difference, which renders a greater sense of teamwork and subsequently stronger results. Perhaps the most important lesson, however, is that the work is not over once culturally relevant leadership is at first achieved. Rather, it is something that needs to be consistently nurtured and adapted, just as the people who are nurturing and adapting it do.

Julie's Instructor Perspective

Leadership Experience offers students a unique opportunity to put their coursework into action to better understand how leadership practices play out in sites and contexts beyond the textbook; thus, contributing to the certificate's mission of theory to practice to theory. My hope in using CRLL is that students will take lessons learned from this framework into their careers and communities after graduation, the way Audrey was able to in her leadership experience course site. At its premise, CRLL honors individuals' unique interactions and embodiment of leadership based on identity, inclusion, and exclusion, so it is a natural fit to use CRLL as students grapple with leadership's complex manifestation in diverse settings. As the Leadership Experience course continues to evolve, I am committed to using CRLL as an impactful framework with which students can see themselves as leaders no matter what their perception of and experiences with leadership have been prior to completing the certificate program. I see the impact of CRLL as a teaching tool as two-fold; primarily, the framework positions students as equity-minded leaders who are aware of differences and are empowered to act inclusively. Secondly, CRLL aspires to transform students' ways of seeing themselves and others in the leadership process as we continue to emphasize leadership rooted in justice.

Cooper and LeBlanc's student and instructor perspectives are rich in demonstrating how CRLL is foundational as a leadership framework in action. They also reflect on how using CRLL as a pedagogical approach allows students to reflect personal leadership learning through experiences outside of the classroom as well as in the classroom. These perspectives inspire how students are able to transform their ways of seeing themselves and others in the leadership process. This is an essential aspect of CRLL, especially as social identities and lived experiences are acknowledged and celebrated in leadership learning.

The narratives in this chapter are insightful in illuminating various ways CRLL supports the development of academic programs. Chung, as a curriculum writer for an academic program, shared how viewing CRLL as both a process and an outcome has provided a more holistic approach to program development. Ford extended the conversation to frame the importance of syllabus development in an overall creation of a culturally relevant course. Providing insight on using CRLL to engage learners with certain theories, Weng shared strategies in providing learning opportunities to develop identity, capacity, and efficacy. Chunoo specifically shared how his development of a Collaborative Leadership course helped him reflect on his own practice as a culturally relevant leadership educator. Also, Cooper and LeBlanc provide insightful perspectives of being a student and instructor in a course where CRLL is used in the development and implementation. These narratives offered insights to using CRLL in program development in an academic context. However, these are applicable beyond academic context with minimal variations. Applying these strategies offered in cocurricular contexts, as well as developing research methodology and personal development is effective to the overall operationalizing of CRLL. We conclude this chapter with Table 8.1 where we offer questions for your consideration as you work on developing academic programs. These questions serve as a foundational starting point for integrating CRLL constructs into programs.

TABLE 8.1 Culturally Relevant Leadership Learning Considerations: Development of Academic Programs

Culturally Relevant Leadership Learning Constructs	Questions for Consideration
Identity	• How can identity be presented as a socially constructed concept throughout the curricula? • How will identity be integrated in all areas of the curricula? • In what ways will leadership identity development be explored and infused with salient social identities?
Capacity	• How will the curricula be scaffolded to best develop competencies needed for leadership? • In what ways is reflection integrated throughout the curricula to assist students' development of this skill? • How will authenticity and self-awareness be at the heart of the curricula?

(continued)

TABLE 8.1   Culturally Relevant Leadership Learning Considerations: Development of Academic Programs (continued)

Culturally Relevant Leadership Learning Constructs	Questions for Consideration
Efficacy	• In what ways will issues of power and dominance be deconstructed and examined? • How will topics of adaptive leadership be explored to sharpen learners' belief in the ability to lead? • In what ways will students' own positionality on various social issues be explored in order for them to develop their sense of being able to enact change?
Historical Legacy of Inclusion and Exclusion	• In what ways will your institutional history be explored and connected to leadership learning? • In addition to institutional history, how will opportunities to confront the legacy of inclusion and exclusion in higher education and leadership be discussed? • How will concepts of power, privilege, and oppression be discussed historically throughout the curricula by exploring it in different contexts?
Compositional Diversity	• Throughout the curricula, will diverse authors be included in required course content? • Will the demographics of instructors and teaching assistants align with institutional, local, state, national, and global demographics? • How can curriculum be developed to include all perspectives, even those whose are not in attendance?
Psychological Dimension	• How will courses situate students as equity-minded leaders who are empowered to act inclusively? • In what ways will opportunities for learners' cognitive dissonance be intentionally included in curricula? • How is critical reflection integrated throughout courses?
Behavioral Dimension	• How will opportunities for learners' reflection on their own cultural socialization and engagement with difference be included in the curricula? • In what ways will your program have theory as foundational, but be centered in practice of diverse individuals? • How will all experiences be included, and elitism be eradicated from the curricula?
Organizational and Structural Dimension	• How can your courses be developed or redesigned to challenge the traditional dominant ways of leading? • In what ways will the curriculum be developed with criticality in mind? • How will feedback on courses' cultural relevance be intentionally collected and incorporated into future curriculum revisions?

9

Academic Program Implementation Using Culturally Relevant Leadership Learning

As Guthrie and Jenkins (2018) summarize, academic programs in leadership studies began in the 1980s and into the 1990s, academic programs began to emerge in both undergraduate and graduate education. Just as these academic programs were emerging, more work on how to execute programs on both a macro and micro level also began to improve. As research began to focus on how individuals learn, instructional and learning assessment strategies also become more sophisticated. When examining the use of culturally relevant leadership learning (CRLL) in the delivery of academic programs, instructional strategies and the use of storytelling are worth highlighting.

Instructional Strategies

Thoughtful pedagogical strategies are critical for intentionally designed leadership programs to be delivered in an appropriate way. Pedagogies put CRLL

Operationalizing Culturally Relevant Leadership Learning, pages 139–160
Copyright © 2021 by Information Age Publishing
All rights of reproduction in any form reserved. **139**

into action by considering how participants develop their identity, capacity, and efficacy while attending to the cultural relevance of the learning environment. In academic programs, it is required that learning outcomes are provided and well communicated to students, typically presented in a course syllabus. To implement appropriate pedagogies and their associated activities, and experiences, it is essential to first look at the articulated learning outcomes related to the program (Guthrie & Jenkins, 2018). Rosch and Anthony (2012) state that for leadership educators to maximize students' leadership learning, they "must be intentional in matching their intended program or course outcomes with relevant student and leadership development theory, and then apply effective strategies for the delivery of material to a diverse student population" (p. 38). Not only is bridging learning outcomes to pedagogies applying appropriate leadership concepts, but also focusing on the learners themselves. The diversity, demographics, and readiness of learners is also essential to consider how learners might receive content.

There are several approaches to consider for aligning pedagogical strategies with learning outcomes using CRLL as a supporting framework. One suggestion may be aligning aspects of CRLL with the appropriate instructional strategies. For example, when centering learning in CRLL, evaluate what instructional strategies will best facilitate growth in the areas of identity, capacity, and efficacy. An effective instructional strategy to teach identity development might differ from efficacy, although all three are intertwined. Another approach might be selecting instructional strategies based on how students might demonstrate growth and achievement of a learning outcome regardless of content (Jenkins & Allen, 2017). This focuses on how pedagogy can provide learning in the experience of the instruction. An example might be incorporation of a simulation based in social justice, which by just participating could develop identity, capacity, and efficacy of participants.

Storytelling

Personal narratives and storytelling are often underutilized in delivering academic programs. Although this instructional and assessment strategy is utilized more in leadership learning than other forms of learning, it is a powerful tool in considering the cultural relevance of leadership learning. Both creating personal narratives, sharing them with others, and listening to diverse stories are powerful for learning about lived experiences, our roles in power and authority, and unveiling the influence of systemic oppression in experiences. We believe in the power of storytelling and narratives, and our use of hearing others' lived experiences with using CRLL in different contexts has been effective in learning how to move toward culturally relevant and socially just leadership education.

In continuing to share narratives, this chapter provides examples of how educators have implemented academic programs with the CRLL model in mind. Jasmine D. Collins shares strategies from teaching a course in leadership ethics, through activities designed for students to reflect on their evolving leader identity and how to develop confidence with ethical leaders who can influence positive change. Specific approaches on operationalizing CRLL are shared by Vivechkanand S. Chunoo, who teaches a course on leadership communication. In two specific examples, he breaks down how identity, capacity, and efficacy are focused on as well as the five dimensions of CRLL in this course. A Latinx leadership development undergraduate course is the focus of the next narrative by Maritza Torres where she provides lessons learned from providing such a course. Aliah Mestrovich Seay and Mac Benavides offer insights into implementing a course on culture and context in leadership at Kansas State University. A global leadership course is also the topic of a narrative by Aoi Yamanaka, where CRLL expands beyond a domestic context. Finally, lessons from implementing a leadership development program for faculty and staff focusing on being academic change agents is provided by Amena O. Anderson.

TEACHING LEADERSHIP AND ETHICS
Jasmine D. Collins

I employ CRLL in my *Leadership Ethics and Social Issues: Addressing Contemporary Challenges* course. The purpose of this course is to help students strengthen their capacity for ethical leadership while recognizing that complex interactions of social identity, culture, power, privilege, and oppression will undoubtedly influence the kinds of challenges and decisions that they will face as emerging leaders. Thus, students receive the explicit message that "leadership is a process that is ultimately concerned with fostering change from wherever we are now to some future place or condition that is different" (Astin & Astin, 2000, p. 8) and that the term "leader" does not refer to a person in position of formal authority, but rather anyone one who fosters change.

It is important to foreground the course in this way in order to help students recognize themselves as leaders. The development of a leader identity—a student's own theory about who they are as a leader—serves as an important gateway to engagement and action for students (Bertrand Jones et al., 2016; Guthrie et al., 2017). I carry this theme throughout the course by leading students through several reflective activities. In one activity, students are tasked with creating a leadership vision statement, which asks them to consider the ways they would like to impact the lives of others and how this vision connects to their core values. In another activity, students are asked to map their spheres of influence, incorporating people and communities who have greatly influenced them in addition to the people and communities they believe they currently influence, or will in the future. Through this exercise, students learn two important lessons. For one, they can see that teachers, coaches, friends, parents, and others have had a profound impact on their lives, oftentimes without possessing a formal leadership title. This leads them to recognize an important second point, which is that they can also affect change in the lives of others with or without a formal leadership title.

Although these activities are designed to help students evolve in their identity as a leader and confidence, they have the power to affect change, CRLL recognizes that individuals may vary in their leadership experiences and desire to identify with the leader label, given their social identities and the broader contexts in which leadership learning takes place (Guthrie et al., 2013; Guthrie et al., 2017). Therefore, a large component of my course centers on the social construction of identity and how these identities are rooted in larger systems of power and privilege (Allen, 2010; Johnson, 2017; Tatum, 2000). In connecting these concepts to ethical leadership, students learn about historical practices such as redlining, and how this institutional policy has contributed to racial wealth disparities that are evident in the United States today. Students also learn about gender bias, intersectionality, and organizational barriers that inhibit women from occupying leadership positions in greater numbers. Suggestions for implementing this include:

- Providing a link between historical influences and present-day outcomes provides important context for students, but as the CRLL framework points out, "there are multiple layers of context, including national, institutional, and curricular/cocurricular" (Guthrie et al., 2017, p. 62). With this in mind, I teach an interactive lesson on racial microaggressions (Sue et al., 2007) using a research study from our own campus. Through a hands-on activity, students match anecdotal experiences shared by students in the report to the type of racial microaggression the anecdote exemplifies. More important than the correct match, however, is the feeling students get when seeing our campus from the perspectives of students who experience discomfort, discrimination, and degradation in the very spaces which students in the class frequent regularly. Here are some examples of strategies used:

- We create guidelines for community conduct as a class, which we then print out and refer to throughout the semester:
  - These guidelines go beyond statements of "respect everyone and their viewpoints" to detailing what respect looks, feels and sounds like, how to use inclusive language and the role of data/evidence in supporting claims about social realities.
- For small-group breakout discussions, I often assign groups ahead of time to cultivate interaction with different people in the class.
- For each exam, the class creates a shared study guide—this reinforces the themes of community, collaboration, and mutual accountability.
- I also begin each class session throughout the semester with an icebreaker. Over time, this allows us to get to know each classmate and can create a lighthearted atmosphere which is useful when getting ready to discuss heavy subject matter.

Indeed, my *Leadership Ethics and Social Issues* course challenges students to think beyond the boundaries of their own experiences to understand the responsibilities they have to lead in ethical and socially responsible ways when in a position of influence or power. However, I also strive to equip students with tools and strategies to communicate and collaborate effectively across differences, which is an important duty of leadership educators (Bertrand Jones et al., 2016).

One of the powerful aspects Collins's example provides is how she integrates the development of leader identity into the course, which supports student engagement in the process of leadership and action as a leader. Collins's use of reflective activities to help students strengthen their capacity for ethical leadership is noteworthy. As she states, acknowledging that complexity in interactions of culture, power, privilege, oppression, and social identities will challenge diverse leaders to lead ethically and inform the decisions they will face as leaders. Working to equip students with strategies to communicate across differences, Chunoo tackles this head on in a leadership communication class, which is highlighted in the next two narratives.

IDENTITY, CAPACITY, AND EFFICACY
IN A LEADERSHIP COMMUNICATION COURSE
Vivechkanand S. Chunoo

At the University of Illinois at Urbana-Champaign, I teach a course in Leadership Communications (LEAD 230). LEAD 230 is required for the organizational and community leadership concentration in the agricultural leadership, education, and communications Bachelor of Science. The course is grounded in transformational leadership and guided by Quintanilla and Wahl's (2018) *Business and Professional Communication, 3rd edition.* As a hybrid lecture and discussion course, students work individually, in small teams, and in larger groups to develop written, visual, and oral communication skills. The course's primary objective is to understand the importance of communication in the practice of leadership. Throughout the course, I leverage constructs of identity, capacity, and efficacy as described by the CRLL model to develop professional and authentic ways of communicating among students.

Students in leadership communications tend to be in their first or second year of study. Therefore, they are less likely than their upperclassmen peers to have well-articulated identities around leading in college, and far fewer hold or have held college-level leadership positions (although many bear leadership responsibilities nonetheless). Therefore, I leverage the Four I's of transformational leadership to augment students' communication skills (Bass, 1985) and use the development of those abilities (written, verbal, and nonverbal) to foster leader identity development. For example, to encourage intellectual stimulation, students plan and deliver training presentations on a topic of personal importance. Additionally, to foster individualized consideration, learners provide one another with written, oral, and/or video recorded feedback on presentations. Finally, to engender inspirational motivation, course members produce mini-TED talks centered on individually salient issues.

Admittedly, there is less of an explicit emphasis on leadership processes in this course; however, a great deal of attention is focused on communication processes and the role of communication in leadership. Additionally, the process nature of leadership is nonetheless integrated into course discussions, lab activities, and reflection assignments. Thus, understanding leadership as a process is mediated by students' understanding of communication as a process and the role(s) those processes play in leadership and professional excellence.

In lecture meetings of LEAD 230, we consider standard practices of professional and business etiquette as well as deconstruct who those practices advantage and who they disadvantage. Students are evaluated on their ability to achieve those standards with respect to authentic expressions of identity. In lab meetings, students practice various communication strategies and provide peer feedback. The teaching team actively challenges students to view these communication strategies and feedback processes with respect to social, personal, and ascribed identities.

Students are regularly challenged to develop the communication skills related to leadership capacity. Often, students share stories about leadership successes and failures as sense-making activities around their own capacity for leadership, as well as to understand the capacities of others. Ample opportunities are provided for learners to refine their storytelling abilities (leadership moments), conduct instructional presentations (train), manage mock team meetings (team up), and deliver motivating speeches (inspire). Each of these activities includes peer feedback (coach), and collectively support leadership capacity development.

As anyone might expect, students can be reluctant to deliver planned and unplanned speeches publicly. However, we scaffold public speaking in labs for students to develop a style and approach to speaking publicly to authentically build that skill set. While every student in the course may not be a polished orator by the end of the semester, each of them makes measurable progress across a variety of dimensions. At the conclusion of the course, students effectively (if not confidently) address their entire lecture section; an exercise that requires significant efficacy building throughout the semester.

Leadership communication skill-building can be a fruitful pathway into CRLL. When activities, assignments, and reflections are constructed to foster identity, capacity, and efficacy, they help students develop authentic ways of leading. Although underclass students may not have as many or as varied experiences as their upper class colleagues, any student can benefit from practicing culturally relevant leadership communication skills. Successful culturally relevant leadership educators strive to match their approach to instruction with their content and context.

Communication is an important aspect in the practice of leadership. CRLL helps deconstruct who those communication practices advantage and who they disadvantage in various situations. As Chunoo shares, in the academic class he teaches students are evaluated on their ability to authentically express their identity rather than conforming to the dominant ways only. Chunoo discusses how students practice various communication strategies and provide peer feedback. Peer feedback is a critical element in supporting and challenging peers in the practice of leadership (Guthrie &

Jenkins, 2018). Chunoo offers how communications strategies with respect to students' identities help them develop authentic ways of leading. Overall, the role of communication in developing identity, capacity, and efficacy of students cannot be overemphasized and is often overlooked. Chunoo continues to explore the way CRLL is used in deconstructing communication habits through the five dimensions in this next narrative.

LEADERSHIP AND COMMUNICATION AND THE FIVE DIMENSIONS
Vivechkanand S. Chunoo

My Leadership Communications course (LEAD 230) prepares students to lead change in organizations, communities, and larger society. LEAD 230 is required for agricultural leadership, education and communications Bachelor of Science students in the organizational and community leadership concentration. It blends concepts from professional etiquette, workplace culture, and transformational leadership as students learn to navigate teams of various sizes. Throughout the course, its activities, and our assignments, I leverage the five dimensions of CRLL model to help my students deconstruct and reconstruct their preferred communication habits into ones designed to promote their success and transform their organizations.

As a course rooted in tenets of professionalism and business etiquette, the leadership communications course naturally lends itself to discussions about how professional ways of being (dress, interaction, power dynamics, etc.) have historically privileged members of certain identity groups. Shifting this conversation toward leadership is fairly easy when students are primed to consider how the norms and values of capitalist organizations have historically excluded individuals from diverse backgrounds. Throughout the semester, the teaching team supports students as they practice professionalism and explore authentic leadership simultaneously. This support includes individual and small group conversations, dynamic changes to course assignments (and creative application of rubrics) in response to feedback, and creative crowdsourced problem-solving around campus and community resources.

As a sophomore-level course with no prerequisites, LEAD 230 is a leadership course with lower barriers to entry at my institution. Having minimized enrollment requirements makes it accessible to a wide array of students with a broad swath of social identities. Although the compositional diversity dimension is not entirely concerned with the number of students from marginalized groups, the quality of course activities nonetheless benefits from having large numbers of diverse learners. Increasing participation is accomplished by highlighting speakers with historically underrepresented identities in leadership, using case examples featuring individuals whose intersecting identities are made explicit, and challenging students to view social dynamics from perspectives different from the ones they usually adopt. Featuring prominent examples of transformative and professional leaders, highlighting complex cases, and encouraging perspective-taking challenges students to strive for excellence in diverse ways. These are ideas students may not have considered prior to attending the course.

Given the emphasis on communication skill development in this course, the teaching team pays great attention to both baseline proficiency and proficiency gains among students across a variety of exercises throughout the semester. As we practice written, spoken, and nonverbal forms of communication, we routinely encounter differential sociocultural values in communicating and leading. Resolving these mismatches among individuals involves critically and collaboratively confronting the assumptions underlying behaviors and patterns of action to move them beyond simple adherence to traditional narratives of leadership and communication. As a result of adopting these strategies, students learn productive ways of engaging across social differences.

For every major assignment with an oral communication component, students work in pairs or triads to give and receive feedback on efficiency and effectiveness. This creates opportunities for students to confront differing worldviews from both content and process perspectives. What one student says about a given topic may vary dramatically from the opinions of their feedback partner or team and the ways in which they choose to deliver those messages (structure, verbiage, tone, etc.) may also be drastically different among partners. Nonetheless, students are expected to provide substantive and actionable feedback to their peers, regardless of opinion alignment. These opportunities to engage differing opinions while encouraging trust through constructive feedback is one of the ways we leverage CRLL's psychological dimensions in leadership communications.

Professional excellence and business etiquette have deeply embedded cultural assumptions. As leadership classrooms (including my own) reflect a wider and deeper range of interconnected social identities, it becomes of paramount importance to help students find themselves in the material, the ideas, the activities, and the discussions essential to learning. I continually engage in a rigorous review of these aspects of LEAD 230 to find innovative and relevant depictions of leaders across social identities, social locations, organizations, communities, and the university itself. I also actively involve students in this search; every semester at least one student shares a resource with me that represents a perspective on leadership communications that I had not previously encountered yet speaks to them and their experiences in profound ways. These resources become part of the course for future cohorts of students to review, critique, and incorporate into their leadership learning. Being flexible and responsive to the examples my leadership students surface for their peers is how we exemplify the ideas within the organizational and structural dimensions of CRLL.

Using leadership communication skills as the vehicle to deliver transformational leadership ideas through a CRLL lens presents a plethora of opportunities for robust leadership learning. Taking a culturally relevant stance on leadership communications means constructing assignments, interactive opportunities, activities, discussions, and course readings to provide meaningful content in a way that empowers students to find authentic ways of leading, rather than shallowly assimilating to the pressures of their peers, the department, or the university. Some may argue students new to college may not be adequately prepared to become culturally relevant leadership communicators; however, without opportunities to practice, we actively hinder their growth in these areas. Even novice students can benefit from a CRLL orientation when instructional strategies are matched to educational content and context.

As stated, the need for leaders to be culturally relevant communicators cannot be overstated. In continuing to explore how a leadership communication class operationalizes the CRLL model, Chunoo further shares how the five dimensions support not only the implementation of this leadership learning opportunity, but actual student development. Chunoo emphasizes how using communication is a vehicle to deliver transformational ideas and can lead to positive change. However, the same is true for oppressive ideas being turned into systemic action. As many scholars suggest, language is important to leadership learning (Dugan, 2017; Guthrie et al., 2013), but how leaders communicate is just as important. Focusing on cultural relevance within a communications framework can lead to more diverse transfer of ideas and acceptance to various methods. Considering the five dimensions, not only in a specific course on leadership communication, but how leadership is communicated can be a powerful way to make sure leadership education is socially just. Expanding our conversation in how CRLL is operationalized in undergraduate leadership courses, Maritza Torres shares insights in teaching a Latinx leadership development course.

LATINX LEADERSHIP UNDERGRADUATE COURSE
Maritza Torres

The Latinx Leadership Development class at Florida State University is a theory-to-practice, interactive, and identity-based leadership course discussing and analyzing components of Latinx leadership development. This course explores the historical and cultural aspects of Latinx culture and how it intertwines with leadership development, learning, and practice. Students are assigned to read *Critical Domains of Culturally Relevant Leadership Learning: A Call to Transform Leadership Programs* by Bertrand Jones, Guthrie, and Osteen (2016). This reading is provided to them midsemester because it is pertinent for students to first understand the foundation of Latinx leadership and have been given opportunities in class to critically analyze and assess their readings.

The model is gone over in detail in class; then students are advised to form groups (in class) and use the CRLL model to analyze their campus environment. A discussion is held after the activity about how the domains are relevant to their current experiences as student leaders on campus and how the university environment influences their leadership practice. The CRLL model is integrated into two assignments: *Testimonio* and defining leadership. Each of these assignments encourages students to apply the principles of Latino leadership presented in the book *The Power of Latino Leadership* by Juana Bordas (2013).

In the beginning of the course students were asked to define "Latinx leadership." As the instructor, I saved the responses and presented them to class again during the last 2 weeks of the course. These last 2 weeks, they are asked again to define Latinx leadership, and the instructor compares their definition to the one they presented during the first few weeks of the course. This assignment touches each domain of the CRLL model because students are providing definitions of Latinx leadership based on their experiences, how they were socialized as leaders, and through their environment. For example, aspects of the historical legacy of inclusion and exclusion are present when students discuss leadership as having a leadership title or role. However, some students acknowledged that one does not have to have a title in order to be a leader. In this specific discussion, students mentioned how being an older sibling or church volunteer is also considered leadership, however, that does not align with the mainstream definitions of leadership. Aspects of the behavioral dimension occur when students are discussing the definition of Latinx leadership with their peers and are engaging in discussion with peers from different backgrounds and experiences.

Testimonio is a unique form of storytelling because it must include the intention of affirmation and empowerment (Reyes & Curry Rodriguez, 2012). The goal of *testimonio* is to have individuals write and speak about their experiences as a form of liberation. By doing this, individuals can form communities in which similar experiences are shared and acknowledged. Students write a three- or four-page *testimonio* responding to prompts regarding Latinx leadership.

Students have a day in class in which they learn about *testimonio* and are presented with different types such as: music, art, spoken word, and writing. This is done because once the students have a strong understanding of the history of *testimonio*, their assignments become reflective of that knowledge. This assignment is connected to the CRLL model through the pathways of identity, capacity, and efficacy (Bertrand Jones et al., 2016). As presented in the model, these pathways provide an opportunity for students to reflect on how they engage in the leadership process. Students go through the identity piece by reflecting on their sense of self and how they identify as a leader as well as their social identities. The capacity piece is implemented when students provide examples of principles and course readings that are most applicable to them. In this portion of the prompt, they must think critically on how they enact leadership and whether they are being congruent with their practice. Lastly, the efficacy is present in the last prompt in which they must think about ways in which they will practice Latinx leadership to better themselves and their community.

These are only just two ways in which the CRLL model has been implemented into a Latinx leadership class. It is suggested that instructors present students with the model once they are knowledgeable of the foundations of leadership and theoretical models. For students who are new to leadership, this may be a little difficult, so it is advised that students with leadership experiences and scholarship can better analyze their current environment using CRLL. Overall, this model provided a great framework in which students learn to critically assess their learning environments and how they align (or not) with their own values and practices in leadership.

Storytelling is a powerful way to provide space for cultural relevance and the sharing of lived experiences to emerge. The power of *testimonio*, as Torres discusses, is that it includes intentional affirmation and empowerment. Whether it is through a story, spoken word, written formats, music, art, and such, sharing stories through various formats is a powerful learning opportunity. *Testimonio* can engage students in their sense of self and how their social identities are celebrated. This supports students in developing communication practices, as Chunoo discussed, and allows for lived experiences to be a source of empowerment and learning rather than perceived deficit or shame. Although Torres' narrative explores how *testimonio* is used for a course focused on Latinx leadership development, storytelling as a pedagogy can be used in all courses to center cultural relevance in the curriculum. Next, Mestrovich Seay and Benavides share how they facilitate discussions on privilege and oppression in a course on culture and context, in which personal storytelling is essential.

CULTURE AND CONTEXT IN LEADERSHIP
Aliah Mestrovich Seay and Mac Benavides

As part of the undergraduate leadership studies minor, the Staley School of Leadership Studies at Kansas State University (K-State) offers the course, Culture and Context in Leadership. Students are taught to understand how cultural identities, life experiences, and worldviews affect leadership relationships in relation to privilege and inclusion. In the Fall 2019 semester, several instructors grounded their curriculum in CRLL. With the five critical domains of this model in mind, we framed the course with the belief that every student has a story to tell; a story representing a composite of their cultural and ethnic histories, relationships with power and privilege on individual and systemic planes and understanding of how they navigate the world based on their intersecting identities and experiences.

To begin the conversation on dismantling oppressive systems, it was necessary to surface the historical legacy of whiteness and other narratives of dominance and normalcy (Jones et al., 2016). Students read about McIntosh's (1989) proverbial invisible knapsack to explore White privilege and then used storytelling and facilitated discussions to consider how other forms of individual and systemic privilege affect access to education, career, and community resources. This learning and development required a commitment to understanding historical, social, and political legacies of exclusion primarily represented within concealed stories of historically underrepresented groups.

Dialogic activities throughout the semester focuses on expanding students' worldviews. Through these activities, students articulate a greater understanding of their cultural selves and practiced perspective-taking and empathy to develop deeper awareness of different cultural frameworks. According to Bennet (2004), this developmental process leads to an ethnorelative capacity for adaptive behavior, which not only appreciates cultural differences but shifts and adapts behavior in culturally appropriate ways. While adaptive behavior is discussed throughout the course, students struggle with developmental barriers as most were in the early stages of understanding their own cultural identity as it relates to power, privilege, and systems of oppression. This is the first time many of them actively recognize and question dominant narratives of exclusion. Due to enrollment constraints at a predominantly White institution, the compositional racial and ethnic diversity of this course was lacking. Although demographics in Kansas have shifted in recent years, the university continues to be predominantly White. This created challenges for instructors to avoid leaning into the practice of focusing on the cultural, ally, and leader identity development of White students at the expense of students of color. One way to address this challenge is to intentionally seek out readings, guest speakers, and other opportunities for students to interact with stories of historically underrepresented and underserved communities in a way that does not tokenize or misrepresent these stories.

To foster a learning community that recognizes and accepts multiple truths, we introduced students early in the semester to the Developmental Model of Intercultural Sensitivity ([DMIS]; Bennett, 2004). Consistent with the behavioral and psychological dimensions of CRLL, the DMIS is a tool focused on mindsets towards interactions across different cultural frameworks. The early learning around the DMIS allowed students to be more acutely aware of how and when they dismiss their own or others' minoritized identities: students named it, unpacked it, and took action to change how they were navigating difference. While several tools exist to measure intercultural competence, we were unable to use many of these due to financial and time constraints. Therefore, students' understanding of how they navigate interculturally relied on critical self-reflection, as well as peer and instructor feedback.

The behavioral domain is best represented by the longstanding collaboration with K-State's English Learning Program. Through this partnership, students engaged with international students over two class periods. Discussions were designed to profoundly explore cultural values, beliefs, behaviors, and perceptions that may be similar or different than their own. Through this experience, students began to realize that they could successfully engage across differences. However, recognizing that behavioral adaptation often requires a higher threshold for intercultural discomfort, this experience may have happened too early in the semester when students still struggle with cross-cultural engagement.

Critically examining systemic oppression and adapting structural processes to be more inclusive are central elements of the curriculum. For example, we assigned a policy project which required students to identify an oppressive local, institutional, or political policy and offer an amended option that addressed current asymmetrical power dynamics. However, many students found these systemic concepts difficult to fully comprehend, likely due to the organizational/structural dimension being beyond our students' developmental level.

While CRLL offers a conceptual framework that greatly benefits the leadership development of students, we suggest that the model is lacking attention to developmentally congruent tasks in each of its critical domains. Models like the DMIS serve as an exceptional overlay to enhance classrooms employing CRLL because they encourage different levels of challenge and support depending on students' current mindsets (Bennett, 2004). These models are grounded in the concept that recognizing, tolerating, accepting, and adapting to cultural difference and commonality are all developmental tasks. By addressing the developmental nature of these areas of learning, instructors can truly prepare students to practice inclusive intercultural leadership as an act of advocacy for social change.

As Mestrovich Seay and Benavides highlight, the Culture and Context in Leadership course they teach offers dialogic activities throughout the semester to support the expansion of students' worldviews. These activities provide students the opportunity to reflect and develop deeper awareness of different cultural frameworks. Using the DMIS (Bennett, 2004) with CRLL enhances course implementation by encouraging different levels of support and challenge depending on students' current cultural mindsets. Mestrovich Seay and Benavides emphasize the developmental nature of learning can assist instructors in preparing students for leadership as an act of advocacy for social change. Considering how cultural relevance is essential to not only intercultural leadership, but global leadership, Yamanaka shares her experiences with using CRLL to support implementation in a global leadership course at George Mason University.

GLOBAL LEADERSHIP COURSE
Aoi Yamanaka

The CRLL model is one of the core materials in the INTS 406 Global Leadership course in the School of Integrative Studies at George Mason University. INTS 406 has been offered for undergraduate upper-level students in a face-to-face format. However, this course will be offered in an online format in the near future. In the global leadership course, the main learning outcomes are the following: (a) explain own definitions of global leadership, (b) recognize philosophy of global leadership in oneself and others, (c) understand ideologies and perspectives different from those in the United States, (d) analyze social justice issues in other cultural contexts, and (e) evaluate the importance of global leaders' ethical decision and social responsibilities. In this sense, this course mainly focuses on the analysis of social justice issues in different cultural contexts (or global contexts) and develops its own global leadership philosophy through global leadership models and CRLL. In INTS 406, global contexts are not necessarily defined as they are in non-U.S. countries; rather, the definitions of global contexts in INTS 406 are broad and include groups of people (even in the United States) who are from another country or whose cultural backgrounds are different from that of the United States.

There are mainly two ways that CRLL is incorporated into INTS 406. First, CRLL's five dimensions are utilized to address issues of "cultural" imperialism in academia and social justice fields as well as to discuss issues of applying U.S. perspectives on social justice issues to social justice issues in other countries. Also, students will analyze social justice issues in an organization in the United States and other countries.

For students to familiarize themselves with CRLL's five dimensions (historical legacy of inclusion and exclusion, compositional diversity, psychological dimension, behavioral dimension, and organizational/structural dimension), students first applied these dimensions to analyze George Mason University. After they became familiar with CRLL's five dimensions, a group of students chose to engage in the following activities:

1. Students chose one social justice issue in one organization in another country (e.g., male students receive "priority" to be admitted to a private medical school in Japan). As a group, they analyzed the historical legacy of inclusion and exclusion, compositional diversity, psychological dimension, behavioral dimension, and organizational/structural dimension by applying CRLL.
2. These domains of CRLL resonate with Sorrells' (2020) micro-, meso-, and macro-frame analyses. Thus, students also analyzed the issue at a micro level (e.g., cultural orientation, communication style, organizational factors, situational factors), meso level (e.g., religion, power differences, history of inclusion and exclusion), and macro level (e.g., economic and political factor and influence of media).
3. After students analyzed the one social justice issue in one organization in another country by applying both CRLL and Sorrells' (2020) micro-, meso-, and macro-frame analyses, they discussed how different contexts (e.g., history, culture, organizational structures, history

of inclusion and exclusion, media, religions, economic and political power/structures) would influence social justice issues.

CRLL is also used as an antidote to deficits of currently available global leadership models. Many global leadership models fail to address leadership identities, efficacy, motivation, capacity, and enactment. Also, they do not usually take contexts (such as CRLL's five dimensions) into consideration as a part of the leadership process. To address these issues, CRLL was used in the following steps:

1. Students first analyzed how their intersectional identities affected their own leadership efficacy, motivation, capacity, and enactment.
2. Then, students analyzed how CRLL's five dimensions influenced their leadership identities, efficacy, motivation, capacity, and enactment.
3. After they increased their understanding of CRLL, students analyzed how their leadership identities, efficacy, motivation, capacity, and enactment may change across different contexts (such as organizations in other countries). This analysis was related to the students' analyses of one social justice issue in one organization in another country.
4. Lastly, students wrote global leadership statements/narratives, reflecting on how their intersectional identities affected their own leadership efficacy, motivation, capacity, and enactment as change agents in a society where people with diverse backgrounds interact and various cultures coexist.

Throughout these activities, students developed not only their understanding of how leadership identities, efficacy, motivation, capacity, and enactment as well as their global leadership narratives might change in a different cultural context, but also the analytical skills to assess non-U.S. perspectives on social justice issues to become a change agent in a context where people with diverse backgrounds interact and various cultures coexist. These are essential components of global leadership because various contexts (history, culture, organizational structures, history of inclusion and exclusion, media, religions, and economic and political power/structures) influence social justice issues in different cultural environments, and U.S. perspectives on social justice issues might not be applicable.

In the global leadership course, Yamanaka teaches, she uses the five dimensions in CRLL to address issues of cultural imperialism. She also uses CRLL to highlight deficits of global leadership models, especially the lack of identity, efficacy, and capacity, as well as motivation and enactment in leadership learning opportunities. Yamanaka highlights how often context is not considered and how CRLL helps provide a usable framework for this learning. Specific examples of not only instructional strategies, but learning assessment strategies are offered. One strategy Yamanaka shares is a project where students analyze social justice issues in both the United States and in other countries. This allows learners to discuss the differences in social justice issues globally and to take context into consideration while embracing the pathways to leadership learning. Yamanaka and colleagues shared several examples of how CRLL is supportive in implementing leadership learning for students in an academic setting. In this final chapter narrative, Anderson shares how CRLL supports training for faculty and staff.

DEVELOPING ACADEMIC CHANGE AGENTS
Amena O. Anderson

Inspired by findings from the author's research on men faculty engagement in gender equity work in STEM (Anderson, 2017), which identified *sense of duty* as both an initial and continuous driver of men faculty's engagement in equity work, the course, Developing Academic Change Agents for Social Justice (referred to throughout as "change agent course"), was created. It serves as a mechanism for the cultivation and mobilization/ preparation of a cadre of faculty and staff with a felt *sense of duty* to address injustice and inequity at both their academic unit and broader institutional levels. The change agent course provides an opportunity to scan the university for faculty who are well positioned to enact social justice change and engage them in a unique leadership development experience that will prepare them to do so.

The CRLL model emphasizes the importance of context in leadership learning (Guthrie et al., 2017). The change agent course reflects this tenet in its attention to the nuances of academic culture across disciplines, schools, and colleges, as well as within the larger institution. At the same time, it acknowledges that these cultures are rarely scrutinized, deeply ingrained, and anchor both constructive and destructive organizational norms. A philosophical underpinning of the course is that for social justice change to occur, academic leaders must consider and confront the cultural realities that resist necessary change. Simultaneously, academic leaders must contemplate their role in the maintenance of oppressive cultural norms, as well as their capacity and commitment to challenge them. Thus, academic culture as context is the pertinent backdrop for leadership learning in the change agent course.

CRLL underscores the dynamic interaction between the individual and the leadership process through one's identity, capacity, and efficacy (Bertrand Jones et al., 2016). This dynamic interaction is manifest in each of the three phases of the change agent course.

Phase 1. Love (2000) asserts that our collective complicity in the maintenance of a "dis-equal" system is due to society's socialization process which assigns us to roles as either dominant or subordinate group members. Whether we intend to or not, Love argues that we enact behaviors that reinforce this dis-equality. Based on this change agent course, participants are assigned activities which press them to interrogate their personal and professional roles/identities. Participants' capacity to engage in this form of "systems thinking" (Guthrie et al., 2017, p. 63) has important early implications for their sense of efficacy to be successful in the course.

Phase 2. Course content and activities tap into the critical connection between identity and worldview. Participants describe their positionalities and are sensitized to the limitations of their individual lenses. Both explicit and implicit biases are explored, and distinctions are made between *genuine* blind spots and *willful* blindness when it comes to acknowledging and addressing injustice/inequities. As participants work through these capacity-building activities, their sense of efficacy to identify instances of injustice/inequity increases.

Phase 3. Course content and activities focus on taking action for social justice, as well as accountability (both individual and collective). In this phase, the accrual of more knowledge about why and how inequities and injustice manifest, increase a sense of efficacy to make change, while simultaneously triggering fears about not getting it right by either overreacting or underreacting. Participants consider the conundrum of a *bias toward action* and *the paralysis of analysis*. This dilemma provides a strategic segue to an important discussion about accountability. Love (2000) proffers awareness, analysis, action, and accountability as "elements" of liberatory consciousness" (p. 471). While all the elements are interconnected, accountability is inextricably linked to action (inaction, too). Love explains, "As liberation workers...we will make mistakes. Rather than self-condemnation or blame from others, it will be important to have the opportunity and the openness to hear an analysis from others that allows us to reevaluate problematic behaviors or positions" (p. 473).

Pre and post surveys of course completers indicate significant increases in knowledge and awareness about injustices and inequities in academia as well as significant increases in course completers sense of efficacy to take social justice action within their academic units and across the university (Lisa Dilks et al.'s unpublished study). Data from personal interviews with course completers indicate that many have enacted/are enacting equity and justice promoting practices and policies within their areas of influence and/or in other facets of the institution. Some positive *unexpected* outcomes also appeared, former participants' discernable pride in identification with the change agent course, as well as their desire to sustain their connection with other former participants is one. This cross-disciplinary coalescence of academic change agents poised to transform their institution for social justice represents what Guthrie et al. (2017) describe as emergence. That is, "the collective, dynamic reformulation of a system that produces something fundamentally different from its previous form . . . an organic and naturally occurring system of power resulting from interdependent relationships among individuals" (p. 63). The beginning of *emergence* is a critical endpoint for the change agent course as it "leads to communities of practice and then influential systems of change" (p. 64).

Providing a course titled "Developing Academic Change Agents for Social Justice" at West Virginia University, Anderson has provided an invaluable example of how training the educator through an academic course can push the academy forwards towards socially just leadership education. Framing leadership as interdisciplinary and multidisciplinary, Anderson operationalizes CRLL by implementing the course using the dynamic interaction between the individual and the leadership process through one's identity, capacity, and efficacy. Activities are assigned to have faculty examine their personal and professional roles and identities. As Anderson highlights, this enhances faculty and staff's capacity to engage in this form of thinking and influences their sense of efficacy to not only be successful in the course, but as a culturally relevant and socially just educator.

Although Anderson focused on a course for faculty in a cross-disciplinary context, these strategies can also be successful with graduate and professional students, as well as undergraduate with appropriate implementation. Just as Collins, Chunoo, Torres, Mestrovich Seay and Benavides, and Yamanaka shared how CRLL is supportive in implementing leadership learning in an academic setting, specifically in undergraduate leadership courses, these can be applied to different populations. Not only in graduate and professional student contexts, but with appropriate framing, professional development for faculty and staff as well. Finally, in conclusion, we offer questions for consideration in Table 9.1. We hope these questions cause you to pause and consider how your academic program can be delivered in a more culturally relevant way.

TABLE 9.1   Culturally Relevant Leadership Learning Considerations: Implementation of Academic Programs

Culturally Relevant Leadership Learning Constructs	Questions for Consideration
Identity	• In what ways will you share your personal identities with students? • How will you use tools, such as the Model of Multiple Dimensions of Identity (MMDI) (Jones & McEwen, 2000), in instructional and assessment strategies? • How will identity be integrated throughout the course rather than a "one and done" topic?
Capacity	• What instructional strategies will be used for students to practice deconstructing complex problems? • How will engaging across differences be developed throughout the course? • How will course learning outcomes center capacity development of diverse students?
Efficacy	• How are diverse voices and experiences represented and modeled intentionally? • How will this course redefine who can be leaders and what leadership is beyond positional? • What assessment strategies will be used to honor diverse voices and experiences?
Historical Legacy of Inclusion and Exclusion	• Will you include a land acknowledgement statement in your syllabus? What will this statement include? • How will your classroom be redesigned from historically White learning environments? • How will historical narratives of diverse leaders and followers be used in the learning of leadership?
Compositional Diversity	• Have you done an audit of identities represented in your classes? If so, what can you determine from who is taking your courses? • How will who is included or excluded from academically based course be addressed? • How will race, class, gender, and sexuality be acknowledged and honored in the academic space and contribute to the learning environment?
Psychological Dimension	• How will space be created for learners and instructors to reflect on their leadership learning? • What opportunities will be provided for students to confront differing worldviews from both content and process perspectives? • In what ways will students be challenged to consider and confront the cultural realities that resist necessary change?

(continued)

TABLE 9.1   Culturally Relevant Leadership Learning Considerations: Implementation of Academic Programs (continued)

Culturally Relevant Leadership Learning Constructs	Questions for Consideration
Behavioral Dimension	• In what ways will behaviors of being a leader be redefined to include diverse individuals? • How will observations of the behavior of current leaders be discussed throughout the course? • How will critical reflection be used both as an instructional strategy and an assessment of learning strategy?
Organizational and Structural Dimension	• How will critical pedagogy be integrated throughout curriculum to challenge dominate ways of being? • In what ways will relevant depictions of leaders across social identities, social locations, and organizations be integrated into the structure of the course? • What opportunities will be given for discussion regarding current oppressive practices in higher education?

10

Applying Aspects of Culturally Relevant Leadership Learning to Theoretical Frameworks in Scholarship

Leadership educators have called for more social justice approaches in leadership education scholarship (i.e., Beatty & Manning-Ouellette, 2018; Chunoo et al., 2019; Guthrie & Chunoo, 2018; Guthrie & Chunoo, 2021); however, Chunoo et al. (2019) called for stronger empirical evidence in order to develop and implement high-impact practices in socially just leadership education. Scholars have noted one's positionality must be acknowledged in the research process because social identities are the product of environments, which are undergirded by systems of power and oppression (Abes et al., 2019; Jones & Stewart, 2016).

Reflexivity is considered an integral aspect of qualitative research. It involves us, as researchers, understanding how processes of doing research shape its outcomes (Hardy et al., 2001), reflecting upon the ways in which the researcher carries out their research design, and explaining to the reader how the researcher moves through research design and implementation

Operationalizing Culturally Relevant Leadership Learning, pages 161–179
Copyright © 2021 by Information Age Publishing
All rights of reproduction in any form reserved.   **161**

processes to arrive at certain conclusions. Beatty, Irwin et al. (2020) not only stressed how identity is socially constructed, but also outlines how this "assertion must contend with questions of by whom and for what ends" (p. 2). By not centering social identities in the context of leadership education research in a culturally relevant way, the research will only maintain and reproduce the structures that privilege some while marginalizing others. Before arriving at theoretical and methodological decisions that prioritize social identities, leadership educators must seriously consider two items: one's positionality to leadership education and one's epistemological commitments when framing and implementing conceptual and theoretical frameworks in leadership education scholarship (Beatty, Irwin et al., 2020).

Conceptually Framing Culturally Relevant Leadership Learning as the Researcher

Positionality as a researcher ultimately means asking the question: "Who am I in relation to my participants and my context?" In Leigh Patel's (2016) *Decolonizing Educational Research: From Ownership to Answerability*, she called on researchers to employ a different way of framing their positionality in the research process through asking themselves three questions: "Why me/us?"; "Why this particular study?"; and "Why now?" This framing aligns with the core of culturally relevant leadership learning (CRLL) and approaching research through a socially just lens.

The narratives shared in this chapter provide insight into how the CRLL model is operationalized when considering researcher identity, researcher reflexivity, and implementing conceptual and theoretical frameworks in leadership education. Jennifer M. Batchelder shares how the CRLL dimensions prompted reflection on her own identity as a Chicana researching generativity in the Latinx community. Brittany Brewster provides how CRLL contributed to framing her scholar activist identity. Pei Hu discusses how she centers international student leader identity through the CRLL model in her research. Cassandra R. Kepple frames a leadership scholar identity through her understanding of the CRLL model and Riccardo Purita outlines how he uses the CRLL model to frame his research on social class in higher education. Finally, Antron D. Mahoney shares his process of collecting and analyzing data collected from the most vulnerable minoritized communities. Antron explores how they develop leadership knowledge, skills, and values that are countercultural/institutional.

FILLING IN LITERATURE GAPS THROUGH THE FIVE DIMENSIONS
Jennifer M. Batchelder

It was in my higher education master's leadership education class that I learned about generativity as the fifth of six stages in the leadership identity development (LID) model by Komives et al. (2005). In the LID research, students in the generative stage "began to accept responsibility for developing others and for regenerating or sustaining organizations" (Komives et al., 2005, p. 607). I felt "seen," as this was something I could recall doing at various levels throughout my life. However, when I learned most college students never meet this phase of the LID model, that lightbulb dulled as I felt something was missing. If I had practiced generativity as a child with my family, how were college students not reaching this stage of leadership? Yearning to understand more, I knew I would have to do further research on this topic to understand it more clearly. This is what drew me to my dissertation research on leadership and generativity at Florida State University.

My program included a focus on social justice within our studies which is where I was first introduced to the CRLL model. As I read through the framework, my heart lifted! It gave me a form of permission to challenge leadership education through my cultural lens. I always had the right to take a cultural approach, yet this model demonstrated the dimensions of systems that prevented me from doing so in the first place. With this consideration, I began exploring my study of generativity and leadership through my Chicana/Latina cultural perspective.

In reflecting on the five dimensionss of CRLL, I found myself agreeing and, once again, feeling "seen." As a scholar, I began to consider what taking on this call for culturally relevant learning would look like in my research. In my review of literature on generativity from a historical perspective, I found that while there were arguments for culture's connection to generativity, very few studies included the perspective of people of color. Further, the literature on generativity has not often been told from the perspective of minoritized populations, leaving out their cultural experiences. This certainly demonstrated a lack of compositional diversity in research participants and called for an exploration of generativity from a diverse perspective. While there is some literature on generativity and its relationship with culture, there still does not seem to be enough data speaking to cultural practices of generativity.

My consideration of the psychological dimension relates to my counter experience with generativity in the context of leadership as identified in the LID model. While the LID model identifies generativity as the fifth stage, my lived experiences were telling me my practices of guiding and mentoring others throughout my life were a cultural way of experimenting and engaging in leadership before I had identified myself as a leader. This did not align with the stage development presented within the LID model; so, there had to be more to consider when culture was brought in. Additionally, as I read more literature on Latin* college students' engagement with leadership, I heard the voice of several study participants also demonstrating a challenge with understanding leadership and seeing themselves as leaders. Yet, they shared how they were intentional about learning how to persist then sharing that information with their peers so the next group would not have to struggle: a practice of generative behavior. These countercultural experiences became the crux of my research purpose.

Though I have focused my first study of generativity and leadership on the Latin* student population, I have been conscious for a while of the community-orientation of the Latin* culture, which I believe is foundational for generative behavior. I hope to look further into cultural generativity and leadership as it relates to other community-oriented cultures with the intention of establishing a base for a leadership approach that is founded in culture. With this approach, I am considering the organizational/structural dimension as I work toward creating a framework that considers the overarching picture of leadership education in a diverse world where student learners from various backgrounds and experiences can find a leadership model relatable and approachable. I further consider the behavioral dimension in my work to offer students a framework that can be discussed and practiced across identities within our leadership education programs.

While it would be nice to say these dimensions come naturally in the development of my study, I believe there is humility involved in using your resources, from peers and family to fellow scholars and literature, to refer to as we constantly develop our work. The CRLL model is one that I keep handy to reflect on in both my scholarship and practice!

Through Jennifer's narrative she outlines her process of reflecting on her own identities and situating herself in the research. Jennifer was intentional about approaching the research process from a CRLL framework. Jennifer's narrative outlines her experience of reviewing the literature on generativity from a historical perspective, and how she found that while there were arguments for connecting generativity to culture, very few studies included the perspective of people of color. Interrogating these histories of representation and legacies of inclusion and exclusion are an important aspect of CRLL. Jennifer concluded after doing her own reflections of her identities, she could name how the literature on generativity has erased the perspective of minoritized populations, leaving out their cultural experiences and how she wants her exploration of leadership education and generativity to be rooted in the cultural backgrounds and experiences of Latin* students. In the next narrative, Brittany Brewster shares her process of cultivating a scholarly identity using a culturally relevant leadership framework.

CULTIVATING A SCHOLARLY ACTIVIST IDENTITY
Brittany Brewster

Stories of perseverance through the deep haze of racism and hard-fought progress shared by my grandparents, natives of rural Alabama and Georgia, taught me early the need to cultivate change rested on my shoulders without choice. Communal household responsibilities mirrored group commitments made within my predominantly-Black community. This broader accountability for the collective was inherited from family members and neighbors who stressed the need for critical voices to amplify the experiences of the marginalized. We strived for a better world, together. Growing up, leadership as I understood it was rarely optional.

The language to understand the seeds of collectivism, radical self-love, justice, and leadership planted deep within my spirit were different at the time. Engaging in leadership and activism has and continues to be ever-present in my life story. In countless spaces, I sought to put into practice what was offered to me. This call placed on my spirit to be in service with others tasked me to imagine and move towards liberatory possibilities. It's no surprise they remain at the core of who I am and give purpose to why and how I do the work inside and outside of the academy. Leadership within this chapter of my life has evolved to include a journey of intellectual curiosity and activism. CRLL as a framework reminds me of the endless possibilities that exists when leadership centers our *identities, capacities,* and *efficacies* (Bertrand Jones et al., 2016). Through this process, I've learned and rediscovered my innate capacity to lead and create change via the cultivation of self, skill development, and belief. I offer these experiences as a source of affirmation for those who too find themselves on a journey towards scholarly activism rooted in leadership.

As a Black cisgender woman preparing to complete a doctoral degree, I've occupied and shook up a fair share of spaces established without me in mind. Before I can utter a word into a space, my Black feminine-presenting body speaks for me. It utters some truths and attempts to tell plenty of lies. Rather than internalizing these social signals as limitations, with time, I've come to both imagine and create new possibilities from my distinctive "outsider within" Black feminist standpoint (Collins, 2002). These barriers exist alongside my privileged financially stable middle-class upbringing, heterosexual, able-body and countless other identities which afford me power. This includes my very status as an instructor, former student affairs practitioner, and scholar.

My leadership capacity and efficacy are deeply intertwined with a vast love, value, and commitment to self. Central to this development as a scholar activist has been the knowledge creation of foremother scholars like Anna Julia Cooper, bell hooks, Patricia Hill Collins, Toni Morrison, and Brittney Cooper. Their perspectives of the world further clarified and affirmed my experiences, strengthening my voice and my efficacy to see my scholarship as activism. Likewise, literary perspectives from a wide-range of minoritized viewpoints continues to support a deeper understanding of self in leadership. The saliency of identity within my experiences makes it a necessary starting point of conversations with others and a north star for program, curriculum, and scholarship development. This dialogue is transformative when in space with other minoritized scholars, especially Black women. In tandem, it disrupts the influence of dominant leadership discourse and drowns out attempts to devalue my worldview. Though it is challenging, this greater sense of identity strengthens my ability to no longer believe or hold space for deficit thinking. It has no home here.

Countless knowledge within the academy fails to reach the communities, people, and individual stories who often serve as muses of inspiration for research, theoretical development and practice. Within my own scholarly activist journey, I am reminded how central these stories and experiences are to better understanding our world and the complexity of experience. The pursuit of a PhD was catalyzed by the rampant number of questions I had as opposed to answers as a leadership and community engagement practitioner. Central to this inspiration were the countless experiences of Black undergraduate women who leveraged their leadership to create or shift spaces to amplify untold stories and empower communities. Their narratives shined a light on the sheer power and influence of Black women's leadership and served as an inroad to my own research agenda.

Scholarly pursuits for the minoritized may occur in search of validation of self through inquiry and theory generation (hooks, 2014). The desire to understand a piece of myself by way of studying Black women brought me to academia and stressed the importance of being in culturally responsive spaces. Scholars with shared or adjacent identities often possess wells of knowledge that further skill development central to my understanding of leadership and scholarly activism in practice. In the community, they've introduced me to critical research methodologies and created space for big and small questions I often am too embarrassed to ask in other spaces.

Some have leveraged their social and cultural capital to provide hands-on experience on writing projects, research teams, and academic presentations. Without these individuals and spaces, my competency and belief as a storyteller and intellectual activist would remain underdeveloped.

As the journey to the doctorate begins its final lap, I am reminded of the cyclical influence of others' leadership and activism on my socialization. When I think about scholarly activism, I often reflect on the individuals and experiences who inform my understanding of it as a concept, action, and identity in concert with leadership. I now see clearly the overlap of each and often reflect on its influence on my own leadership story. I share this not to oversimplify a complex journey, but to give you a glimpse into how I continue to evolve as a leadership educator and aspiring intellectual activist.

Brittany's narrative highlights how her cultivating a scholarly activist identity through rediscovering her innate capacity to lead and create change. Brittany shares that her process of becoming and being a scholar activist is rooted in the cultivation of self, skill development, and belief. She addresses how wanting to understand a piece of herself through studying Black women brought her to academia and the importance of being in culturally responsive spaces. Through her narrative, Brittany offers her experiences as a source of affirmation for leadership educators and those who identify as scholars who find themselves reimagining leadership through their engagement in activism and scholarship that advances leadership education. In the reflection that follows, Pei Hu, also offers a personal narrative rooted in her identity as an international student and how engaging in leadership research is rooted in this lived experience.

NARRATIVES OF INTERNATIONAL STUDENT LEADERSHIP DEVELOPMENT
Pei Hu

I am an international doctoral student in the higher education program and work within the Leadership Learning Research Center on campus. My scholarly work has been focused on international student engagement and their leadership development since I started my doctoral program of study. This year, when I was designing a qualitative research project to explore international students' experiences in U.S. higher education institutions, I experienced challenges to find relevant literature either from the fields of international student studies or leadership education. As leadership development for all college students is a commonly stated outcome in U.S. higher education mission statements (The National Task Force on Civic Learning and Democratic Engagement, 2012), "Why is the literature on international students' leadership development so scarce?"; "Should leadership research and scholarship include international student populations?"; and "How?"

I had many conversations regarding my research project and limited literature on my topic with professors in my department, current and graduated PhD students, international students, and scholars. They all think international student leadership development is an important topic deserving of more scholarly attention instead of just mentioning it in institutional missions, but never acting on leadership development for all college students. The professional and personal perspectives my professors and friends shared on my research topic encouraged me to develop my research project on international student leadership development. But at the same time, I was still questioning—if scholars around me all noticed and understood the significance of research on international student development, more people outside of my world may have already noticed that—so why have so few scholars conducted research on this topic?

I did not have solid and structured answers for my aforementioned questions until I read Guthrie et al. (2016) scholarly work on CRLL model, which not only addressed my confusion on why few scholars want to research on international student leadership development, and also provided me with possible approach that I can continue my research on this topic. I wrote a book chapter titled *International Student Leadership Development: Honoring Cultural Identities to Create Inclusive Environments* based on the insights from the CRLL model, in which I explained the diverse and complex identities represented by international student population (i.e., from different countries, different beliefs) that make it challenging to understand leadership development of this diverse student group (Pei, in press). While many leadership educators have agreed that leadership is a socially constructed concept, the CRLL model provided more specifics to help leadership educators understand how individuals from diverse cultural backgrounds may define or perceive leader, leadership, and their efficacy differently. Three dimensions of the CRLL model, identity, capacity, and efficacy, remind leadership educators of their understanding of students' leadership development from a culturally values-based lens. More importantly, it provides directions for leadership educators to support their students' leadership development with the fourth-dimension exterior component of the CRLL model—contextual dimension of campus climate.

In another of my future dissertation work the conceptual framework for the study is formed by combining the CRLL model with the traditional student development outcome assessment model—Astin's (2012) "input-environment-outcome" (I-E-O) model. I used the CRLL model to replace the "environment" component originally in the I-E-O model as presented in Figure 10.1. As the CRLL model mainly focuses on institutional environment and how students from diverse backgrounds may experience leadership development in different contexts, it is reasonable to insert the whole CRLL model to specify the environmental component in the overarching I-E-O model. The CRLL model combined with the I-E-O model makes it possible for leadership educators to explore international student leadership experiences in a comprehensive way by taking both individual student cultural identities and their leadership development in institutional environments into account.

The CRLL model underscores the need for leadership educators to challenge old paradigms of leader and leadership in the context of diversity.

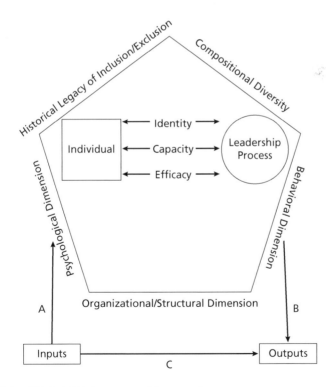

Figure 10.1   CRLL & I-E-O conceptual framework.

In addition, this model helps explain how students with different identities from diverse backgrounds define and experience leadership in the campus environments (Guthrie et al., 2016). Institution's environmental factors could be a possible approach for leadership educators to understand and support leadership development of international students from culturally diverse backgrounds. Five dimensions of the campus climate described in the CRLL model include historical legacy of inclusion/exclusion, compositional diversity, behavioral dimension, organizational/structural dimension, and psychological dimension. Each of these dimensions implies multiple ways we can support international student engagement and further leadership development.

Take the historical legacy of inclusion/exclusion as an example, international students may be not familiar with a foreign country's institutional buildings, statues, or institutional culture, such as homecoming and football. It does not necessarily need to change the historical legacy and transitions of the institution, but it is important to share these historical and culture related information with international students (through campus visits, orientations, online introductions) to make these students feel engaged physically and mentally within their institutions. Sometimes, campus environments may need more transformational change, such as creating new spaces to value international students' religions. It is our responsibility to be aware of the unique needs of international students and do our best to support their culture identity expression and leadership exploration through creating inclusive and safe campus environments for them. The CRLL model makes it possible to promote leadership for all college students including international students, and I am committed to these practice responsibilities.

Pei shares how salient her identity is as an international student engaging in research on international students' leadership development. Pei offers how she often uses a conceptual framework, where she combines the CRLL model with the traditional student development outcome assessment model—Astin's (2012) "input-environment-outcome" (I-E-O) model. Through the narrative, Pei explains how the CRLL model combined with the I-E-O model could be a tool for leadership educators to explore international student leadership experiences in a more culturally applicable way. Pei notes how the combination of the frameworks allows for researchers to center both individual student cultural identities and their leadership development, in the context of the institutional environments. Next, in Cassandra Kepple's narrative, she shares how CRLL aides in her scholar identity development.

USING CULTURALLY RELEVANT LEADERSHIP LEARNING TO DEVELOP A LEADERSHIP-BASED SCHOLAR IDENTITY
Cassandra R. Kepple

As a student scholar preparing to lead my own research in just a few years, I actively work to find various opportunities for me to work with diverse student populations. While I identify as a White female in education and recognize I hold identities that have been traditionally overrepresented in scholarship, I also hold the identity of a first-generation student from Appalachia. As someone who is the first person in their family to ever extensively navigate the postsecondary world, I often find spaces that accept me but are not set up to show me the way. Just as first-generation and lower SES students need colleges to support their sense of belonging (Ardoin, 2018), I hope to use my experiences to increase access and success in college to all students.

Coming into a higher education program, I knew I wanted to work to make college spaces more accessible, so they are meant to exist for students of differing abilities. I am able to do this work and grow in my own leadership capabilities by using the CRLL model. As I reflect on my own development as a leader, I focus on the three processes within CRLL of identity, capacity, and efficacy (Bertrand Jones et al., 2016).

As I look to developing my identity, I focus on how my experiences as a first-generation student have developed my initiatives to increase access to college spaces to anyone who wants to be in them. I act on these ideas using CRLL through my work as a research assistant studying the needs of college students with autism. College students with autism are a historically underserved population who increasingly plan on attending college (Anderson et al., 2016; VanBergeijk et al., 2008). I use the process of identity formation in CRLL to help me understand I can be an advocate for these students and increase accessibility for them just as I wished someone could have helped me. I connect with the idea of an activist leader identity as described by Guthrie et al. (2013), as I try to engage with getting rid of the oppressive structures that are upheld on college campuses today. I continue to define myself as a culturally relevant leader as I work to help raise the voices of students with autism so they may be able to succeed in their postsecondary endeavors.

Exploring my capacity, I also often look at my background and my current experiences in a graduate program focused on student success, leadership, and social justice. I use my degree and experiences in the field of psychology to inform my leadership development by recognizing that neurodiverse students belong in college just as much as any other student. In order to provide them with the best education possible, we must directly find out from the students what they need to succeed, and then actively seek out ways to meet those needs. As I am able to recognize that leaders are needed to help this student population, I design my coursework and experiences in graduate school so I may be able to serve diverse student populations in the best way possible. I specifically build my capacity as a culturally relevant leader by working on a research team that aims to ensure students with autism have the support they need. We do this through studies of college support programs as well as by disseminating recent scholarship about college students' autism through short infographics that are free to the public. As I continue throughout my studies, I aim to continue to build my capacity as a leader through lifting the voices of college students with autism, as well as other underrepresented students, so they may be able to succeed in any college setting.

Defining my identity and capacity contributes heavily to my development in the area of efficacy as well. As efficacy is all about the belief that I am able to succeed in my endeavors, my identity as a first-generation student and my capacity as someone who has worked directly with neurodiverse students and who has studied specifically how we can help students from diverse backgrounds, provide the foundation for my self-efficacy as a leader. Every day, I use my experiences and knowledge base to inform my actions in advocating for colleges to truly be accessible and supportive for all students. As a student scholar, there are plenty of days when my self-efficacy as a leader is not strong. I often doubt if I have enough experience or knowledge to be a successful advocate for diverse student populations. This is where the CRLL model is vital because it shows me that leadership learning is a continuous work in progress, and that I should rely on who I am, and who I want to be, to inform the actions that I take to lead on college campuses.

I use the CRLL model in my daily life as a graduate student working to develop her own leadership identity. I built upon my identity as a first-generation student who often felt disconnected, and sometimes unwelcomed, in the spaces around me throughout college. I work so that we can ensure students do not feel that way on campus. Taking inspiration from my identity, I build my capacity as a leader by seeking out coursework and experiences in research and practice to help open access to all students. In my work as a scholar, this manifests as helping college students with autism have access and success throughout their time in college. I continue to develop my leadership identity through reinforcing my efficacy on a daily basis. I try to identify what I am capable of doing and act upon it. When I identify what I am yet to be capable of, I seek out other scholars and practitioners to help me learn so that I can then be comfortable in action. The CRLL model continues to help me develop my leadership identity as a student, a scholar, and a future professional who is focused on making college a space that is accessible and supports all students.

Cassandra's narrative outlines her process of identity development using CRLL to help her understand that she can be an advocate for students and increase accessibility for them just as she wished someone would have done for her. Cassandra shares how she connects with the idea of an activist leader identity as described by Guthrie et al. (2013), because she works to get rid of the oppressive structures that are upheld on college campuses. She continues to define herself as a culturally relevant leader as she works to help amplify the voices of students with autism so they may be able to succeed in their postsecondary goals. Riccardo outlines his approach to social class identity research in the next narrative.

CULTURALLY RELEVANT LEADERSHIP LEARNING APPROACH TO SOCIAL CLASS IDENTITY RESEARCH
Riccardo Purita

Throughout my life, my immigrant parents have relied on me to take their thoughts and feelings and convey them in an organized manner; whether it was a formal email, a resume for employment, or a business notice. Since English is not their first language, they are less confident in written communication. There is also a lot of cultural capital involved in producing these documents. I have always readily accepted a writing request from my parents in part because of the responsibility I feel towards using my education to help others.

There have been times throughout my 20 years of formal education that I have questioned what the purpose of school was, beyond social mobility. With regular instances of discrimination and oppression happening across this nation, I have found myself uncomfortable being in an academic bubble of privilege. The moments that motivate me to keep going in my education are when I can use it to help others in a tangible way.

This foundation began with my responsibility to my parents and has inspired how I approach my research in higher education. I have been involved in research on food and housing insecurity at campuses. Through that project, we have been able to better understand the college experiences of low-income students and help advance the national conversation on these issues, especially during the COVID-19 pandemic. I helped to build a digital collection of information so students can more easily access local resources to directly support them. With every research project I am involved with, I purposely lay out how it will be used to tangibly help college students in the immediate future.

During my first semester at FSU, I learned about the minimal studies that have been conducted on social class in higher education. There is also yet to be an established theoretical framework for how college students develop their social class identity. From this exploration, I reflected on my own social class and college experiences. In the last year, I have worked to learn as much as I can regarding issues on social class and how to best support low-income students specifically.

I have learned this mentality directly applies to CRLL. The pedagogy in which this theory is modeled (Ladson-Billings, 1995), calls attention to focusing on the interests of marginalized populations like low-income students and responding in ways that directly addresses their interests. My research on low-income students works to honor their identity, capacity, and efficacy. By better understanding the development of social class identity, I hope to promote the learning dimensions of identity and efficacy. I can then use that insight to help programs and offices develop these students' leadership efficacy. It is also important to continue to critically review support programs for low-income students and ensure they celebrate the capacity and assets this population already brings to college.

Developing a social class identity development theory will also encompass the five dimensions of the model: historical legacy of inclusion/exclusion, compositional diversity, psychological dimension, behavioral dimension, and organizational/structural dimension. By creating a theoretical framework, I am validating a major aspect of many students' lives that is often unacknowledged on college campuses and excluded from formal discussion. I hope to draw attention to the importance of having social class diversity at universities. While the number of low-income students at colleges has increased over the years (Smith, 2019), students as a whole need to be intentionally given opportunities to discuss social class with each other. Identity development directly pertains to the psychological and behavioral dimensions by understanding how students view and behave towards others of the same social class and those from different class groups. Higher education promotes middle-class values (Ostrove & Long 2007), which affects how low-income students develop and go through college. Overall, using the aspects of the CRLL model in my research will help guide how I consider social class identity and the way it develops on college campuses.

Over the next few years, I hope to understand the experiences of food and housing insecurity for international students, how to discuss class consciousness with upper-class students, and how to build programs for low-income students that develop leadership efficacy. With all of these initiatives, I will always make sure that I am giving back directly to the communities I work with. This will include partnering with students to finally create a development theory on social class identity. Growing up, I focused on using my education to help my parents. Now, I am ready to share that responsibility with college students around the world through the framework of CRLL.

Riccardo's narrative frames his approach to research through stressing that developing a social class identity development theory also encompasses the five CRLL dimensions of the model. Riccardo's research on low-income students works to honor their identity, capacity, and efficacy. Riccardo hopes to promote the learning and development of these students, focusing on their leader identity and efficacy. Riccardo's goals are to design research that offers insights to support campus programs and offices in developing low-income students' leadership efficacy. Through this research approach, Riccardo also hopes to highlight support programs for low-income students and ensure that the programs celebrate the capacity and assets that this population already brings to college. In the final narrative for this chapter, Antron Mahoney frames the concept as deviance through a CRLL lens.

DEVIANCE AS CULTURALLY RELEVANT LEADERSHIP LEARNING
Antron D. Mahoney

In her seminal essay, "Deviance as Resistance," Cathy Cohen (2004) proposes a paradigm shift in how scholars study Black politics. Specifically, Cohen is concerned with "who" and "what" scholars regard worthy of study, positing "scholars must take up the charge to highlight and detail the agency of those on the outside, those who through their acts of nonconformity choose outsider status" (p. 27). Cohen is referring to those who society deems deviant, racialized subjectivity situated beyond the boundaries of state-affected, normalizing institutions predicated on White capitalist cis-heteropatriarchy. For Cohen, this charge is not simply about an increased representation of vulnerable populations, but a fundamental transformation of what we know and believe to be Black politics, as she states:

> I am suggesting that through a focus on 'deviant' practice we are witness to the power of those at the bottom, whose everyday life decisions challenge, or at least counter, the basic normative assumptions of a society intent on protecting structural and social inequalities under the guise of some normal and natural order to life. (p. 33)

In considering CRLL in leadership research and scholarship, I have found a focus on deviance fully enables CRLL's transformative possibilities.

As the architects of CRLL suggests, this model works to transform leadership programs by addressing how leadership can often be a tool of inequitable power relations (Bertrand Jones et al., 2016). Historically, the scholarship on leadership has been constructed over and against those outside of institutional boundaries, including gender minorities and people of color (Mahoney, 2016). As minority difference has been incorporated into institutions like the academy, that difference has typically been recognized by a set of logics that conform and regulate its neoteric articulations to institutional standards (Ferguson, 2012), thus placing emphasis on exceptional forms of minoritized difference. In leadership studies, this has meant the inclusion of minoritized subjects but typically those who are bodily, most intelligible and utilize recognizable or legitimate forms of leadership, whether that's engagement in formal organizational roles, community service, or even acceptable forms of activism. As Cohen (2004) writes, "Lost in this analysis are the agency and actions of those under surveillance, those being policed, those engaged in disrespectable behavior" (p. 32). Therefore, if CRLL is to address all the ways "advantages and disadvantages difference creates" (Bertrand Jones et al., 2016, p. 10), leadership studies must go low and consider the leadership inherent in the disorderly and disrespectful.

Just as CRLL acknowledges the influence of institutional climate/culture on students' agency for social change, CRLL employed in research and scholarship must also acknowledge the power of institutional climate/culture on leadership scholars' capacity to study and affirm the type of leaders and leadership that may exist in-between and alongside institutionalized structures and ways of being. It is in these alternative life-worlds, where CRLL may truly harness its most transformative possibilities in how we understand leadership. Thus, in my recent study of Black Greek-lettered fraternities and higher education, I took the low road to produce a critical historical analysis of Black fraternalism by centering Black queer fraternal formations, specifically examining those seemingly unruly subjectivities that rest beyond the sights of the university. This approach took me to the underground and private spaces of the nightclub, behind dorm-room doors, and off-campus houses, to uncover a history of Black queer students whose forms of leader self-efficacy and leadership encompass a type of resistance and community building centered around reconfiguring institutional logics of manhood and womanhood.

In this case, the most vulnerable in minoritized communities, those that are not exceptional nor fully included within institutional regimes, develop leadership knowledge, skills, and values that are countercultural/institutional. Cohen (2004) writes, "These so-called deviants have chosen and acted differently, situating their lives in direct contrast to dominant normalized understandings of family, desire, and sex" (p. 30). Cohen articulates what I found to be true in this study. That is, for those with limited agency, there is a leadership capacity to challenging institutional norms that are situated at the intersections of pleasure, desire, recognition, and subjectivity. Consequently, by taking up deviance as CRLL, we must contend with the following questions: "What bodies designate leaders?" And, "What movements qualify as leadership?" For CRLL to truly be a transformative analytical tool, it therefore must seek and contend with subjugated knowledges, those disqualified by institutional logics, which Michel Foucault (1980) insist is where "criticism performs its work" (p. 82).

Antron weaves in the concept of deviance and how he accepts Cohen's (2004) charge of highlighting the agency of those on the outside of the dominant narrative of leadership learning. Antron's narrative outlines how he does this through the key components of the CRLL model. His narrative leaves leadership educators and leadership education researchers with questions to contend with for the purpose of CRLL truly being a transformative analytical tool.

Although Batchelder, Brewster, Kepple, and Purita focused on their scholarly identity as it intersects with their social identities, their strategies are practical reflective tools for considering one's positionality, reflexivity, and conceptual frameworks when designing research from a CRLL lens. Hu and Mahoney, both offer key reimagining possibilities for applying CRLL for research on international students, racially minoritized students, and all students on the margins of leadership learning. Finally, we offer questions for consideration in Table 10.1. We hope these questions cause you to reflect and consider your positionality and approach to leadership education research through a culturally relevant framework.

TABLE 10.1   Culturally Relevant Leadership Learning Considerations: Conceptual/Theoretical Framework in Scholarship

Culturally Relevant Leadership Learning Constructs	Questions for Consideration
Identity	• How can identity and positionality be presented a socially constructed concepts throughout the research process? • How will positionality be negotiated in all areas of the research process? • In what ways will leadership identity development be researched while centering minoritized social identities?
Capacity	• How will leadership theoretical and conceptual frameworks be critiqued and analyzed through a culturally relevant leadership learning lens? • In what ways is reflection integrated throughout the research process to assist the researchers in interrogating their own identity? • What strategies will you employ in order to center identity and self-awareness through the research process?
Efficacy	• In what ways will issues of privilege and structural inequities be deconstructed and examined in the leadership process? • How will topics like deviant practice be explored in leadership learning research? • In what ways will leadership educators' own positionality and intersecting social identities be explored in order for them to develop their sense of researcher identity?
Historical Legacy of Inclusion and Exclusion	• In what ways will your context and environmental history be explored and connected to the theoretical and conceptual framework guiding the research? • In addition to history and environmental context, how can theoretical frameworks confront the legacy of inclusion and exclusion in leadership education research? • How will concepts of socially just leadership education be discussed historically throughout the research design in different contexts?
Compositional Diversity	• How will minoritized experiences be explored through leadership learning research? • Will research participant identities align with the environmental contexts being explored in the research questions? • How can leadership learning research be developed to include more culturally relevant approaches?

(continued)

TABLE 10.1 Culturally Relevant Leadership Learning Considerations: Conceptual/Theoretical Framework in Scholarship (continued)

Culturally Relevant Leadership Learning Constructs	Questions for Consideration
Psychological Dimension	• How can leadership educators also be scholar-activist who are empowered to center socially just research outcomes? • In what ways can leadership learning researchers constantly frame their positionality statements in identity, capacity, and efficacy? • How is socially just reflection integrated throughout the research process?
Behavioral Dimension	• How will researchers' reflection on their own leader identity, capacity, and efficacy be included in the theoretical framework? • In what ways will your research be grounded in a socially just theoretical foundational and center minoritized individuals? • How can oppressive systems be addressed and navigated through the research design?
Organizational and Structural Dimension	• How can leadership education research approaches be redesigned to challenge the traditional dominant ways of inquiry? • In what ways will the theoretical framework and research design be developed with CRLL in mind? • How can research peer debriefing and triangulation be more culturally relevant?

11

Socially Just Research Methods in Operationalizing Culturally Relevant Leadership Learning

Scholars advocating for more socially just leadership education have outlined how undergraduate leadership programs, both curricular and cocurricular, have been built on ideologies and practices of dominant and privileged conceptualizations of leadership (Beatty & Manning-Ouellette, 2018; Dugan, 2017; Guthrie & Chunoo, 2018, 2021; Tapia-Fauselier & Irwin, 2019; Wiborg, 2018). These leadership underpinnings, amongst many others, are equated to individualistic cultures and western ways of knowing and are measures of success or failure. This chapter contributes to the discussion by offering narratives about designing research rooted in addressing dominant ideologies of leadership education. Throughout this section of the book, we offer these narratives from leadership educators that call for those engaged in leadership education to consider pedagogies, practices, and research approaches that decenter dominant ideologies for more socially just, relational ways of knowing. Socially just leadership education

Operationalizing Culturally Relevant Leadership Learning, pages 181–197
Copyright © 2021 by Information Age Publishing
All rights of reproduction in any form reserved.

consists of acts of cognition, not transference of information (Frerie, 1973). For example, "What would leadership learning research look like when using indigenous ways of learning, dialogue, testimonies, storytelling, remembering and reframing to make new meanings of what leadership education research is and can be (Collins, 2000)?"

Bell and Adams (2016) point to social justice education that should be rooted in understanding power, oppression, and socialization, as well as working toward changing oppressive systems. The most effective and efficient ways of meeting these demands is through leadership education centered on liberatory pedagogy (Chunoo et al., 2019), in order to reimagine the possibilities of leadership learning outcomes. This can also be achieved through leadership education taking a more critical social justice approach rooted in CRLL. We recommend centering indigenous and decolonizing perspectives, counternarratives, and socially just research methods with the goal of disrupting the dominant narratives of undergraduate leadership learning research.

The narratives included in this chapter provide critical reflections from leadership educators on how they frame research and assessment from a CRLL approach. Brittany Devies acknowledges the importance of intentionally creating curricular and cocurricular leadership learning experiences using CRLL but calls for that same intention in crafting assessment tools for such leadership experiences. Lori Kniffin shares her dissertation research process and how frameworks like CRLL are not just helpful, but imperative when engaging in community-based leadership. Julie Owen offers insights from her process of writing her book on women and leadership learning for undergraduate students grounded in CRLL. Josephine Shikongo shares her research process of studying Namibian women in leadership and how culture influences women's career progression. The final narrative from Erica Wiborg outlines her call for confronting the systems of oppression that influence the models, theories, ideas, structures, and relationships in leadership programs in order to inform assessments and approaches to research.

FROM INFORMING PRACTICE TO EVALUATING THE WORK: RESEARCH AND ASSESSMENT OF CRLL
Brittany Devies

CRLL was developed as a conceptual tool to help leadership educators to "begin transforming their leadership programs, and thus institutions" (Bertrand Jones et al., 2016, p. 19). As this conceptual framework to leadership learning has become more widely used and implemented in practice, students across the country are experiencing evolved leadership education curriculum as a result. As it continues to be used as a framework to deliver leadership knowledge and provide leadership development, training, and engagement opportunities to students, it also must be researched and assessed to see the ways it is influencing student leadership learning. As much as this framework is used to craft curriculum and frame pedagogical delivery, it must also inform our assessment and research practices. While the original charge called for leadership educators to collectively redesign leadership learning programs with CRLL as a framework, I argue we must also collectively reenvision our assessment and research of these newly redesigned programs.

In most instances, CRLL is used to inform practice, not necessarily as content delivered directly to participants. This means many students in CRLL spaces may not be learning what the historical legacy of inclusion/exclusion domain entails, but are likely learning about the historic traditions of their institutions and instances of oppression against historically marginalized populations. This means as we craft assessments of our leadership learning curriculum, we may not be able to ask "How well did this program help you understand the historical legacy of inclusion/exclusion in the CRLL model?"; but rather "How well did this program prepare you to identify institutional historic events that impact how you learn leadership on campus?"

Being a pedagogical and curricular framework does mean the model influences the leadership learning within the curriculum and therefore, CRLL cannot be left out of our research and assessment practices. CRLL should frame our learning outcomes and curriculum, and therefore must also be the foundation on which we build our post-program, post-course, and postexperience assessments. CRLL influences the practices, pedagogy, reflections, and questions posed by leadership educators to participants. That makes it worthy of research and assessment to see how participants benefit from its tenets.

As we intentionally craft curricular or cocurricular leadership learning experiences using CRLL, we must also carry that same intention in crafting our assessment tools. For example, when making space for leadership learning, you are likely thinking of compositional diversity and its impact on who is in the room. When it comes to assessment, we must also strongly consider who is in our sample and the impact that may have on the leadership learning outcomes we are measuring.

Within research, not only can questions be crafted with CRLL as their foundation, but analysis of findings can also be done with CRLL as a framework. If students talk about a campus policy that made them feel excluded from a space where leadership was happening, it can be deductively coded as an element of the organizational/structural dimension that inhibited their leadership learning. If you are researching leadership educators creating CRLL grounded classrooms, you may hear stories about realizing the importance of sociocultural conversations in the classroom that could be classified as an element of behavioral dimension operationalization.

Beyond assessing and studying the influence of the five domains on leadership learning, it is imperative to the work of leadership education to be studying a student's leader identity, capacity, and efficacy, which are the centric core of the CRLL model. Developing and increasing a student's leader identity, capacity, and efficacy is a center of many leadership education and learning experiences in the curricular and cocurricular spaces. "The combination of identity, capacity, and efficacy describes a student's way of understanding self as an agent of change through interpersonal and intrapersonal development" (Bertrand Jones et al., 2016, p. 12). The beautiful complexity of those three moving between the leader and leadership process and their two-way arrows shows the reciprocal relationship of the leader and leadership process in development (Bertrand Jones et al., 2016). Those rich complex arrows are the human experience in leadership learning that we should be trying to better understand with our research and assessment. The piece that makes this model unique in leadership learning is that it acknowledges that those three arrows do not happen in a bubble. Student learning happens within many layers of context and environment, which we can begin to understand through the five domains: historical legacy of inclusion/exclusion, compositional diversity, psychological dimension, behavioral dimension, and organizational/structural dimension (Bertrand Jones et al., 2016). In operationalizing CRLL to our leadership education experiences, it is critical we also continue to use CRLL as a tool and conceptual framework in our research and assessment practices.

Brittany's narrative applies the CRLL model, and especially gives examples of the environmental dimensions when making space for leadership learning when it comes to assessment. For example, compositional diversity asks us to consider who is in the research or assessment sample and the impact that may have on the leadership learning outcomes being measured. Brittany's examples allow for leadership educators to interrogate their assessment tools and analysis methods from a critical culturally relevant lens. Next, Lori offers insights from her dissertation and outlines the role CRLL can play in community-based research methods.

CULTURALLY RELEVANT LEADERSHIP LEARNING AND COMMUNITY-BASED RESEARCH
Lori E. Kniffin

My journey to using CRLL started with the challenge of creating a zine—a self-published, low circulation booklet with specialized subject matter—as part of a critical pedagogy course. I was in a doctoral program rooted in critical theory and my classmates and I were asked to demonstrate how critical pedagogy intersected with another area of interest. My professional background is in leadership studies, which I had somewhat ignored in my first year of graduate school in order to fully immerse myself in a new scholarly area of critical theory. After finding out that two of my classmates were also interested in the intersections of critical pedagogy and leadership education (in different contexts), we searched for literature at this intersection. CRLL quickly rose to the top of our list as a key framework that focused on leadership education with attention to power, privilege, and social change. The zine opened a door for me to (a) consider the benefit of studying critical theory and leadership together, (b) focus my dissertation inquiry at this intersection, and (c) explore my identity as a critical leadership scholar.

My passion for leadership education stems from my desire to have more people in the world who actively contribute to making progress on our world's complex social issues. There is a heavy focus in leadership education on action. The relationship between the individual and leadership process in CRLL illustrates this desire for individuals to apply leadership learning. I do not believe there is much value to teaching people to lead if there is no "engagement in the leadership process" (Bertrand Jones et al., 2016, p. 12). Yet, sometimes leadership action occurs too quickly and might benefit from consideration of more diagnosis (Heifetz et al., 2009). Therefore, my study of critical theory brought to the fore practices of analyzing power and oppression, reading the world critically (Kincheloe, 2008), and asking questions... lots and lots of questions. The five domains of CRLL illustrate this type of critical work. Sometimes, however, I would get frustrated that this critical practice would get stuck in diagnosis. Through the compilation of the zine, I had my ah-ha moment—that bringing these two worlds together might actually lead to action that is informed by a critical thought.

From the stance of a critical leadership scholar, I began forming my dissertation by asking questions about leadership education:

- Who has access to formal leadership education?
- Whose ideas of leadership are represented in current leadership theories?

- How can leadership development be made accessible in meaningful ways outside of higher education?
- What does the practice of civic leadership look like, and how might this inform civic leadership development?

I focused my dissertation on members of a community coalition who participated in a leadership development grant. I sought to better understand their leadership process within the context of their community work. Without using this language specifically, I included questions about their historical legacy of inclusion/exclusion, compositional diversity, and organizational/structural dimensions (Bertrand Jones et al., 2016; Milem et al., 2005). My findings suggest exercising leadership in civic contexts is deeply contextual and connected to one's intersectional identities. Therefore, frameworks like CRLL are not just helpful but imperative in community-based leadership.

My hope is to extend the thinking of CRLL and other models within critical leadership studies to consider leadership learning in civic contexts for two reasons: (a) leadership is occurring within culturally diverse communities and leadership learning may enhance the practice of civic leadership, and (b) students in higher education are also community members who might be actively practicing leadership in their communities outside of higher education. In short, CRLL is a model at the forefront of understanding intersections of leadership action and critical thought particularly in higher education, and I believe it has value for community leadership development contexts.

Lori shares in her narrative how CRLL is a model that centers the understanding of leadership action and critical thought particularly in higher education, and how this understanding can be useful for community leadership development contexts. Lori breaks down how CRLL and other models within critical leadership studies consider leadership learning in civic contexts. She highlights how leadership is occurring within culturally diverse communities and leadership learning may enhance the practice of civic leadership. She also notes how students in higher education are also community members who might be actively practicing leadership in their communities outside of higher education. Lori concludes that her goal is to extend CRLL thinking into community-based research methods. Next, Julie brings insights from her book and the use of counter-narratives in CRLL research methods.

COUNTER-NARRATIVES AND COURAGEOUS CONVERSATIONS
Julie E. Owen

Many stories matter. Stories have been used to dispossess and to malign. But stories can also be used to empower, and to humanize. Stories can break the dignity of a people. But stories can also repair that broken dignity.

—Chimamanda Ngozi Adichie

In my scholarly work, I have found the use of narratives, or telling stories, to be a profound tool for self-revelation, reflection, and healing. The process of autoethnography helps illicit internal truths and values and can be a useful pathway for all, especially those from historically marginalized communities. This narrative describes how I, along with a talented student research team, used autoethnography to develop narratives and counter-narratives in our shared leadership research and scholarship.

As part of the book, *We are the Leaders We've Been Waiting For: Women and Leadership Development in College* (Owen, 2020a), I invited a group of undergraduate and graduate women of color to undertake a collective auto-ethnographic process, grounded in the CRLL model, to explore how their intersectional identities affect their own leadership efficacy, motivation, capacity, and enactment. The research process included learning about auto-ethnographic research, the CRLL model and its enactment, writing individual auto-ethnographic narratives, sharing those narratives, echo reflections, and editing for publication.

Because leadership is a socially-constructed phenomenon, I consider it essential to center conversations about identity, social location, efficacy, and agency in leadership education (Bertrand Jones et al., 2016; Dugan, 2017; Owen, 2020a). By using narrative, or telling stories, participants and readers alike apply meaning-making and critically reflective frames to leadership. Stories are powerful because they allow others to access our thoughts, feelings, and experiences, and hopefully to find connections. Autoethnography "refers to a particular form of writing that seeks to unite ethnography (looking outward at a world beyond one's own) and autobiographical (gazing inward for a story of one's self) intentions" (Schwandt, 2001, p. 13). I encourage all leadership educators to learn the philosophy, approaches, and skills of autoethnography in order to enhance courageous conversations and leadership learning.

While narratives are powerful, counter-narratives can be transformative. Counter-narratives refer to the telling and listening to stories from those who have been historically marginalized. The goal of counter-narratives is to create opportunities for voices and unique experiences of marginalized populations to be centered rather than being obscured by dominant narratives (Delgado & Stefancic, 2012). The sharing of narratives and counter-narratives has the potential to create empowerment and agency to those who may previously have been silenced. Surfacing counter-narratives is not a new idea, indigenous communities have rich traditions of oral histories. For thousands of years, Aboriginal people have used stories to pass on ecological knowledge, historical events, and spiritual traditions, even when telling such stories was forbidden or outlawed. Latin communities have used *testimonio* as a form of witnessing of oppression and social and political inequality. Myles Horton and colleagues founded the Highlander Folk School in the 1930s to use storytelling to solve community problems which evolved to address civil rights and desegregation in the United States (Horton & Freire, 1990).

If we as leadership educators are committed to creating more emancipatory and equitable spaces, it stands to reason that the use of storytelling, counter-narratives, and autoethnography are crucial scholarly tools. I find that autoethnography allows for participant voice in ways often overlooked in post-positivist research (van Manen, 2018). It allows for learner reflexivity and for the connection of multiple intersectional identities to the theory and practice of leadership education (Jones et al., 2012; McClellan, 2012).

Yet, many educators resist using narratives as part of scholarly pursuits, perhaps because they have not been trained on the philosophy, methodology, and approaches to enacting these processes. Others may critique autoethnography as non-rigorous (La Roux, 2016) or worry about centering student voices in research and scholarship. The CRLL model helped me and my team address these critiques by providing a scholarly foundation for auto-ethnographic work. My belief is that CRLL is an antidote to the proliferation of leadership theories and approaches that do not take identity into account.

Since the *We Are the Leaders* text follows the vast majority of the women's leadership canon and is written by a White woman, I place high value on the collective auto-ethnographic process which provides space for students to name their own experiences and author their own stories. These narratives are embedded in each chapter, not as an ideal for readers to aspire to (though many are worthy of emulation), but as an authentic expression of the lived experiences of dynamic individual college women and gender nonconforming people. I find some of the stories difficult to read as they describe incidents of sexual violence, harassment, and other challenges. Others are uplifting and life-affirming. All of them situate intersectional identities, critical consciousness, and hope as core aspects of leadership. Since one of my goals in writing the book is to foster more just and equitable spaces for all people within leadership, students' narratives and counter-narratives provide liberatory examples of how readers might address systemic oppression and apply aspects of the CRLL model. They also allowed research team members to think critically about their own leadership identities, capacities, and efficacy.

Julie gives some background information on her recent book and shares how she invited a group of undergraduate and graduate women of color to participate in a collective auto-ethnographic process, grounded in CRLL. Through this part of her book, Julie aimed to explore how these women of color and their intersectional identities affect their own leadership efficacy, motivation, capacity, and enactment of leadership. Julie's goal for writing the book was to foster more just and equitable spaces for all people within leadership through students' narratives and counter-narratives addressing systemic oppression and applying aspects of the CRLL model. Similarly, Josephine shares her research of engaging in leadership education research with women from Namibia.

BACK TO THE ROOTS THROUGH CULTURALLY RELEVEANT LEADERSHIP LEARNING
Josephine Shikongo

People learn in different ways. This difference results from the environment they were raised in, the education received, as well as the culture in which they are raised. Oftentimes, these learnings are interconnected and inform each other, as the environment an individual is raised in can influence the education they receive as well as the career they end up with. Underpinning all of this is the notion of culture, which is often hard to explain but so crucial to the very idea of being humans. The United Nations Educational, Scientific and Cultural Organization (UNESCO), defines culture "the set of distinctive spiritual, material, intellectual and emotional features of society or a social group, that encompasses, not only art and literature, but lifestyles, ways of living together, value systems, traditions and beliefs (Pessoa et al., 2009, p. 9). This broad definition shows how culture is at the center of everything we do. Gloria Ladson-Billings (2014) describes "culture as an amalgamation of human activity, production, thought, and belief systems" (p. 75). Since culture informs everything, it is also logical to explore how it influences career choices and ideas of leadership

In my study *Namibian Women in Leadership, How Culture Influences Women's Career Progression*, I interviewed women of different cultural backgrounds, who received different types of education but all ended up lucrative careers in different industries within the country. Speaking with these women to understand their backgrounds, I could not have imagined how differently they understood the concept of leadership and how their upbringing influenced where they are now. Some of the women grew up well aware of their identity, deeply rooted in their culture, others were not able to identify growing in one set culture as they were from mixed families, whereas, some came from a minority-perceived culture in the country.

How they viewed themselves as children differed greatly, which for the most part also influenced their leadership path. There were women who were raised as girls and told they could not achieve everything a man could and only their male siblings could achieve great careers, while they should aspire for blue collar jobs and marriage. A larger group of women were raised as the ones who do all the work, serving the men and boys in the family and doing all chores because that is what women do. Meanwhile, a few numbers were raised as the strong girl who can achieve and be anything, often to their own detriment. All these types of women overcame their adversities in different ways to become leaders in their industries. The strength to persevere and pursue education even when you are told it is not for you, it is beyond your reach and you should not aspire for it can be said to be deeply rooted in self-efficacy. Being labeled as the helper of the family, taking care of everyone somehow inspires a woman to become even greater and serve a larger purpose at a national level.

These women's identities and self-efficacy motivated their leadership behaviors and predicted their capacity (Bertrand Jones et al., 2016) beyond their own imagination. What would appear to be hindrances to career progression resulted in leadership advancement. They overcame all the barriers their cultural communities enforced upon them from a young age and made great strides in their careers to become respected members of the community, including the same ones that raised them. During interviews, the participants were known friends, so I had to navigate the power dynamics to ensure the conversation remains relevant to the study. Keeping them on course further included ensuring they dig deep to reflect on their experiences, some of which they may have chosen to forget as they progressed in their careers. Taking them back to their childhood, reliving memories of a cultural system which they have since left behind was necessary to add richness to the study.

The definition of "leadership" differs across settings. My study was focused on positional leadership; however, many related the leadership to their backgrounds and how they were raised.

In carrying out this study, I had to be aware of my own experiences and identity growing as I listen to their stories, which helped guide the interview, and will be useful in data analysis. I intend to use CRLL during data analysis, in being aware of my bias as I code the data. As a woman who was raised in a patriarchal society and had to work extra hard to make a mark in the corporate world, I know firsthand how it feels to be in the minority. Sitting on a company board as the only Black and the only female, with White men, some who are almost double my age, I have faced identity and self-efficacy issues, as well as an intrinsic bias on what it takes to make it as a woman in leadership in Namibia. The women I interviewed however could have different experiences, and CRLL model as a tool will guide my analysis to bring out their experiences of their own identities and self-efficacies.

Josephine shares her process of interviewing women of different cultural backgrounds, who received different types of education, but all ended up in lucrative careers in different industries within Namibia. Through her reflection, Josephine shares the role CRLL can play in the data analysis of analyzing the women's stories and understanding her own bias as the researcher with her own experiences of oppressive systems and leadership. Josephine acknowledges that the CRLL model is a tool that will guide her analysis to bring out participants' experiences of their own identities and self-efficacies. Next, Dorsey outlines the role narrative inquiry can play when grounded in CRLL in amplifying minoritized voices.

AMPLIFYING VOICES THROUGH NARRATIVE INQUIRY AND CULTURALLY RELEVANT LEADERSHIP LEARNING
Dorsey Spencer, Jr.

Leadership scholarship has historically labeled the leadership experiences of communities of color as service or activism (Guthrie et al., 2013) and has thereby had a profound impact on leadership learning. Students from marginalized populations do not see themselves or representatives of their communities as leaders, nor do they read work written by or about their perspectives in the leadership canon. Narrative inquiry provides a vehicle for disrupting this issue as it is meant to study experiences through stories being told by the participant in collaboration with the researcher (Johnson & Christensen, 2014). In my dissertation study, I used narrative inquiry guided by CRLL to amplify the stories of 15 undergraduate Black men who were student leaders at a predominately White institution (PWI). Previous research has given minimal attention to how Black male undergraduates learn leadership. The goal of this dissertation was to gain a comprehensive understanding of how Black men at higher education institutions learn and understand leadership and the experiences that contribute to them seeing themselves as leaders.

The CRLL model was integral to this study's framework and data analysis. At the center of the CRLL model is a vibrant interaction between the individual and the leadership process through a leader's identity, capacity, and efficacy (Bertrand Jones et al., 2016). Since leadership learning does not occur in a vacuum, the interaction between the student and the leadership process is influenced by five domains that are representative of the campus' climate. Due to CRLL still being an emerging model, for this study it was supplemented with the experiential learning theory (Kolb, 1984). The result was a new conceptual framework called experiential CRLL. In the framework, the campus environment influences the experiential learning process which in turn directly impacts the individual's interaction with the leadership process.

The adaptation of CRLL into the conceptual framework shaped the data analysis by providing a culturally relevant lens for exploring how the participants describe themselves as leaders, how what they learned from their experiences informed who they are as a leader, and how their institutional environment may influence both the prior items. In examining the interview data, inductive coding was used to allow for themes to emerge rather than assessing preconceived hypotheses. While this study employed three different types of coding, the use of *invivo* (Saldaña, 2013) provides the most evidence of the presence of CRLL in the data analysis process. With *invivo* coding, the participant's actual words from the transcript were used as codes (Miles et al., 2014). Using this approach amplified the voices of a group of people often left out of leadership research.

CRLL was also prevalent in the data collection of this study. The model accounts for leadership's history of policing who is a leader and what qualifies as leadership, especially as it pertains to people of color. To disrupt this practice, the participants self-identified as leaders and were involved in both formal and informal leadership experiences. I used purposeful sampling (Creswell, 2013) strategies, specifically maximum variation, snowball, and convenience sampling (Miles et al., 2014). To select participants, I contacted various departments and offices, including athletics, student activities, Greek life, student government, leadership, service and identity centers, the center for first-generation students, the initiative focused on Black men, and the leadership certificate program. I aimed to capture variations that surfaced due to the specific conditions each student was immersed in while engaging in leadership learning. Participants were also asked if they knew of other Black men who met the criteria of the study that they could connect me with. This sampling approach gave the participants the opportunity to identify other students that they felt were leaders which provided further insight into who Black men saw as leaders on campus.

Semi-structured interviews allowed for the participants to give an in-depth and accurate account of their experiences, which is key for a narrative inquiry. Grounded in the conceptual framework, the interview questions focused on the participants' curricular and cocurricular experiences at the university, the environment of a PWI, their experiences with leadership prior to college, and how they see themselves as leaders. The interviews assisted me with collecting data on how Black male student leaders' experiences at PWIs influence their understanding and learning of leadership as well as their leader identity.

Based on the findings of the study, there are several implications and recommendations for addressing campus climate for Black male student leaders. Most of the men acknowledged their involvement in student organizations or sports in high school was a component of them seeing themselves as leaders. High school and higher education educators should develop partnerships to streamline students' development as leaders as they transition to college (Dugan & Komives, 2007). This would allow for secondary school students to see a clear connection between their involvement and leadership and what it looks like in a postsecondary environment and develop positive relationships with each other and college mentors. By enhancing leadership learning in secondary school, students will come to colleges and universities with a better understanding of leadership, leader identity, and leadership capacity.

Faculty and staff who work with leadership learning programs are encouraged to adopt CRLL (Bertrand Jones et al., 2016). Practitioners should investigate whether Black men see themselves reflected in courses or program curriculum. Some recommendations include identifying books that reflect the leadership experiences of Black men. Adopt leadership theories and frameworks that are conducive to the manner that Black people, but more specifically Black men, understand and practice leadership. Discussing historical and contemporary Black male leaders is also highly recommended to show that Black people engage in leadership and are recognized for it.

Studies suggest some Black men in college are enabled to engage in introspection and identity progression because of their relationships with faculty (Brooms, 2014, 2016; Brooms & Davis, 2017; Moore & Toliver, 2010). Higher education institutions need to create an environment where this connection is possible by intentionally developing formal or informal events, programs, and initiatives that encourage Black students to develop meaningful relationships with trained faculty and staff. Some overarching themes in the study regarding challenges Black male student leaders face are related to life skills and well-being. Ideally institutions should develop a culturally competent first-year experience course that covers these areas and provides students with resources to seek out additional support and services (Porter & Swing, 2006).

Dorsey's research example of narrative inquiry and implementing CRLL into the conceptual framework guides the data analysis process by providing a culturally relevant lens for exploring how minoritized participants describe themselves as leaders. CRLL and narrative inquiry also allows for a protocol to explore how what students learned from their experiences informed who they are as a leader, and how their institutional environment may influence their identity, capacity, and efficacy for leadership. Dorsey stresses the importance of CRLL and the role the model can play in amplifying the voices of minoritized students. In the final narrative, Erica offers thoughts on centering CRLL in research methods when assessing leadership programs.

CONSIDERING RESEARCH METHODS WHEN ASSESSING PROGRAMS USING CULTURALLY RELEVANT LEADERSHIP LEARNING
Erica R. Wiborg

When researching and assessing student programming—curricular and cocurricular—it can be challenging to identify what to ask or what to create to understand if a program is culturally relevant. In general, most leadership and student affairs educators are taught to start with the learning and program outcomes to determine how to assess a leadership program (e.g., what will students be able to know, be, or do after participating in the program). This discourse sounds familiar; however, the CRLL model presents a process of leader and leadership identity, capacity, and efficacy taking into consideration the influence of campus climate on both the individual leader and the process of engaging with others. As an educator, it certainly can seem complex on how to assess the ways CRLL is integrated into a leadership program. This narrative will share considerations of approaching leadership program assessment, research, and CRLL, informed by culturally responsive education and indigenous research methods.

Although learning does not feel linear, for the purposes of starting, it is important to challenge your overall approach to knowledge, research, and assessment. We often are deeply rooted and engrained in a dominant set of values in approaching research. For example, you may have been taught collecting data requires a certain level of formality (Wilson, 2008). Instead of a conversation with students, we conduct a focus group with specific boundaries of confidentiality we cannot necessarily promise. A second dominant value is to approach your research with an open-mind, rather than fixed; allowing the learning of the students to be the primary focus of your research (i.e., "to emerge"). However, you as the researcher or educator are looking for specific outcomes, challenging objectivity as a possibility or goal. Further, research on CRLL is not objective, a goal is to understand how systemic oppression is named as a problem and challenged through leadership learning. Indigenous research methods challenge formality and dominant ways of knowing, recognizing all knowledge is culture, and research is focused on relationality, with people, communities, and ideas (Wilson, 2008).

Leadership learning is already biased on years of historical and social conditions. When leadership learning is done in higher education institutions, it can be difficult to separate the oppressive system of education from the programs and actors funded to work for said institution. In the research I have conducted on racism and Whiteness in leadership learning, educators asked how to prioritize anti-racist education in a system that centers Whiteness (Wiborg, 2020). Examining who the research and assessment is for, balanced with honesty and grace, as you answer it can be helpful in approaching CRLL assessment. Who or what are you accountable to by doing the research? Are you accountable to the students who participated in the leadership learning program? To the university who employs and funds your position? To the donor who is funding your program? As described by Wilson (2008), "The research must accurately reflect and build upon the relationships between the ideas and participants" (p. 101).

These questions ask us to consider the five campus climate dimensions at your specific institution and program—the campus and local community culture will matter to how you respond to these questions. Confronting the systems of oppression that influence the models, theories, ideas, structures, and relationships in your program is crucial to inform your assessment purpose and approach.

Erica offers questions for leadership educators to consider within their specific institutional contexts and programs because the campus and local community culture will matter to how you respond to these questions. By confronting the systems of oppression that influence the models, theories, ideas, structures, and relationships in leadership programs, CRLL can inform leadership program assessments design and approach. Similarly to Wiborg, Devies offered key consideration when implementing CRLL and framing curricular and cocurricular leadership program assessments. Kniffin, Owen, Shikongo, and Spencer share practical examples as researchers and how CRLL can be used as a research tool when approaching research methods from a culturally relevant lens. Finally, we offer questions for consideration in Table 11.1. We hope these questions cause you to reflect as you consider methods and approaches to leadership education research through a culturally relevant framework.

TABLE 11.1   Culturally Relevant Leadership Learning Considerations in Research Methods

Culturally Relevant Leadership Learning Constructs	Questions for Consideration
Identity	• How can positionality statements be written to address biases and power dynamics throughout the research process?
	• How will leader identity be negotiated in respect to research design and culturally relevant research methods?
	• In what ways can counternarrative methods be centered in culturally relevant ways?
Capacity	• How will traditional research methods be critiqued through a culturally relevant leadership learning lens?
	• In what ways can traditional understandings of culture be integrated throughout the research methods?
	• What strategies can researchers adapt that are rooted in culturally relevant research approaches?

(continued)

TABLE 11.1   Culturally Relevant Leadership Learning Considerations in Research Methods (continued)

Culturally Relevant Leadership Learning Constructs	Questions for Consideration
Efficacy	• In what ways will dominant narratives be disrupted by socially just research methods?
	• How will counternarratives of minoritized educators and learners be explored in leadership learning research?
	• In what ways will current research and theories be interrogated and critiqued in literature reviews and theoretical frameworks explored in order for them to develop their sense of researcher identity?
Historical Legacy of Inclusion and Exclusion	• Whose ideas of leadership are represented in current leadership theories?
	• In what ways can context and environmental history be centered throughout the research methods?
	• How can disrupting and naming dominant approaches to research methods confront the legacy of inclusion and exclusion in leadership education research?
Compositional Diversity	• How does who has access to formal leadership education determine the research findings of leadership education research?
	• How can research recruitment methods be more inclusive and culturally relevant?
	• How can leadership learning research be more inclusive of researchers who hold minoritized identities?
Psychological Dimension	• How can researchers continue to educate themselves on critical methods and culturally relevant approaches to research methodology?
	• How can your epistemological approach be more culturally relevant?
	• How can research reflexivity be guided with prompts that are rooted in CRLL?
Behavioral Dimension	• How can leadership researchers apply the National Leadership Educators Research Agenda (Beatty et al., 2020; Pierre et al., 2020) to their modes of inquiry?
	• How can researchers constantly answer for themselves, "what makes this research design culturally relevant?"
	• How can culturally relevant approaches be more explicit in the research design?
Organizational and Structural Dimension	• How can leadership education train reviewers to critique studies framed from traditional and dominant ways of inquiry?
	• How can leadership development be made accessible in meaningful ways outside of higher education?
	• What does the practice of civic leadership look like, and how might this inform civic leadership development and research outcomes?

12

Processing Where to Start

Engaging in the Work

As Chapters 4–11 have highlighted, there are various ways to operationalize culturally relevant leadership learning (CRLL). As we continue to work towards socially just leadership education, we must also persist in interrogating how various CRLL constructs not only inform our practice, but how they should be integrated throughout all our work. At the end of Chapters 4–11, questions were provided using the diverse experiences of educators as guideposts to help us all continue to engage in this work. This chapter synthesizes the questions highlighted in the contexts of self-work, cocurricular, academic, and scholarship and provides overarching questions by the CRLL constructs to help us all move towards culturally relevant and socially just leadership education. The synthesis of questions previously offered will help guide us in deconstructing and reformulating leadership education within our own institutional and program contexts.

Operationalizing Culturally Relevant Leadership Learning, pages 199–208
Copyright © 2021 by Information Age Publishing
All rights of reproduction in any form reserved.
199

CRLL Constructs: Synthesizing Guiding Questions

By organizing our synthesis of questions derived from narratives, we hope to offer a starting or continuing point for leadership educators to engage in culturally relevant and socially just leadership education. The social construction of leadership and how different aspects of context influence how we design leadership learning opportunities is important to consider. The various CRLL constructs of identity, capacity, efficacy, historical legacy of inclusion and exclusion, compositional diversity, psychological, behavioral, and organizational structure may offer numerous ways to not only reflect but engage in this work. As seen in Figure 12.1, the image of the CRLL model provides a visual of the constructs and how they interact.

───

Identity

Leadership educators can apply pedagogical tools, design curriculum, and develop cocurricular programs that consider asking students: (a) "Who are they as a leader?"; (b) "What conceptual frameworks and/

Figure 12.1 Culturally relevant leadership learning model. *Source:* Reprinted with permission from Guthrie, Bertrand Jones, & Osteen, 2019.

or strategies can be utilized to help participants make sense of themselves and their leadership contexts?"; and (c) "How does my content and pedagogical choices represent and support expanding views of self and leadership (i.e., personal, relational, collective)?" (Priest & Middleton, 2016). Integrating both leader and social identity development through all aspects of program curriculum is vital and a key component of the CRLL model. Centering minoritized identities is also an aspect of CRLL that moves beyond just thinking of one type of identity as leader and starts to take a more socially just approach to leadership education. This can be done by allowing for representation of minoritized identities in examples of leader and leadership embedded in curriculum for both academic programs and cocurricular programs.

The previous chapters call for reflection of personal identity and sharing with others through storytelling, counter-narratives, *testimonios*, and so on. Approaching identity development from a more culturally relevant lens allows for learners to consider their own culture and how they make meaning of themselves in relation to leadership. One's identity should not be and is not disconnected from how they understand and engage in the leadership process. The extent to which a student defines themselves as a leader and considers the leader role as a central part of who they are refers to their leader identity (Day et al., 2009). Leadership educators should consider modeling this process for leadership learners. Chapter 4 outlines why we see the need for understanding one's positionality as a leadership educator and relationship to power, privilege, and oppression. Socially just leadership education must acknowledge its history of centering dominant identities and narratives over others and what this communicates to learners regarding who is considered a leader and who is not (Beatty & Manning-Ouellette, 2018; Guthrie & Chunoo, 2018; Chunoo et al., 2019; Owen, 2020b). We as leadership educators play a role, both actively and passively, in perpetuating inequities in leadership education, and we must start with ourselves to address these socially just issues.

We intentionally developed questions and themes that highlight and analyze the contexts and importance of identity development for both leadership learners and leadership educators. We offer the following questions as reflective prompts when centering culturally relevant and socially just ways of considering leadership identity within your own work in leadership education:

- What strategies and reflection tools can you apply for thinking about your own identities and positionality when designing curricular and cocurricular leadership programs as a leadership educator?

▪ In what ways will students explore their identity and leader identity, and how will minoritized identities be centered in their leadership learning?

Capacity

Integration of knowledge, skills, and attitudes which lead to the ability to engage effectively in the leadership process is the focus of capacity. As seen through the diverse experiences of educators highlighted in the narratives provided, engaging in development skills, and intentionally creating opportunities for students to develop their capacity is apparent across contexts. Skill development is critical not only for educators' capacity to engage in professional contexts, but also in personal development and in scholarship. Similarly, scaffolding the development of students' skills will flourish in both academic and cocurricular contexts.

Synthesizing the questions across contexts provided insight into themes that emerged in the need for developing capacity. One emergent theme was the importance of focusing on self-awareness as a skill. Increased self-awareness expands emotional intelligence, which leads to better engagement in the leadership process and the further development of others. Another important aspect to consider is ensuring that with an increased self-awareness, students' skills in engaging across differences is also a focus of development throughout the program curriculum. Developing these skills gives students the agency to sustain their own growth in cultural competence Remembering that cultural competence is a lifelong and ongoing process is critical to centering leadership learning in cultural relevance.

Analyzing questions offered across contexts can provide guidance in deconstructing and reformulating how we currently provide leadership capacity development opportunities for students. The questions below give educators an opportunity to reflect on how they ground culturally relevant and socially just ways of leadership capacity development within their own leadership development program offerings:

▪ As a leadership educator, what strategies will you employ to center self-awareness in your own personal and professional development and throughout the research process?

▪ In what ways will skill development, both as a leader and engagement in the leadership process, be offered and scaffolded for increased ability to engage across differences?

Efficacy

When engaging in the leadership process, one's leadership self-efficacy is the belief that one has the capacity to perform leadership. This personal belief can change based on different contexts and environments. One's efficacy can also be affected by how a person learns behaviors throughout their development, which influences their judgment and decision-making process (Bandura, 1997). Leadership educators' narratives highlighted through personal and professional examples of building efficacy through leadership education. Developing leadership efficacy by centering a socially just lens and CRLL approach allows learners and educators to redefine leadership and reimagine who can be a leader.

Focusing intentional reflection on beliefs and building leadership capacity was a theme that emerged from the leadership educators' narratives. Developing learning outcomes for curricular and cocurricular programs is a key component for CRLL because learner's must be prompted to reflect on their own beliefs regarding their capacity to engage in the leadership process in order to make change. Leadership educators must remind learners that CRLL is not an end destination, but a journey. If committed to socially just approaches and equitable outcomes, we must also be committed to the ongoing work of maintaining our cultural competence with our ever-changing environmental contexts.

Interrogating how one enacts a CRLL approach allows for space to reflect on ways leadership efficacy might come easy for some learners and be more difficult for others, depending on contexts. As the previous sections shared, the questions that follow offer reflection prompts for leadership educators to consider how they center culturally relevant and socially just ways of leadership efficacy development within their own leadership learning contexts:

- How will you help learners explore what they believe about themselves as leaders and their capacity to engage in the leadership process?
- In what ways will you model the lifelong learning process in response to the shifting times, environments, and contexts and the need that therein lies for reflecting on one's leadership efficacy?

Historical Legacy of Inclusion and Exclusion Dimension

A theme that emerged for leadership educators engaging in CRLL was that they must be honest about the context of including and excluding narratives of leaders, followers, and educators when developing curriculum and programs. Another theme highlighted was that as leadership educators, we must show our commitment to socially just and CRLL by integrating global, local, and institutional historical perspectives throughout programs. By centering contextual and environmental dimensions and connecting history to present day, leadership educators take responsibility for disrupting dominant narratives of leadership and legitimizing who is framed as a leader on campus, in the community, in our nation, and globally.

The ongoing interrogation of values, actions, and beliefs around leadership learning is crucial for socially just leadership education. Through the power of language and tradition, dominant narratives around what is leadership, who are leaders, where can leadership take place, and when is leadership appropriate have been perpetuated. Interrogating who defines values and determines what actions are meaningful is important for disrupting dominant narratives of leadership. Knowing the historical context of place and space is an important dimension to reflect on when engaging in CRLL.

Questions leadership educators can consider when interrogating and disrupting historical dominant narratives of leadership are shared as leadership educators approach this work through a socially just lens. The questions below are not an exhaustive list for reflection, but aim to prompt the consideration of historical context in leadership learning spaces:

- How does interrogating contextual history ensure that leadership educators do not further perpetuate dominant narratives in our leadership learning spaces?
- How can leadership educators think about their own programs' histories of inclusion and exclusion for the purpose of disrupting dominant narratives of leadership and leader?

Compositional Diversity Dimension

The compositional diversity dimension acknowledges that centering the participation and representation of historically underrepresented racial/ethnic groups, women, transgender, gender non-binary, and other marginalized student populations is needed in leadership education. Interrogating *who*, *how*, and *why* individuals are included or marginalized in campus leadership programs and the campus community more broadly, can start to acknowledge the ways in which the historical legacy of inclusion and exclusion is perpetuated in the present day. Additionally, this interrogation of who is represented and who is marginalized in the campus community provides an opportunity to increase the exposure of diverse perspectives for all students.

CRLL calls for the framing of diversity to include, but not be limited to -isms (including race, gender, class, sexuality, ability, and socioeconomic status). Moving beyond simply numbers of those in attendance and representation, but actually addressing what are the experience once marginalized learners are represented in the space is an important theme that the leadership educators' narratives addressed in this book. Socially just leadership education and CRLL call leadership educators to move beyond who is and who is not in the room. If leadership education is truly socially just, then acknowledging who is trying to get in the room and what barriers are being maintained to exclude some and include others must be interrogated for the purpose of dismantling.

The reflective questions we offer here are prompts for leadership educators to continuously interrogate the compositional diversity of their own campus environments and leadership programs. The reflective questions are also for leadership educators to interrogate their own understandings of compositional diversity in the programs they facilitate:

- In contexts where compositional diversity is not immediately possible, due to constraints like enrollment, how can we achieve compositional diversity?
- In what ways can leadership educators seek to understand who, how, and why individuals are included or left out/marginalized in leadership programs? Once you have an understanding, what can you enact to address the needs of marginalized and minoritized participants engaged in leadership programs?

Psychological Dimension

The psychological aspect of CRLL encompasses the attitudes about difference, perceptions of discrimination, and individual views about group dynamics in various contexts. It is worth noting that all various factors, including the other constructs of CRLL discussed here, contribute to the psychological aspect of leadership learning. Although we are focusing on specific factors related to developing opportunities for CRLL, we acknowledge and honor this dimension is more complex than we can discuss here. By concentrating on facets leadership educators can control, although not perfect, we can move towards more socially just leadership learning spaces.

Continuing to reflect on the questions previously offered to guide educators in the deconstructing of traditional ways of delivering leadership learning opportunities, CRLL challenges educators to reconstruct them in more culturally relevant and socially just ways. The importance of what and how language was used in all aspects of leadership education was noted. From marketing to program delivery to learning assessment, use of language has a powerful influence on whether creating a positive learning environment where students feel welcomed and able to engage in learning or an inequitable one that clearly favors certain types of students and therefore excludes some students.

Another theme that emerged from the various contexts discussed is the need for intentional reflection on differing worldviews. Integrating various pedagogies and assessment strategies throughout a curriculum related to differing worldviews not only develops students' self-awareness and skills in engaging across differences but provides diverse students the opportunity to share their own beliefs with others. Finally, addressing the context of campus is critical to the psychological aspect of a CRLL environment. Interrogating inherited beliefs that are passed down in formal and informal ways that are oppressive in nature can be difficult but is necessary. Oftentimes oppressive ideology can be masked as tradition on college campuses and having conversations to challenge socialization are critical in moving towards culturally relevant and socially just leadership education.

Reflective questions offered across contexts can aid in continual examination of how educators create leadership learning environments in consideration of the psychological domain:

- How is culturally relevant and socially just reflection on leadership, especially on differing worldviews, integrated throughout leadership educator development in which influences leadership learning program development and implementation, and scholarship?
- In what ways is the current campus context being interrogated to deconstruct the ways oppressive ideology may be masked as tradition, both formally and informally?

Behavioral Dimension

Simply put, the behavioral dimension encompasses the interactions and the quality of interaction across diverse individuals in various contexts. The behavior of all involved in a learning environment includes both the educators and the learners, and in the scholarly context it includes both the researchers and participants. Although behavior is often outwardly seen through interactions, oftentimes educators, scholars, and learners hesitate in distinguishing oppressive behavior, if recognizable, as a result of having been socialized in contexts that labeled it acceptable.

To deconstruct traditional oppressive behavior, often asking simple questions and honestly reflecting on them can reveal such behaviors. One critical question found in the narratives of diverse educators' experiences considers how leadership educators' behaviors are influential in creating culturally relevant and socially just leadership learning environments. Although this seems obvious, it is a critical aspect that cannot be overlooked and instead critically analyzed from as many aspects as possible. One way is acknowledging and disrupting behaviors, of students and other educators, that minimize culturally relevant and socially just leadership learning outcomes. Another theme to consider is how the behaviors of diverse leaders are celebrated instead of judged, especially if they are not in alignment with traditional ways of being.

Synthesizing questions offered across contexts can provide guidance in deconstructing and reformulating how we currently provide leadership learning opportunities. The questions we offer hopefully provide an opportunity for educators to pause and reflect on how to center culturally relevant and socially just avenues to leadership development, through examining behavioral dimensions of environments. Educator behavior is observable, influential, and therefore critical in setting up CRLL environments:

- In what ways is reflection integrated throughout the curriculum to deconstruct obvious oppressive behaviors?
- How do you, as a leadership educator, model behaviors in culturally relevant and socially just ways, including acknowledging and celebrating diverse student behaviors and disrupting behaviors that minimize inclusivity?

Organizational and Structural Dimension

The processes that guide the daily operation of institutions, departments, and programs are the organizational and structural constructs of the CRLL model. Not only being aware of, but interrogating how policies, procedures, and processes can create inequity is essential for leadership educators to consider. Revealing inequities and organizational and structural barriers not only allows for students to learn in a more culturally relevant way, but also supports access to a learning environment that provides the opportunity as fully as they can. Focusing on organizational and structural aspects also models for future leaders how influential operational processes and the importance of constant assessment are in creating socially just environments in all situations.

Synthesis of questions previously offered provided insight into how we can move toward more CRLL by specifically focusing on organizational structures. One emergent theme is that organizational structure must be interrogated at all levels to move toward more culturally relevant and socially just leadership education. Although program and department processes are more accessible, processes at the division and institutional level must also be questioned. Another theme is that gathering feedback must be intentional and consistent at all levels of organizational structure and then incorporated. The feedback gathered should then lead to reimagining policies, procedures, and processes that center culturally relevant and socially just frameworks. This is a multistep process that includes constantly gathering feedback and then rethinking and executing changes in operating systems.

Two broad questions are offered in hopes of provoking your reflection of deconstructing and reformulating the organizational structure of the specific context you are currently situated in:

- How are current standards of organizational operation interrogated at all levels and from various perspectives?
- In what ways is feedback intentionally collected, analyzed, and utilized for revision of organizational policies, procedures, and processes in efforts of a more equitable environment?

Summary

Through this chapter, we offered processing questions as a starting point for operationalizing CRLL. The reflective questions are also framed to interrogate the CRLL model and consider socially just approaches to leadership learning. The narratives highlighted in Chapters 4–11 are examples of how leadership educators operationalize CRLL. Working towards socially just leadership education must be connected to interrogating how various CRLL constructs cannot only inform our practice and pedagogy, but also how they should be implemented in intentional ways with the purpose of socially just outcomes. These reflective questions were provided using the wide range of experiences of educators as guiding lights for those engaged in this personal and professional work.

13

Resources to Move Forward

Foundational and Enrichment Activities

As we have shared in previous chapters, we acknowledge culture is central to learning for both students and educators. Acknowledging, responding to, and celebrating cultures offers equitable access to leadership education for all students. Modeling the use of intentional language, applying how context and cultural backgrounds affect students' leadership learning, and prioritizing how socially just and equitable practices inspire greater student engagement in the leadership process all contribute to culturally relevant leadership learning (CRLL). The ongoing process of interrogating CRLL allows for leadership educators to continue to imagine possibilities to operationalize socially just leadership education. This can be done through self-work, engaging in professional associations and conferences, and continuing to move research forward that addresses identity and inequities in leadership education. Professional associations and professional development opportunities like the Association for Leadership Educators, the International Leadership Association, the Association for Student Affairs Administrator's, Student Leadership Programs Knowledge Community, College

Operationalizing Culturally Relevant Leadership Learning, pages 209–221
Copyright © 2021 by Information Age Publishing
All rights of reproduction in any form reserved.

Student Educators International's Commission on Student Involvement, and the Leadership Educators Institute are all places to continue engaging with interrogating CRLL in practice, pedagogy, and scholarship.

Resources for Leadership Educator Professional Development

In this final chapter, we offer resources for leadership educators to continue building from the narratives offered in Chapters 4–11 and continue operationalizing CRLL in their spaces. While this chapter is not exhaustive of resources, it offers leadership educators pedagogical tools that center the growth and development of students' leadership identity, capacity, efficacy, and their environmental dimensions. The pedagogical tools shared here can engage learners at foundational levels of understanding components of the CRLL model. These tools can also take learners through an *enrichment activity* to support going deeper in more socially just ways for more equitable and just outcomes of leadership education. In the next section, we offer broad strategies and activities to create opportunities for learning with each construct. Additionally, we provide a *foundational activity* as a starting place for understanding each of the CRLL constructs and an enrichment activity to go deeper once a general understanding of CRLL is achieved. These activities are great pedagogical tools for leadership educators to engage learners, but the activities can also be useful reflective tools for leadership educators' own process of developing their capacity for CRLL.

Identity

Having leadership educators create space for learning with activities, models reflection and exploration of leader identity development. Chapter 12 synthesized and offered additional interrogating prompts developed from the themes across leadership educators' narratives that employ strategies of counter narratives and storytelling. An additional skill that can support leadership educators and learners' engagement with their own leader identity is reflection (Volpe White et al., 2019). Reflection activities can be designed to facilitate contemplation on a core value that connects to one's leader identity through engaging in the leadership process. Reflection is an important skill, not only for understanding self in relation to context, but for engaging in the process of CRLL.

Torres (2020) outlined an activity using *testimonio*, a form of storytelling rooted in Latinx culture with an emphasis on intentional inclusion of affirmation and empowerment (Latina Feminist Group, 2001; Reyes & Curry

Rodríguez, 2012). *Testimonio* provides space for reflection where learners share their experiences with others in various forms such as writing, speaking, or visual aid (Reyes & Curry Rodríguez, 2012). For this foundational activity, Torres (2020) shared the process of learners writing the *testimonio* of their chosen leader. Leadership learners are given the opportunity to practice *testimonio* by creating a leader profile and presenting it in small and large groups. The goals of the activity are to learn the practice of *testimonio* and become knowledgeable of a person's leadership journey. This application of *testimonio* allows students to practice reflecting on someone else's leadership journey before doing critical reflection of their own leadership journey and the role their identities play in that journey.

An example of an enrichment activity for identity development is one shared by Teig (2020), titled *What's in my Leader House?* This guided reflective writing activity provides learners the opportunity for thinking and processing their leader identity in relationship to interpersonal, intrapersonal, and societal constructs. Leadership learners who progress in ownership of a leader identity require examples of ongoing critical reflective processing to understand their past experiences in learning leadership, how they were framed within historical contexts, and how institutional structures still perpetuate historical legacies of inclusion/exclusion based on identity (Teig, 2020; Kelly & Bhangal, 2018). Learners are guided through a written reflection to consider the evolution of their leader identity through the lens of the CRLL model (Bertrand Jones et al., 2016). Next, learners identify *how, where,* and *why* they have been influenced in their understanding of leader and leadership. Students are then instructed to provide specific institutional examples of historically gendered/racialized conceptions of leadership. This is then followed by prompting students to recognize the institutional examples of perpetuating leadership outside of historically gendered/racialized understandings. The reflection activity ends with students creating an action plan to disrupt historically gendered/racialized conceptions of leadership in their own organizations.

Capacity

Intentionally creating opportunities for development of leadership capacity is essential for overall student development. As shared in Chapter 12, emerging priorities for capacity development include increasing self-awareness and skills to engage across differences. One skill that can support such engagement is empathetic listening. Spencer (2020) offers a learning activity that allows participants to practice empathetic listening skills, as well as observe others and give feedback in the process. In this activity, participants learn how to use specific techniques of different levels of listening (Crawley, 2018). In groups of three, students take turns telling a story, listening, and observing. Listening is an important skill, not only for engaging across differences, but for engaging in the whole process of leadership.

Morante (2020) shares an activity designed to ask big questions that incite thoughtful reflection regarding topics of life. This foundational activity provides space for students to reflect on their identity, authenticity, and purpose, which increases their self-awareness and may further lead to capacity development. To set up this activity, educators introduce the three concepts of identity, authenticity, and purpose while co-creating community guidelines with students for conversation. First, individually, students reflect how identity, authenticity, and purpose interact with each other. Morante (2020) provides specific prompts which can be used for this activity, but we encourage you to create your own that fits your specific context. Magazines, newspapers, markers, and crayons are provided for students to draw, write, and cut out images or phrases that represent these reflections. After approximately 15 minutes of individual reflection, students are asked to pair with one or two peers to share, and then join into a larger group to continue processing. This foundational activity focuses on increasing self-awareness, which is a critical skill for culturally relevant and socially just capacity development.

An enrichment activity for capacity development could be similar to one offered by Grospitch and Gleason (2020) titled *You Think What?: Utilizing Reflection to Enhance Understanding of Self and Comfort with Differing Perspectives*. This activity provides students with various opportunities to reflect on initial results from an inventory given and to discuss different worldviews with others. Although Grospitch and Gleason (2020) provide examples of inventories that could be utilized, choosing a self-assessment is dependent on the context of the leadership program. The flexibility of choosing the assessment tool allows for it to be focusing on cultural competence or highlighting differing worldviews. Once the self-assessment tool is completed, individuals reflect on their results by answering prompts focused on their perceived strengths, weaknesses, and roles in change. Next participants will be asked to share their initial reflections with a small group, and group members are asked to share feedback and present tough interpretations (O'Malley & Cebulla, 2015), which are explanations of thoughts that can be uncomfortable. How to give and receive critical feedback are learned skills. Both verbal and nonverbal communication is critical in developing an environment in which this processing can be successful. Once small group processing concludes, additional time is given for large group reflection.

Efficacy

Building on capacity, leadership educators must connect opportunities for development for leadership efficacy. Believing in the skills and abilities that encompass leadership capacity in order to engage in the leadership process is an important aspect of CRLL. The concept of efficacy has theoretical foundations to learning and development. Learners' beliefs about their ability determines whether they practice their leadership knowledge and skills in relation to their context when engaging in the leadership process. The process of building one's leadership efficacy entails interrogating and examining internalized marginalization and addressing dominance in the leadership process. Developing leadership efficacy reimagines leaders as ordinary people who do extraordinary things with others when working towards change and engaging in the leadership process.

Beatty, Brown et al., (2020) shared *Mind Mapping and Exploring the "Leader Box."* This foundational activity is reflection and discussion-based with focus on facilitated reflection through mind mapping and exploring the who and what is considered a leader. The goal of this activity is for leadership learners to consider their preconceived understandings of the definition of leader and what/who informed those understandings. The activity asks students to define leader and follower by drawing a mind map. The mind map is made up of concepts, generally represented by words/phrases, bubbles, and branches with the lines connecting the concepts. On the branches are words or short phrases to explain the connection between two concepts. The activity also asks students to create a map for both *follower* and *leader*. Students then create branches that stem to concepts, feelings, behaviors, and thoughts associated with the main idea. Participants can create more branches off of each new bubble they create. When learners have completed their mind map, they then share it through a pair and share activity. Finally, the activity concludes with a large group discussion consisting of prompts like, *"How do we know how a leader is supposed to act or look? Where do these messages come from?"* As the facilitator of the activity, the leadership educator provides space for learners to discuss and reflect. Through this foundational activity mind mapping is used as a pedagogical tool for reflection when considering the process of developing leadership efficacy in culturally relevant and socially just ways.

An example of an enrichment activity for efficacy is offered by Wiborg (2018), *In My Feelings: Individual and Collective Capacities for Emotional Intelligence*. This activity is rooted in reflection based on the *Emotionally Intelligent for Students: Inventory* (Shankman et al., 2015). This activity requires students to interpret their strengths in relation to the emotionally intelligent leadership capacities, as demonstrated by their ability to apply these capacities to their current leadership contexts. Learners then discuss opportunities for success, challenges, and learning by reflecting on their strengths. Learners are then requested to engage in collaborative work for developing a collective action plan by debriefing and building connections. Through reflection, learners consider their strengths and application of their own understanding of their emotional intelligence in connection to their leadership capacity and efficacy.

Historical Legacy of Inclusion and Exclusion Dimension

When starting with the historical legacy of the inclusion/exclusion aspect of CRLL, leadership educators recognize and redesign historically White learning environments that constitute dominance in space and contexts. Leadership educators also disrupt dominant narratives of leadership that have been passed down in the environment. The historical legacy of inclusion/exclusion offers a framework for leadership educators to start identifying and amplifying marginalized voices, authors, theories, and practices in curricular and cocurricular programs. Leadership educators need to be prepared to call out how exclusion specifically occurs for marginalized and minoritized groups. Beatty and Manning-Ouellette (2018) offered reflective questions for leadership educators to consider the history of leadership education and the ways leadership education has erased some voices and amplified others. The reflective questions from Beatty and Manning-Ouellette can be a good activity for leadership educators to engage with when thinking about their own self-work before facilitating activities, like the activities that follow, with learners.

Phillips (2020) activity, *Communities as Assets,* is a foundational activity example to help students consider how their leader identity influences how they think about and approach working with communities. This is an opportunity for participants to understand how their assumptions influence their perception of what "help" is needed in a community. The activity also highlights the need for participants to understand the importance of entering communities ready to learn and support existing efforts from those who intimately understand existing needs and past efforts. The goals of the activity are to explore how students' leadership identity influences their perception of community needs. The activity is designed to support learners in understanding the influence their perception has on identifying community needs. The activity also focuses on understanding the community's history, context, and relationship to the present. The activity opens with a discussion focused on how our identity as leaders impacts how we view communities and community needs. The activity also asks students to reflect on how our assumptions about the history, what is needed, and what is not needed in a community impacts how we are received into the community.

Morgan Acosta's (2020) activity, *The Big Picture*, encourages leadership learners to think about how their actions (e.g., goals, organization, leadership) are connected to the bigger picture and the world beyond their current reality. By this enrichment activity connecting daily actions to larger entities (historical context, social change movements, etc.) and reflecting upon campus culture, organizational goals, and personal goals, learners are able to understand the scope and purpose of their work and realize they are not alone in their efforts. The goals of the activity are to: (a) understand the history of their organization(s), including any connections to institutional or social history, movements, other groups, reflect upon personal goals; (b) link aligned activities and goals to their local and global communities; and (c) commit to action.

Compositional Diversity Dimension

As mentioned in Chapter 12, the compositional diversity aspect of CRLL encourages leadership educators to confront the answers of who, how, and why certain individuals are included or excluded from campus programs. Focusing on understanding the compositional diversity and representation of historically minoritized and marginalized student populations, allows for students to critically think about who is represented in their own organizations and who is trying to engage with their group, but are not represented. Mills's (2020) activity, *Community Dialogue*, provides guidelines for "achieving mutual understanding during a dialogic process" and discussion on difference (p. 67). Through this activity, leadership educators can not only demonstrate dialogic conversations, but also acknowledge representation and the reasons for the demographic given the context. Compositional diversity allows for real conversations regarding who is in the room, who is missing from the room, and what are the power structures in place that allow this to happen.

A creative foundational activity offered by Priest et al. (2020) called *T.I.P.S. for Leadership Learning* is a letter writing exercise. This letter writing activity is based on Anu Taranath's (2014) book, *T.I.P.S. to Study Abroad: Simple Letters for Complex Engagement*. T.I.P.S. stands for *thing, idea, person, or self.* The method, developed by Taranath (2014), is intended to support global travelers to "reflect on how moving from one context to another invites questions about identity, society, and the meaning of travel itself" (p. 3). Priest et al. adapted the activity for a reflection exercise as part of academic service-learning work, in this case around the social issue of food security. However, it can be used more broadly to reflect on experiences that contribute to leadership learning and compositional diversity. First, students identify and compose a letter that demonstrates their reflection process and articulates learning. The educator then asks students to choose a thing, idea, person, or self-learning that impacted them the most. The letter should follow this general format: introduction, body, and conclusion. The narrative should demonstrate *reflection and application* as students elaborate on one to three key points representing their most significant learning (e.g., the history of the idea, their attitude to the idea, how they chose actions steps). Finally, allowing leadership learners to voluntarily read their letters aloud creates space for multiple perspectives and deeper conversation about their shared experience. This also allows you as the leadership educator to dig deeper regarding representation and the compositional diversity of the context they chose in their letter.

The enrichment activity for the compositional diversity aspect of CRLL is from Manning-Ouellette (2020), *Game On! Using Barnga to Facilitate Cultural Awareness in Leadership Education.* Manning-Ouellette uses the card game Barnga, created by Thiagarajan and Thiagarajan (2006), to encourage students to confront histories and cultural assumptions in order to intentionally confront these assumptions and reflect on them when considering who is represented in a group and who is not. The activity is facilitated as a simulation to deconstruct cultural assumptions, the roots of these assumptions, engage in facilitated examples of representation and inclusion/exclusion, and have large group discussion around the experience of compositional diversity. The large group discussion following the simulation also sparks reflection and opportunities to make connections of the compositional diversity and assumptions students make in their own context.

Psychological Dimension

In offering learning opportunities for students with the psychological domain in mind, the use of language and integrating reflection on differing worldviews is central to working towards CRLL. Honoring the power language has on not only creating supportive learning environments, but also how we engage in discussion about differing worldviews is essential. It is worth considering how pedagogical tools are used in programs focused on this learning. Ford (2020) offers a learning activity that facilitates discussion highlighting diverse views on leadership and emphasizes how influential language is. In this activity, participants take a piece of paper and draw a picture of their understanding of leadership on one side and on the other side, write a description of the picture. Each participant should post one side of the paper, whichever side they choose, around the room. Next, participants are to observe peer's pictures and descriptions. A debriefing session on what was observed, how differing views of leadership emerged, and how language was used in the description supports activities in developing students' awareness of differing worldviews and their learning of how to engage in conversation around this.

The complexity of the psychological construct and honoring that there are many aspects in which the social construction of leadership influences various aspects of learning is important to consider. Integrating various ways to reflect on our differing worldviews is essential in not only creating a supportive environment but supporting student's development. Additional pedagogical tools include Owen's (2020a) use of Chimamanda Ngozi Adichie's TED Talk: *The Danger of a Single Story* in an activity to also highlight differing worldviews and how it is important to honor authentic expression of self and others. Chung (2020) encourages creativity in journaling and shares how reflecting through artistic means can allow for students to make meaning in new and different ways. By being creative in reflection, this can mirror the artistry of leadership. Although we are often encouraged to journal in a written format, by using art, various learning styles that may be less linear may be given the opportunity to emerge.

A foundational activity in supporting the psychological aspect of CRLL can be supported by video clips as Chapman and Kaya (2020) share. This activity guides students in the exploration of how socialization has influenced their understanding of leadership. Having students first reflect on words they associate with the concepts of "leader" and "leadership" uncovers possible assumptions they may have. Directing students to do a Google search on the words "leader" and "leadership" can illuminate how unknowingly messages of who can be a leader and what leadership is has influenced personal beliefs. Chapman and Kaya (2020) offer discussion prompts and sharing of specific video clips as counter narratives. Video clips include Radical Monarch (http://radicalmonarchs.org/support-us/), Video Project 562 (https://www.youtube.com/watch?v=GIzYzz3rEZU), Young Women's Freedom Center (https://www.youtube.com/watch?v=_9VRjZRLXoc), and Building a Caring America: TEDxMiddlebury (https://www.youtube.com/watch?v=ColFFPNgtK4).

Bruce and Collins (2020) offer an enrichment activity using photography to capture and share the various ways they see leadership in the world around them. This activity allows for flexibility in framing the activity around a specific leadership theory, concept, cultural competency, or a current contested issue. By nature of having diverse individuals participate, differing worldviews will emerge from the photography, explanation, and reflection of the pictures they share. Students will need to be reminded that pictures need to be taken in public spaces and private citizens need to give their permission to be photographed. The ability to dig deep into differing worldviews is in the discussion of the picture and prompting of how individuals make meaning of our world through their personal lens, definition of leadership, and socialization.

Behavioral Dimension

As shared in Chapter 12, emerging priorities for behavioral development for students include being aware of educators' behaviors, disrupting inappropriate behavior, and celebrating diverse leaders' behaviors that model inclusivity. Deconstructing oppressive behavior is the type of action that needs to occur as well as celebrating diverse behaviors. Disrupting inappropriate behavior is as essential as acknowledging behaviors that celebrate diverse students. Deconstructing and disrupting such behaviors can be uncovered during learning activities and assessment. Kaufman (2020) provides direction for facilitating case study development that can support student reflection of behaviors and analysis of multiple leadership concepts in real world contexts. Guiding students in case study development can not only be a pedagogical tool, but an assessment tool as well. This can highlight both diverse student behaviors and an opportunity to disrupt behaviors that minimize culturally relevant leadership.

Watkins (2020) offers a foundational activity titled *Theater of Bad Leadership*. This learning activity provides students an opportunity to connect their lived experiences with leadership concepts in a one act play. Watkins (2020) frames the play development in Kellerman's (2004) types of bad leadership, although any leadership theory, concept, skill, or cultural competency could be used as a guiding framework. This activity requires groups of three to five individuals, although any size could work depending on context. Each group has time to plan, write, and practice their scene in which they perform for the entire group. Once performances have concluded, discussion of the behaviors portrayed in the scenes can both celebrate and disrupt behaviors that either contribute to or minimize culturally relevant and socially just ways of being.

An example of an enrichment activity focused on the behavioral construct is provided by Osteen (2020). In this activity the social change model of leadership development (Higher Education Research Institute [HERI], 1996) is used to frame reflection on daily choices and behaviors and the resulting alignment or misalignment of core values. To begin this activity, the social change model of leadership development and how individuals, groups, and community are centered on change needs to be highlighted. Next, students are asked to reconsider the model as a tree and draw it on a piece of paper. The roots should be reconsidered as the individual context and how we choose to act, the trunk as the group context and how we act, and the branches, the crown of the tree, as the community context and what the vision of change is. Once intentional reflection is completed with specific prompts along the development of the tree, students are asked to share and focus on how their actions either align or misalign with their values. This activity can be done with several modifications to fit the participants' needs and the context in which it is being delivered. Connecting the tree metaphor with how a tree grows in the direction of its roots is powerful. As Osteen (2020) beautifully states, "Everyday there are moments to act, when you have the opportunity to lead and/or follow through the choices you make . . . you are not alone, this is not a single tree, this is a forest of possibilities" (p. 39).

Organizational and Structural Dimension

Organizational and structural aspects of creating environments that are culturally relevant and socially just for leadership learning is a critical consideration. Ensuring that organizational structure is interrogated at all levels is essential, as is developing skills for reflection on current oppressive practices, intentionally gathering feedback, and being able to engage in change. Volpe White (2020) offers a brief activity for individuals to experience a 1-minute reflection. This can be used by having stakeholders write for 1 to 5 minutes on what they believe to be organizational practices that both support and hinder engagement of diverse individuals and being situated in culturally relevant practice. This activity can allow participants to write their thoughts individually as well as give them a space to deconstruct current organizational practices. Miller (2020) offers an activity that gives space for leaders to practice dealing with rapidly changing conditions within organizations. This game provides an opportunity for reflection on how adaptability is essential in leadership, especially when reimagining policies, procedures, and processes.

A foundational activity in exploring the organizational and structural construct of the CRLL model is taken from Seemiller (2020). She provides guidance on developing an organizational change case study where a project is formed as a team-based organizational consulting scenario. This project is designed to simulate a consulting team whose task is to diagnose organizational issues, which in focusing on CRLL environments could be what oppressive policies, practices, and processes are currently being used.

Developing strategies of how to address the organizational issues is also included in the group's charge. Although Seemiller (2020) frames this as a fictional organization and is used for an academic course, this project can be specifically focused on an organization project which participants are engaged with.

Priest (2020) offers an activity titled *Zoom: A Visual Reflection Tool,* that can be considered for an enrichment activity to dig deeper into organizational structure considerations. Zoom is a graphic children's book by Istvan Banyai (1995) that gradually "zooms" out to see other perspectives and provides interesting visuals and moments to reflect on learning and leadership. This book can serve as a frame for organizational structure through reflection of multiple perspectives (self, others, system). Priest (2020) suggests taking the Zoom book and disassembling it into a deck of 30 images and having students reflect on what they are seeing and how they make meaning of what they are seeing in the context of leadership, or specifically in this construct, organizational structure. Bringing in a children's book with powerful images can be influential in developing learning opportunities for both students and colleagues, especially when working towards the deconstruction of systems we have been socialized to be a part of.

Conclusion

This chapter provides resources to move forward in our collective effort in creating more culturally relevant and socially just leadership learning opportunities. Through this book we have interrogated leadership education through CRLL and socially just leadership education (See Figure 13.1). As this book interrogated and offered applications of the CRLL model,

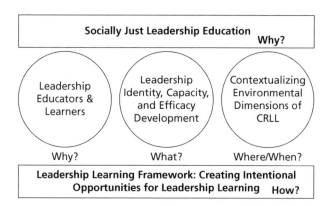

Figure 13.1 Interrogation of leadership education.

reflective questions were shared as starting points for the continued efforts to lead the charge in breaking down the obstacles that hinder socially just leadership education (Chunoo et al., 2019; Guthrie & Jenkins, 2018). As we noted throughout the book our *why* is rooted in avoiding leadership learning without the framing of being culturally relevant from a socially just lens, because that only perpetuates inequities and dominant narratives for our *who*, leadership educators and learners. The environmental aspects of the CRLL dimensions establish the *where/when* and the *how* is the process the leadership learning framework creates for intentional opportunities for leadership learning.

We appreciate you joining this journey in interrogating CRLL, learning from brilliant educators on ways to operationalize this model, and reflecting on how we each personally have our own path into practicing leadership and creating more equitable and just environments and opportunities. As we have acknowledged throughout the book, this work is challenging and as educators we will not always get it right. We cannot undervalue the need for lifelong learning and surrounding ourselves with colleagues and friends who will give us the feedback to enhance our practice. As we engage in this work, we must remember our *why* and focus on preparing the next generation of socially just change makers. Thank you for reimagining leadership education with us. We are honored to do this work with you.

References

Abes, E. S., Jones, D. R., & McEwen, M. K. (2007). Reconceptualizing the model of multiple dimensions of identity: The role of meaning-making capacity in the construction of multiple identities. *Journal of College Student Development, 48*, 1–22.

Abes, E. S., Jones, S. R., & Stewart, D.-L. (Eds.). (2019). *Rethinking college student development theory using critical frameworks.* Stylus.

Abes, E. S., & Kasch, D. (2007). Using queer theory to explore lesbian college students' multiple dimensions of identity. *Journal of College Student Development, 48*, 619–636.

Ahmed, S. (2012). *On being included: Racism and diversity in institutional life.* Duke University Press.

Aiken-Wisniewski, S. A., Taub, D. J., & Whitney, R. (2020). *The missing competency: An integrated model for program development for student affairs.* Stylus.

Allen, B. J. (2010). *Difference matters* (2nd ed.). Waveland Press.

Allen, S. J., & Shehane, M. R. (2016). Exploring the language of leadership learning and education. In D. M. Roberts & K. J. Bailey (Eds.), *Assessing student leadership (No. 151). New directions for student leadership* (pp. 35–49). Jossey-Bass.

Anderson, A. O. (2017). *Men faculty engagement in gender equity work in STEM: The radicalization of "doing the right thing."* [Doctoral dissertation]. West Virginia University. https://www.proquest.com/openview/09522017acf6 d664c4097d7df867212b/1?pq-origsite=gscholar&cbl=18750

Anderson, K. A., McDonald, T. A., Edsall, D., Smith, L. E., & Taylor, J. L. (2016). Postsecondary expectations of high-school students with autism spectrum disorders. *Focus on Autism and Other Developmental Disabilities, 31*(1), 16–26.

Operationalizing Culturally Relevant Leadership Learning, pages 223–240
Copyright © 2021 by Information Age Publishing
All rights of reproduction in any form reserved.

Anthony, M. (2018). Intersecting activism and social justice in leadership education. In K. L. Guthrie & V. S. Chunoo (Eds.), *Changing the narrative: Socially just leadership education* (pp. 41–56). Information Age Publishing.

Ardoin, S. (2018). Helping poor- and working-class students create their own sense of belonging. In G. L. Martin & B. Elkins (Eds.), *Social class identity in student affairs (Vol. 218, No. 162). New directions for student services* (pp. 75–86). Jossy-Bass.

Arminio, J., Carter, S., Jones, S., Kruger, K., Lucas, N., Washington, J., Young, N., & Scott, A. (2000). Leadership experiences of students of color. *NASPA Journal, 37*(3), 496–510.

Astin, A. W. (1993). *What matters in college? Four critical years revisited.* Jossey-Bass.

Astin, A. W. (2012). *Assessment for excellence: The philosophy and practice of assessment and evaluation in higher education.* Rowman & Littlefield Publishers.

Astin, A. W., & Astin, H. S. (2000). *Leadership reconsidered: Engaging higher education in social change.* W. K. Kellogg Foundation.

Avolio, B. J., & Hannah, S. T. (2008). Developmental readiness: Accelerating leadership development. *Consulting Psychology Journal: Practice and Research, 60*(4), 331–347.

Ayman, R., Adams, S., Fisher, B., & Hartmen, E. (2003). Leadership development in higher education institutions: A present and future perspective. In S. E. Murphy & R. E. Riggio (Eds.), *The future of leadership development* (pp. 201–222). Lawrence Erlbaum.

Bandura, A. (1977). *Social learning theory.* Prentice Hall.

Banyai, I. (1995). *Zoom.* Puffin Books.

Bass, B. M. (1985). *Leadership and performance beyond expectations.* Free Press.

Baxter Magolda, M. B. (2001). *Making their own way: Narratives for transforming higher education to promote self-development.* Stylus.

Beatty, C. C., Brown, A. M., & Hall, T. (2020). Mind mapping and exploring the "leader box." In J. M. Volpe White, K. L. Guthrie, M. Torres, & Associates, *Thinking to transform: Facilitating reflection in leadership learning* (p. 66). Information Age Publishing.

Beatty, C. C., Irwin, L., Owen, J. E., Tapia-Fuselier, N., Guthrie, K. L., Cohen-Derr, E., Hassell-Goodman, S., Rocco, M., & Yamanaka, A. (2020). A call for centering social identities: Priority 1 of the National Leadership Education Research Agenda 2020–2025. *Journal of Leadership Studies, 14*(3), 39–44.

Beatty, C. C., & Manning-Ouellette, A. (2018). The role of liberatory pedagogy in socially just leadership education. In K. Guthrie & V. Chunoo (Eds.), *Changing the narrative: Socially just leadership education* (pp. 229–244). Information Age Publishing.

Bell, L. (2010). *Storytelling for social justice: Connecting narrative and arts in anti-racist teaching.* Routledge.

Bell, L. A., & Adams, M. (2016). Theoretical foundations for social justice education. In M. Adams & L. A. Bell (Eds.), *Teaching for diversity and social justice* (pp. 21–44). Routledge.

Bennett, M. J. (2004). Becoming interculturally competent. In J. S. Wurzel (Ed.), *Toward multiculturalism: A reader in multicultural education* (pp. 62–77). Intercultural Resource Corporation.

Bernstein, J. H. (2015). Transdisciplinarity: A review of its origins, development, and current issues. *Journal of Research Practice, 11*(1), Article R1. http://jrp.icaap.org/index.php/jrp/article/view/510/412

Bertrand Jones, T., Guthrie, K. L., & Osteen, L. (2016). Critical domains of culturally relevant leadership learning: A call to transform leadership programs. In K. L. Guthrie, T. Bertrand Jones, & L. Osteen (Eds.), *Developing culturally relevant leadership learning (No. 152). New directions for student leadership* (pp. 9–21). Jossey-Bass.

Bloom, J. L., Weiser, S. G., & Buonocore, V. (2012). An appreciative approach to diversity training. *Journal of Appreciative Education, 1*(1), 25–34.

Bok, D. (2011). *Our underachieving colleges: A candid look at how much students learn and why they should be learning more.* Princeton University Press.

Bolman, L. G., & Deal, T. E. (2013). *Reframing organizations: Artistry, choice, and leadership* (5th ed.). Jossey-Bass.

Bordas, J. (2007). *Salsa, soul, and spirit: Leadership for a multicultural age.* Berrett-Koehler Publishers.

Bordas, J. (2012). *Salsa, soul, and spirit: Leadership for a multicultural age.* Berrett-Koehler Publishers.

Bordas, J. (2013). *The power of Latino leadership: Culture, inclusion, and contribution.* Berrett-Koehler Publishers.

Bordas, J. (2016). Leadership lessons from communities of color: Stewardship and collective action. In K. L. Guthrie, T. Bertrand Jones, & L. Osteen (Eds.), *Developing culturally relevant leadership learning (No. 152). New directions for student leadership* (pp. 61–74). Jossey-Bass.

Brooms, D. R. (2014). Mapping pathways to affirmative identities among Black males: Instilling the value and importance of education in K–12 and college classrooms. *Journal of African American Males in Education, 5*(2), 196–214. https://jaamejournal.scholasticahq.com/article/18455-mapping-pathways-to-affirmative-identities-among-black-males-instilling-the-value-and-importance-of-education-in-k-12-and-college-classrooms

Brooms, D. R. (2016). Encouraging success for Black male collegians: Support, brotherhood and bonding on campus. *Issues in Race & Society: An International Global Journal, 4*, 36–61. https://doi.org/10.1177/0021934717692520

Brooms, D. R., & Davis, A. R. (2017). Staying focused on the goal: Peer bonding and faculty mentors supporting Black males' persistence in college. *Journal of Black Studies, 48*(3), 305–326. https://doi.org/10.1177/0021934717692520

Bruce, J., & Collins, D. (2020). Photographing leadership: Making meaning of our world. In K. L. Guthrie, D. M. Jenkins, & Associates (Eds.), *Transforming learning: Instructional and assessment strategies for leadership education* (pp. 40–41). Information Age Publishing.

Brungardt, C., Greenleaf, J., Brungardt, C., & Arensdorf, J. (2006). Majoring in leadership: A review of undergraduate leadership degree programs. *Journal of Leadership Education, 5*(1), 4–24.

Brunsma, D., Brown, E., & Placier, P. (2012). Teaching race at historically White colleges and universities: Identifying and dismantling the walls of Whiteness. *Critical Sociology, 39*(5), 717–738.

Burkhardt, J. C., & Zimmerman-Oster, K. (1999). How does the richest, most widely educated nation prepare leaders for its future? *Proteus, 16*(2), 9.

Campbell, C. M., Smith, M., Dugan, J. P., & Komives, S. R. (2012). Mentors and college student leadership outcomes: The importance of position and process. *The Review of Higher Education, 35,* 595–625.

Carson, G. (2018, October 29). Inflammatory email spreads through DU. *DU Clarion.* https://duclarion.com/2018/10/inflammatory-email-spreads -through-du/

Carter-Black, J. (2007). Teaching cultural competence: An innovative strategy grounded in the universality of storytelling as depicted in African and African American storytelling traditions. *Journal of Social Work Education, 43*(1), 31–50.

Chapdelaine, R. F., & Alexitch, L. R. (2004). Social skills difficulty: Model of culture shock for international graduate students. *Journal of College Student Development, 45*(2), 167–184.

Chapman, N. H., & Kaya, N. (2020). Leadership: Changing the narrative. In K. L. Guthrie, D. M. Jenkins, & Associates (Eds.), *Transforming learning: Instructional and assessment strategies for leadership education* (pp. 121–122). Information Age Publishing.

Cheung-Judge, M. Y. (2001). The self as an instrument. *OD Practitioner, 33*(3), 11–16.

Chrislip, D. D. (2002). *The collaborative leadership fieldbook* (Vol. 255). John Wiley & Sons.

Chung, J. (2020). Encouraging creative reflection through journaling. In K. L. Guthrie, D. M. Jenkins, & Associates (Eds.), *Transforming learning: Instructional and assessment strategies for leadership education* (pp. 122–123). Information Age Publishing.

Chunoo, V. S., Beatty, C. C., & Gruver, M. D. (2019). Leadership educator as social justice educator. In K. L. Priest & D. M. Jenkins (Eds.), *Becoming and being a leadership educator (No. 164). New directions for student leadership* (pp. 87–103). John Wiley & Sons.

Chunoo, V. S., & Callahan, K. (2017). Pedagogy in action: Teaching culturally relevant leadership. *Journal of Leadership Studies, 11*(3), 42–47.

Chunoo, V. S., & French, G. E (2021). Socially just leadership education in action: Applying the culturally relevant leadership learning model. In K. L. Guthrie & V. S. Chunoo (Eds.), *Shifting the mindset: Socially just leadership education* (pp. 207–219). Information Age Publishing.

Chunoo, V. S., & Osteen, L. (2016). Purpose, mission, and context: The call for educating future leaders. In K. L. Guthrie & L. Osteen (Eds.), *New directions for higher education: No. 174. Reclaiming higher education's purpose in leadership development* (pp. 9–20). Jossey-Bass.

Church, A. T. (1982). Sojourner adjustment. *Psychological Bulletin, 91*(3), 540–572.

Cohen, C. J. (2004). Deviance as resistance: A new research agenda for the study of Black politics. *Du Bois Review: Social Science Research on Race, 1*(1), 27–45.

Collier, D. A., & Rosch, D. M. (2016). Effects associated with leadership program participation in international students compared to domestic students. *Journal of Leadership Education, 15*(4), 33–49.

Collins, P. H. (2000). *Black feminist thought: Knowledge, consciousness, and the politics of empowerment* (2nd ed.). Routledge.

Collins, P. H. (2002). *Black feminist thought: Knowledge, consciousness, and the politics of empowerment.* Routledge.

Cote-Meek, S. (2014). *Colonized classrooms: Racism, trauma and resistance in post-secondary education.* Fernwood Publishing.

Crawley, D. (2018). The five levels of listening. *The Compassionate Geek Blog.* https://www.doncrawley.com/the-five-levels-of-listening-how-to-be-a-better-listener/

Crenshaw, K. (1991). Mapping the margins: Intersectionality, identity politics, and violence against women of color. *Stanford Law Review, 43,* 1241–1299.

Creswell, J. W. (2013). *Qualitative inquiry & research design: Choosing among five approaches.* Sage.

Crosby, B. C. (2017). *Teaching leadership: An integrative approach.* Routledge.

Cross, Jr., W. E. (1991). *Shades of Black: Diversity in African-American identity.* Temple University Press.

Crotty, M. (1998). *The foundations of social research: Meaning and perspective in the research process.* SAGE.

Danowitz, M. A., & Tuitt, F. (2011). Enacting inclusivity through engaged pedagogy: A higher education perspective. *Equity & Excellence in Education, 44,* 40–56.

Darling-Hammond, L., Rosso, J., Austin, K., Orcutt, S., & Martin, D. (2001). *Session 1: How people learn: Introduction to learning theory.* Stanford University.

Davis, T., & Harrison, L. M. (2013). *Advancing social justice: Tools, pedagogies, and strategies to transform your campus.* Jossey-Bass.

Day, D. V. (2001). Leadership development: A review in context. *Leadership Quarterly, 11*(4), 581–613.

Day, D. V., Harrison, M. M., & Halpin, S. M. (2009). *An integrative approach to leader development: Connecting adult development, identity, and expertise.* Routledge.

Delgado, R., & Stefancic, J. (2012). *Critical race theory.* New York University Press.

Denzine, G. (1999). Personal and collective efficacy: Essential components of college students' leadership development. *Concepts & Connections, 8*(1), 1.

dschool. (n.d.). *Steps in design thinking process.* dschool.stanford.edu/resources

Dugan, J. P., & Komives, S. R. (2007). *Developing leadership capacity in college students: Findings from a national study.* National Clearinghouse for Leadership Programs, Multi-Institutional Study of Leadership. https://citeseerx .ist.psu.edu/viewdoc/download?doi=10.1.1.462.9299&rep=rep1&type=pdf

Dugan, J., Komives, S. R., & Segar, T. (2008). College student capacity for socially responsible leadership: Understanding norms and influences of race, gender, and sexual orientation. *NASPA Journal, 45*(4), 475–500.

Dugan, J. P. (2017). *Leadership theory: Cultivating critical perspectives.* Jossey-Bass.

Dugan, J. P., Kodama, C., Correia, B., & Associates. (2013). *Multi-institutional study of leadership insight report: Leadership program delivery.* National Clearinghouse for Leadership Programs.

Dugan, J. P., & Komives, S. R. (2011). Leadership theories. In S. R. Komives, J. P. Dugan, J. E. Owen, C. Slack, W. Wagner, & Associates (Eds.), *The handbook of student leadership development* (2nd ed., pp. 35–58). Jossey-Bass.

Dugan, J. P., & Velázquez, D. (2015). Teaching contemporary leadership: Advancing students' capacities to engage with difference. In S. K. Watt (Ed.). *Designing transformative multicultural initiatives: Theoretical foundations, practical applications, and facilitator considerations* (pp. 105–118). Stylus.

Escudero, B. (2019, January). How to practice culturally relevant pedagogy. *Teach for America.* https://www.teachforamerica.org/stories/how-to-engage -culturally-relevant-pedagogy

Ferguson, R. A. (2012). *The reorder of things: The university and its pedagogies of minority difference.* University of Minnesota Press.

First Story Toronto App and Bus Tour. (n.d.). https://ncct.on.ca/programs/ first-story-toronto-app-bus-tour/

Ford, J. (2020). Diversifying the vision of leadership. In K. L. Guthrie, D. M. Jenkins, & Associates (Eds.), *Transforming learning: Instructional and assessment strategies for leadership education* (pp. 100–101). Information Age Publishing.

Foucault, M. (1980). *Power/knowledge: Selected interviews and other writings 1972–1977.* Vintage Books.

Freire, P. (1973). *Pedagogy of the oppressed.* Penguin Books.

Francovich, C. (2020). Leadership studies at the crossroads. *Journal of Leadership Education, 19*(4), 163–174.

Greenblatt, S. (2005). International students and diversity in American higher education: Implications for internationalization. *International Journal of Diversity in Organizations, Communities and Nations, 5*(2), 163–171.

Griffin, C. (2006). Didacticism: Lectures and lecturing. In P. Jarvis (Ed.), *The theory and practice of teaching* (2nd ed., pp. 87–103). Routledge.

Grospitch, E., & Gleason, M. (2020). You think what? Utilizing reflection to enhance understanding of self and comfort with differing perspectives. In K. L. Guthrie, D. M. Jenkins, & Associates (Eds.), *Transforming learning: Instructional and assessment strategies for leadership education* (pp. 45–46). Information Age Publishing.

Guthrie, K. L., Beatty, C. C., & Wiborg, E. (2021). *Engaging in the leadership process: Identity, capacity, and efficacy for college students.* Information Age Publishing.

Guthrie, K. L., Bertrand Jones, T., & Osteen, L. (Eds.). (2016). *Developing culturally relevant leadership learning (No. 152, Winter). New directions for student leadership.* Jossey-Bass.

Guthrie, K. L., Bertrand Jones, T., & Osteen, L. (2017). The teaching, learning, and being of leadership: Exploring context and practice of the culturally relevant leadership learning model. *Journal of Leadership Studies, 11*(3), 61–67.

Guthrie, K. L., Bertrand Jones, T., Osteen, L., & Hu, S. (2013). *Cultivating leader identity and capacity in students from diverse backgrounds: ASHE Higher Education Report, 39,* 4. John Wiley & Sons.

Guthrie, K. L., & Chunoo, V. S. (2017). Transforming leadership learning for inclusion and cultural relevance. *Journal of Leadership Studies, 11*(3), 39–41.

Guthrie, K. L., & Chunoo, V. S. (Eds.). (2018). *Changing the narrative: Socially just leadership education.* Information Age Publishing.

Guthrie, K. L., & Chunoo, V. S. (Eds.). (2021). *Shifting the mindset: Socially just leadership education.* Information Age Publishing.

Guthrie, K. L., & Jenkins, D. M. (2018). *The role of leadership educators: Transforming learning.* Information Age Publishing.

Guthrie, K. L., & Osteen, L. (2012). Editors' notes. In K. L. Guthrie & L. Osteen (Eds.), *Developing students' leadership capacity (No. 140). New directions for student services* (pp. 1–3). Jossey-Bass.

Guthrie, K. L., & Rodríguez, J. M. (2018). Creating cocurricular socially just leadership learning environments. In K. L. Guthrie & V. S. Chunoo (Eds.), *Changing the narrative: Socially just leadership education* (pp. 245–258). Information Age Publishing.

Guthrie, K. L., Teig, T. S., & Hu, P. (2018). *Academic leadership programs in the United States.* Leadership Learning Research Center, Florida State University.

Hall, D. T. (2004). Self-awareness, identity, and leader development. In D. V. Day, S. J. Zaccaro, & S. M. Halpin (Eds.), *Leader development for transforming organizations: Growing leaders for tomorrow* (pp. 153–176). Erlbaum.

Hall, E. T. (1983). *The dance of life, the other dimension of time.* Doubleday.

Hammer, M. R. (2012). The intercultural development inventory: A new frontier in assessment and development of intercultural competence. In M. Vande Berg, R. M. Paige, & K. H. Lou (Eds.), *Student learning abroad* (pp. 115–136). Stylus.

Hardiman, R., & Jackson, B. W. (1997). Conceptual foundations for social justice courses. In M. Adams, L. A. Bell, & P. Griffin (Eds.), *Teaching for diversity and social justice.* Routledge.

Harding, H. E. (2011). *"A place of becoming" Leadership educators' experience teaching leadership: A phenomenological approach* [Unpublished doctoral dissertation]. University of Nebraska-Lincoln.

Hardy, C., Phillips, N., & Clegg, S. (2001). Reflexivity in social studies: A study of the production of the research subject. *Human Relations, 54*, 3–32.

Hartz, G. A. (1998). Why corporeal substances keep popping up in Leibniz's later philosophy. *British Journal for the History of Philosophy, 6*(2), 193–207.

Harvey, M., & Riggio, R. E. (Eds.). (2011). *Leadership studies: The dialogue of disciplines.* Edward Elgar.

Heifetz, R., Grashow, A., & Linsky, M. (2009). *The practice of adaptive leadership: Tools and tactics for changing your organization and the world.* Harvard Business Review.

Hellman, Y. (2014). *Learning for leadership: A facilitative approach for training leaders.* American Society for Training and Development.

Helms, J. E. (1984). Toward a theoretical explanation of the effects of race on counseling: A Black and White model. *The Counseling Psychologist, 12*, 153–165.

Higher Education Research Institute (HERI). (1996). *A social change model of leadership development: Guidebook Version III.* National Clearinghouse for Leadership Programs.

hooks, b. (1994). *Teaching to transgress: Education as the practice of freedom.* Routledge.

hooks, b. (2014). *Teaching to transgress: Education as the practice of freedom.* Routledge.

Horton, M., & Freire, P. (1990). *We make the road by walking: Conversations on education and social change.* Temple University Press.

House, R. J., Hanges, P., Javidan, M., Dorfman, P. W., & Gupta, V. (2004). *Culture, leadership and organizations: The GLOBE study of 62 countries.* SAGE.

Hu, P. (in press). International student leadership development: Honoring cultural identities to create inclusive environments. In K. L. Guthrie & K. L. Priest (Eds), *Complexities in leadership learning.* Information Age Publishing.

Hudson, J., Acosta, A., & Holmes, R. C. (Eds.). (2018). *Conduct and community: A residence life practitioner's guide.* Association of College and University Housing Officers–International.

Hurtado, S., Milem, J., Clayton-Pedersen, A., & Allen, W. (1999). *Enacting diverse learning environments: Improving the climate for racial/ethnic diversity in higher education. ASHE-ERIC Higher Education Report, 26*, 8. ERIC Clearinghouse on Higher Education. (ED430514)

Hurwitz, M., & Thompson, R. (Eds.). (2020). *Followership education (No. 167). New directions for student leadership.* John Wiley & Sons.

Jenkins, D. M. (2019). Exploring the lived experiences of becoming and being a leadership educator: A phenomenological inquiry. *Journal of Leadership Education, 18*(3).

Jenkins, D. M., & Allen, S. J. (2017). Aligning instructional strategies with learning outcomes and leadership competencies. In C. Seemiller (Ed.), *A competency-based approach for student leadership development (No. 156). New directions for student leadership* (pp. 43–58). Jossey-Bass.

Johnson, A. G. (2017). *Privilege, power, and difference* (3rd ed.). McGraw Hill.

Johnson, B., & Christensen, L. (2014). *Educational research: Quantitative, qualitative, and mixed approaches* (2nd ed.). Sage.

Jones, S. R. (2016). Authenticity in leadership: Intersectionality of identities. In K. L. Guthrie, T. Bertrand Jones, & L. Osteen (Eds.), *Developing culturally relevant leadership learning (No. 152). New directions for student leadership* (pp. 23–34). Jossey-Bass.

Jones, S. R., & Abes, E. S. (2013). *Identity development of college students: Advancing frameworks for multiple dimensions of identity.* Jossey-Bass.

Jones, S. R., Choe Kim, Y., & Skendall, K. (2012). (Re-) framing authenticity: Considering multiple social identities using autoethnographic and intersectional approaches. *The Journal of Higher Education, 83*(5), 698–724.

Jones, S., & McEwen, M. (2000). A conceptual model of multiple dimensions of identity. *Journal of College Student Development, 41*(4), 405–414.

Jones, S. R., & Stewart, D-L. (2016). Evolution of student development theory. In E. S. Abes (Ed.), *Critical perspectives on student development theory* (pp. 17–28). Jossey-Bass. https://doi.org/10.1002/ss.20172

Jones, S. R., Torres, V., & Arminio, J. (2013). *Negotiating the complexities of qualitative research in higher education: Fundamental elements and issues* (2nd ed.). Routledge.

Josselson, R. (1996). On writing other people's lives: Self-analytic reflections of a narrative researcher. In R. Josselson (Ed.), *The narrative study of lives, Vol. 4. Ethics and process in the narrative study of lives* (pp. 60–71). SAGE.

Kaufman, E. (2020). Cracking the case: Learning through student-written teaching case studies. In K. L. Guthrie, D. M. Jenkins, & Associates (Eds.), *Transforming learning: Instructional and assessment strategies for leadership education* (pp. 29–30). Information Age Publishing.

Kellerman, B. (2004). *Bad leadership: What it is, how it happens, why it matters.* Harvard Business Press.

Kellerman, B. (2012). Cut off at the pass: The limits of leadership in the 21st century. *Governance Studies at Brookings Institution,* 1–11. https://www.brookings.edu/wp-content/uploads/2016/06/0810_leadership_deficit_kellerman.pdf

Kelly, B. T., & Bhangal, N. K. (2018). Life narratives as a pedagogy for cultivating critical self-reflection. *New Directions for Student Leadership, 2018,* 41–52. https://doi.org/10.1002/yd.20296

Kendi, I. X. (2019). *How to be antiracist.* Penguin Books.

Kezar, A. J., Chambers, T. C., & Burkhardt, J. C. (Eds). (2005). *Higher education for public good: Emerging voices from a national movement.* Jossey-Bass.

Kim, E. (2012). An alternative theoretical model: Examining psychosocial identity development of international students in the United States. *College Student Journal, 46*(1), 99–113.

Kincheloe, J. L. (2008). *Critical pedagogy primer* (2nd ed.). Peter Lang Publishers.

Kolb, D. A. (1984). *Experiential learning: Experience as the source of learning and development.* Prentice-Hall.

Komives, S. R. (2011). Advancing leadership education. In S. R. Komives, J. P. Dugan, & J. E. Owen (Eds.), *The handbook for student leadership development* (pp. 1–19). Jossey-Bass.

Komives, S. R., Dugan, J. P., Owen, J. E., Slack, C., Wagner, W., & Associates. (2011). *The handbook for student leadership development* (2nd ed.). Jossey-Bass.

Komives, S. R., Owen, J. E., Longerbeam, S. D., Mainella, F. C., & Osteen, L. (2005). Developing a leadership identity: A grounded theory. *Journal of College Student Development, 46*, 593–611.

Komives, S. R., & Wagner, W. (Eds.). (2016). *Leadership for a better world: Understanding the social change model of leadership development.* John Wiley & Sons.

Komives, S. R., Wagner, W., & Associates (Eds.). (2017). *Leadership for a better world: Understanding the social change model of leadership* (2nd ed.). Jossey-Bass.

Kotter, J. (1990). *A force for change: How leadership differs from management.* Free Press.

Ladson-Billings, G. (1992). Culturally relevant teaching: The key to making multicultural education work. In C. A. Grant (Ed.), *Research and multicultural education* (pp. 106–121). Falmer Press.

Ladson-Billings, G. (1994). *The dreamkeepers: Successful teachers of African American children.* Jossey-Bass.

Ladson-Billings, G. (1995). Toward a theory of culturally relevant pedagogy. *American Educational Research Journal, 32*(3), 465–491.

Ladson-Billings, G. (2006). From the achievement gap to the education debt: Understanding achievement in U.S. schools. *Educational Researcher, 35*, 3–12.

Ladson-Billings, G. (2014). Culturally relevant pedagogy 2.0: Aka the remix. *Harvard Educational Review, 84*(1), 74–84.

Ladson-Billings, G. (2017). The r(evolution) will not be standardized: Teacher education, hip hop pedagogy, and culturally relevant pedagogy 2.0. In J. Paris & H. S. Alim (Eds.), *Culturally sustaining pedagogies: Teaching and learning for justice in a changing world* (pp. 141–156). Teachers College Press.

Lancaster, J. M., & Waryold, D. M. (Eds.). (2008). *Student conduct practice: The complete guide for student affairs professionals.* Stylus.

Latina Feminist Group. (2001). *Telling to live: Latina feminist testimonios.* Duke University Press.

Lee, J. J., & Rice, C. (2007). Welcome to America? International student perceptions of discrimination. *Higher Education, 53*, 381–409.

Le Roux, C. S. (2016). Exploring rigour in autoethnographic research. *International Journal of Social Research Methodology, 20*(2), 195–207.

Lorde, A. (1988). *A burst of light: Essays.* Firebrand Books.

Love, B. J. (2000). Developing a liberatory consciousness. In M. Adams, W. J. Blumenfeld, R. Castaneda, H. W. Hackman, M. L. Peters, & X. Zuniga (Eds.), *Readings for diversity and social justice* (pp. 470–474). Routledge.

Lucas, C. J. (1994). *American higher education: A history.* St. Martin's Press.

Mahoney, A. D. (2016). Culturally responsive integrated learning environments: A critical displacement approach. In K. L. Guthrie, T. Bertrand Jones, & L. Osteen (Eds.), *Developing culturally relevant leadership learning (No. 152). New directions for student leadership* (pp. 47–59). Jossey-Bass.

Mahoney, A. D. (2017). Being at the heat of the matter: Culturally relevant leadership learning, emotions, and storytelling. *Journal of Leadership Studies, 11*(3), 55–60.

Manning-Ouellette, A. (2020). Game On! Using Barnga to facilitate cultural awareness in leadership education. In K. L. Guthrie, D. M. Jenkins, & Associates (Eds.), *Transforming learning: Instructional and assessment strategies for leadership education* (pp. 81–82). Information Age Publishing.

Martin, G. L., Linder, C., & Williams, B. M. (Eds.). (2018). *New directions for student leadership: No. 160. Leadership learning through activism.* John Wiley & Sons.

Maslow, A. H. (1970). *Motivation and personality.* Harper & Row.

McClellan, P. (2012). Race, gender, and leadership identity: An autoethnography of reconciliation. *International Journal of Qualitative Studies in Education, 25*(1), 89–100.

McEwen, M. K. (2003). The nature and uses of theory. In S. R. Komives & D. Woodard (Eds.), *Student services: A handbook for the profession* (4th ed., pp. 153–178). Jossey-Bass.

McIntosh, P. (1989). White privilege: Unpacking the invisible knapsack. *Peace and Freedom*, 10–12.

Meichenbaum, D. (1985). Teaching thinking: A cognitive-behavioral perspective. In S. F. Chipman, J. W. Segal, & R. Glaser (Eds.), *Thinking and learning skills, Vol. 2: Research and open questions.* Lawrence Erlbaum.

Meriwether, L. (2018). Getting in formation to lead: Black female student leadership development. In K. L. Guthrie & V. S. Chunoo (Eds.), *Changing the narrative: Socially just leadership education* (pp. 93–108). Information Age Publishing.

Merriam, S. B., & Caffarella, R. S. (1999). *Learning in adulthood: A comprehensive guide.* Jossey-Bass.

Milem, J. F., Chang, M. J., & Antonio, A. L. (2005). *Making diversity work on campus: A research-based perspective.* Association American Colleges and Universities.

Miles, M. (1997). *Art, space and the City: Public art and urban futures.* Routledge.

Miles, M. B., Huberman, A. M., & Saldaña, J. (2014). *Qualitative data analysis* (3rd ed.). Sage.

Miller, M. (2020). Game change management. In K. L. Guthrie, D. M. Jenkins, & Associates (Eds.), *Transforming learning: Instructional and assessment strategies for leadership education* (pp. 114–115). Information Age Publishing.

Mitra, A. M. (2011). Learning how to look: The art of observation and leadership development. In M. Harvey & R. E. Riggio (Eds.), *Leadership studies: The dialogue of disciplines* (pp. 184–196). Edward Elgar.

Moore, P. J., & Toliver, S. D. (2010). Intraracial dynamics of Black professors' and Black students' communication in traditionally White colleges and universities. *Journal of Black Studies, 40,* 932–945. https://eujournal.org/index.php/esj/article/viewFile/5068/4840

Morante, C. (2020). Invitation to intentionality: An exploration of our purpose and authentic selves. In J. M. Volpe White, K. L. Guthrie, M. Torres, & Associates (Eds.), *Thinking to transform: Facilitating reflection in leadership learning* (pp. 63–64). Information Age Publishing.

Morgan Acosta, D. (2018). Infusing leadership education in advising identity-based organizations. In K. L. Guthrie & V. S. Chunoo (Eds.), *Changing the narrative: Socially just leadership education* (pp. 259–276). Information Age Publishing.

Morgan Acosta, D. (2020). The big picture. In J. M. Volpe White, K. L. Guthrie, M. Torres, & Associates (Eds.), *Thinking to transform: Facilitating reflection in leadership learning* (p. 84). Information Age Publishing.

Museus, S. D., & Griffin, K. A. (2011). Mapping the margins in higher education: On the promise of intersectionality frameworks in research and discourse. In K. A. Griffin & S. D. Museus (Eds.), *Using mixed-methods approaches to study intersectionality in higher education (No. 151). New directions for institutional research* (pp. 5–13). John Wiley & Sons.

Nicolescu, B. (2008). *Transdisciplinarity: Theory and practice.* Hampton Press.

O'Malley, E., & Cebulla, A. (2015). *Your leadership edge: Lead anytime, anywhere.* KLC Press.

Ospina, S., & Foldy, E. (2009). A critical review of race and ethnicity in the leadership literature: Surfacing context, power and the collective dimensions of leadership. *The Leadership Quarterly, 20,* 876–896.

Osteen, L. (2012). Considering context: Developing students' leadership capacity. *New Directions for Student Services, 140,* 5–15. https://doi.org/10.1002/ss.20028

Osteen, L. (2020). Tree of alignment. In J. M. Volpe White, K. L. Guthrie, M. Torres, & Associates (Eds.), *Thinking to transform: Facilitating reflection in leadership learning* (pp. 38–39). Information Age Publishing.

Osteen, L., Guthrie, K. L., & Bertrand Jones, T. (2016). Leading to transgress: Critical considerations for transforming leadership learning. In K. L. Guthrie, T. Bertrand Jones, & L. Osteen (Eds.), *Developing culturally relevant leadership learning (No. 152). New directions for student leadership* (pp. 95–106). Jossey-Bass.

Ostick, D., & Wall, V. (2011). Considerations for culture and social identity. In S. R. Komives, J. Dugan, J. Owen, C. Slack, W. Wagner, & Associates (Eds.), *The handbook for student leadership development* (pp. 339–368). Jossey-Bass.

Ostrove, J. M., & Long, S. M. (2007). Social class and belonging: Implications for college adjustment. *The Review of Higher Education, 30*(4), 363–389.

Owen, J. E. (2012). Using student development theories as conceptual frameworks in leadership education. In K. L. Guthrie & L. Osteen (Eds.),

Developing students' leadership capacity (No. 140). New directions for student services (pp. 17–35). Jossey-Bass.

Owen, J. E. (2020a). Personal narratives as authentic expression. In J. M. Volpe White, K. L. Guthrie, & M. Torres (Eds.), *Thinking to transform: Facilitating reflection in leadership learning*. Information Age Publishing.

Owen, J. E. (2020. *We are the leaders we've been waiting for: Women and leadership development in college*. Stylus.

Owen, J. E., Devies, B., & Reynolds, D. J. (2021). Going beyond 'add women then stir': Fostering feminist leadership. In K. L. Guthrie & V. S. Chunoo (Eds.), *Shifting the mindset: Socially just leadership education* (pp. 89–99). Information Age Publishing.

Owen, J. E., Hassell-Goodman, S., & Yamanaka, A. (2017). Culturally relevant leadership learning: Identity, capacity, and efficacy. *Journal of Leadership Studies, 11*(3), 48–54.

Palmer, P. J. (2007). *The courage to teach: Exploring the inner landscape of a teacher's life* (2nd ed.). Jossey-Bass.

Parks, S. D. (2005). *Leadership can be taught: A bold approach for a complex world*. Harvard Business Review Press.

Patel, E. (2016). Preparing interfaith leaders: Knowledge base and skill set for interfaith leaders. In K. L. Guthrie, T. Bertrand Jones, & L. Osteen (Eds.), *Developing culturally relevant leadership learning (No. 152). New directions for student leadership* (pp. 75–86). Jossey-Bass.

Patel, L. (2015). *Decolonizing educational research: From ownership to answerability*. Routledge.

Pessoa, J., Deloumeaux, L., & Ellis, S. (2009). *The 2009 UNESCO framework for cultural statistics (FCS)*. UNESCO Institute for Statistics.

Phillips, J. (2020). *Communities as assets*. In J. M. Volpe White, K. L. Guthrie, M. Torres, & Associates (Eds.), *Thinking to transform: Facilitating reflection in leadership learning* (p. 55). Information Age Publishing.

Pierre, D., Dunn, A., Barnes, A. C., Moore, L. L., Seemiller, C., Jenkins, D. M., Priest, K. L., Guthrie, K. L., Beatty, C. C., Britton, A. L., Duran, A., Bailey, K. J., & Odom, S. F. (2020). A critical look at leadership educator preparation: Developing an intentional and diverse approach to leadership learning and development: Priority 4 of the national leadership education research agenda 2020–2025. *Journal of Leadership Studies, 14*(3).

Piaget, J. (1972). The epistemology of interdisciplinary relationships. In Centre for Educational Research and Innovation (CERI), *Interdisciplinarity: Problems of teaching and research in universities* (pp. 127–139). Organisation for Economic Co-operation and Development.

Porter, S. R., & Swing, R. L. (2006). Understanding how first-year seminars affect persistence. *Research in Higher Education, 47*(1), 89–109. https://doi.org/10.1007/s11162-005-8153-6

Poyrazli, S., & Grahame, K. M. (2007). Barriers to adjustment: Needs of international students within a semi-urban campus community. *Journal of Instructional Psychology, 34*(1), 28–45.

Priest, K. L. (2020). ZOOM: A visual reflection tool. In J. M. Volpe White, K. L. Guthrie, M. Torres, & Associates, *Thinking to transform: Facilitating reflection in leadership learning* (pp. 40–41). Information Age Publishing.

Priest, K. L., Bauer, T., & Finnegan, J. (2020). *T.I.P.S. to study abroad: Simple letters for complex engagement*. In J. M. Volpe White, K. L. Guthrie, M. Torres, & Associates (Eds.), *Thinking to transform: Facilitating reflection in leadership learning* (pp. 90–92). Information Age Publishing.

Priest, K. L., & Jenkins, D. M. (2019). Developing a vision of leadership educator professional practice. In K. L. Priest & D. M. Jenkins (Eds.), *Being and becoming leadership educators (No. 164). New directions for student leadership* (pp. 9–22). Jossey-Bass.

Priest, K. L., & Middleton, E. (2016), Exploring leader identity and development. *New Directions for Student Leadership, 2016,* 37–47. https://doi.org/10.1002/yd.20160

Quintanilla, K. M., & Wahl, S. T. (2018). *Business and professional communication: Keys for workplace excellence.* Sage Publications.

Reichard, R. J., & Walker, D. O. (2016). In pursuit: Mastering leadership through leader developmental readiness. In R. J. Reichard & S. E. Thompson (Eds.), *Leader developmental readiness: Pursuit of leadership excellence (No. 149). New directions for student leadership* (pp. 15–25). Jossey-Bass.

Reyes, K. B., & Curry Rodríguez, J. E. (2012). Testimonio: Origins, terms, and resources. *Equity & Excellence in Education, 45*(3), 525–538.

Reynolds, A. L., & Pope, R. L. (1991). The complexities of diversity: Exploring multiple oppression. *Journal of Counseling and Development, 70,* 171–180.

Riggio, R. E. (2020). Why followership? In M. Hurwitz & R. Thompson (Eds.), *New directions for student leadership: No. 167. Followership education* (pp. 15–22). John Wiley & Sons.

Riggio, R. E., Ciulla, J. B., & Sorenson, G. J. (2003). Leadership education at the undergraduate level: A liberal arts approach to leadership development. In S. E. Murphy & R. E. Riggio (Eds.), *The future of leadership development* (pp. 223–236). Lawrence Erlbaun.

Roberts, D. C. (2007). *Deeper learning in leadership: Helping college students find the potential within.* Jossey-Bass.

Roberts, D., & Ullom, C. (1989). Student leadership program model. *NASPA Journal, 27*(1), 67–74.

Rosch, D. M. (Ed.). (2017). *The role of student organizations in developing leadership.* Jossey-Bass.

Rosch, D. M., & Anthony, M. D. (2012). Leadership pedagogy: Putting theory to practice. In K. L. Guthrie & L. Osteen (Eds.), *Developing students' leadership capacity (No. 140). New directions for student services* (pp. 53–64). Jossey-Bass.

Rosch, D. M., & Collins, J. (2017). The significance of student organizations to leadership development. In D. M. Rosch (Ed.), *The role of student organizations in developing leadership (No. 155). New directions for student leadership* (pp. 9–20). Jossey-Bass.

Rose-Redwood, C. A., & Rose-Redwood, R. S. (2013). Self-segregation or global mixing? Social interactions and the international student experience. *Journal of College Student Development, 54*(4), 413–429.

Rost, J. C. (1991). *Leadership for the twenty-first century*. Praeger.

Ruderman, M. N., & Ernst, C. (2004). Finding yourself: How social identity affects leadership. *Leadership in Action, 24*(3), 3–7.

Saldaña, J. (2013). *The coding manual of qualitative researchers* (2nd ed.). SAGE.

Sawyer, K. (2017). *Group genius: The creative power of collaboration*. Basic Books.

Schrage, J. M., & Giacomini, N. G. (Eds.). (2009). *Reframing campus conflict: Student conduct practice through a social justice lens*. Stylus.

Schwandt, T. A. (2001). *Dictionary of qualitative inquiry* (2nd ed.). SAGE.

Seemiller, C. (2020). Organizational change case study project. In K. L. Guthrie, D. M. Jenkins, & Associates, *Transforming learning: Instructional and assessment strategies for leadership education* (pp. 48–50). Information Age Publishing.

Seemiller, C., & Priest, K. L. (2015). The hidden 'who' in leadership education: Conceptualizing leadership educator professional identity development. *Journal of Leadership Education, 14*(3), 132–151.

Seemiller, C., & Priest, K. L. (2017). Leadership educator journeys: Expanding a model of leadership educator professional identity development. *Journal of Leadership Education, 16*(2), 1–22.

Sessa, V. I., Alonso, N., Farago, P., Schettino, G., Tacchi, K., & Bragger, J. D. (2017). Student organizations as avenues for leader learning and development. In D. M. Rosch (Ed.), *New Directions for Student Leadership: No. 155. The role of student organizations in developing leadership* (pp. 21–32). Jossey-Bass.

Shankman M. L., Allen, S. J., & Haber-Curran, P. (2015). *Emotionally intelligent leadership: A guide for students* (2nd ed.). Jossey-Bass.

Shenberger, M. A., & Guthrie, K. L. (2021). Leader activists: Connecting leadership learning and student resistance. In K. L. Guthrie & V. S. Chunoo (Eds.), *Shifting the mindset: Socially just leadership education* (pp. 193–206). Information Age Publishing.

Sinek, S. (2009). *Start with why: How great leaders inspire everyone to take action*. Penguin Books.

Smith, A. A. (2019, May 23). Study finds more low-income students attending college. *Inside Higher Ed.* https://www.insidehighered.com/news/2019/05/23/pew-study-finds-more-poor-students-attending-college

Solorzano, D., Ceja, M., & Yosso, T. J. (2000). Critical race theory, racial microaggressions, and campus racial climate: The experiences of African American college students. *The Journal of Negro Education, 69*(1/2), 60–73.

Sorrells, K. (2020). *Intercultural communication: Globalization and social justice*. SAGE.

Sowcik, M., & Komives, S. R. (2020). Emerging themes in disciplinary based leadership education. In M. Sowcik & S. R. Komives (Eds.), *How academic disciplines approach leadership development (No. 165). New directions for student leadership* (pp. 163–181). Wiley.

Spencer Jr., D. (2019). *"Like a Unicorn:" A narrative inquiry exploring the leadership experiences of undergraduate Black men* [Unpublished doctoral dissertation]. The Florida State University.

Spencer, G. (2020). Empathic listening triads. In K. L. Guthrie, D. M. Jenkins, & Associates (Eds.), *Transforming learning: Instructional and assessment strategies for leadership education* (pp. 93–95). Information Age Publishing.

Stryker, S., & Burke, P. J. (2000). The past, present, and future of an identity theory. *Social Psychology Quarterly, 63,* 284–297.

Sue, D. W., Capodilupo, C. M., Torino, G. C., Bucceri, J. M., Holder, A. M. B., Nadal, K. L., & Esquilin, M. (2007). Racial microaggressions in everyday life: Implications for clinical practice. *American Psychologist, 62*(4), 271–286.

Sutherland, L., Howard, S., & Markauskaite, L. (2010). Professional identity creation: Examining the development of beginning preservice teachers' understanding of their work as teachers. *Teaching and Teacher Education, 26*(3), 455–465.

Tapia-Fuselier, N., & Irwin, L. (2019). Strengths so White: Interrogating StrengthsQuest education through a critical Whiteness lens. *Journal of Critical Scholarship on Higher Education and Student Affairs, 5*(1), 30–44. https://ecommons.luc.edu/cgi/viewcontent.cgi?article=1113&context=jcshesa

Taranath, A. (2014). *T.I.P.S. to study abroad: Simple letters for complex engagement.* Flying Chickadee.

Taylor, L., & Brownell, E. (2017). Building inclusive leaders: A framework for leadership education. In A. Boitano, R. L. Dutra, & H. E. Schockman (Eds.), *Breaking the zero-sum game: Transforming societies through inclusive leadership.* Emerald Publishing.

Tecnológico de Monterrey (2020). Diversidad e Inclusión. Instituto Tecnológico y de Estudios Superiores de Monterrey. https://tec.mx/sites/default/files/2020-10/reporte-diversidad-e-inclusion-oct2020.pdf

Teig, T. (2020). What's in my leader house. In J. M. Volpe White, K. L. Guthrie, M. Torres, & Associates (Eds.), *Thinking to transform: Facilitating reflection in leadership learning* (p. 92). Information Age Publishing.

Terry, R. (1993). *Authentic leadership: Courage in action.* Jossey-Bass.

The National Task Force on Civic Learning and Democratic Engagement. (2012). A crucible moment: College learning & democracy's future. Association of American Colleges and Universities.

Thelin, J. R. (2011). *A history of American higher education.* JHU Press.

Torres, M. (2019). *Ella creyó que podía, así que lo hizo: Exploring latina leader identity development through testimonio* [Unpublished doctoral dissertation]. The Florida State University.

Torres, M. (2020). Testimonio: Leader profile. In J. M. Volpe White, K. L. Guthrie, M. Torres, & Associates (Eds.), *Thinking to transform: Facilitating reflection in leadership learning* (p. 80). Information Age Publishing.

AU: Cite or delete.

Treviño, R. (2020, September 7). Social leadership in action! Winners of the Eugenio Garza Sada award. *Conecta news desk.* https://tec.mx/en/news/national/institution/social-leadership-action-winners-eugenio-garza-sada-award

Truth and Reconciliation Commission of Canada. (2015). *Final report of the truth and reconciliation commission of Canada: Summary: Honouring the truth, reconciling for the future.* Truth and Reconciliation Commission of Canada.

Turner, Y. (2009). "Knowing me, knowing you," is there nothing we can do? Pedagogic challenges in using group work to create an intercultural learning space. *Journal of Studies in International Education, 13*(2), 240–255.

University of Toronto. (2017). Wecheehetowin: Final report of the steering committee for the University of Toronto response to the truth and reconciliation commission of Canada. https://www.provost.utoronto.ca/wp-content/uploads/sites/155/2018/05/Final-Report-TRC.pdf

VanBergeijk, E. O., Klin, A., & Volkmar, F. R. (2008). Supporting more able students on the autism spectrum: College and beyond. *Journal of Autism and Developmental Disorders, 38*(7), 1359–1370.

Van Manen, M. (2018). *Researching lived experience: Human science for an action sensitive pedagogy* (2nd ed.). Routledge.

Villanueva, A. (2018, September 5). 13 facts you might not know about Tec de Monterrey's past. *Conecta news desk.* https://tec.mx/en/news/national/institution/13-facts-you-might-not-know-about-tec-de-monterreys-past

Volpe White, J. M. (2020). One-minute reflection paper. In J. M. Volpe White, K. L. Guthrie, M. Torres, & Associates (Eds.), *Thinking to transform: Facilitating reflection in leadership learning* (pp. 89–90). Information Age Publishing.

Volpe White, J. M., Guthrie, K. L., & Torres, M. (2019). *Thinking to transform: Reflection in leadership learning.* Information Age Publishing.

Wagner, W. (2007). The social change model of leadership: A brief overview. *Concepts & Connections, 15*(1), 8–10.

Watkins, S. R. (2020). Theater of bad leadership. In K. L. Guthrie, D. M. Jenkins, & Associates (Eds.), *Transforming learning: Instructional and assessment strategies for leadership education* (pp. 120–121). Information Age Publishing.

Watt, S. K. (2016). The practice of freedom: Leading through controversy. In K. L. Guthrie, T. Bertrand Jones, & L. Osteen (Eds.), *Developing culturally relevant leadership learning (No. 152). New directions for student leadership* (pp. 35–46). Jossey-Bass.

Waryold, D. M., & Lancaster, J. M. (Eds.). (2013). *The state of student conduct: Current forces and future challenges: Revisited.* Association for Student Conduct Administration.

Weber, L. (2001). *Understanding race, class, gender, and sexuality: A conceptual framework.* McGraw-Hill.

Werner, L., Hellstrom, D., Chung, J., Kessenich, K., Taylor Jr, L., & Capeder, A. (2016). Bridging theory and practice in the leadership classroom: Intentional emergence as a modern pedagogy. *Journal of Leadership Education, 15*(4), 206–216.

White, J. V. (2012). Students' perception of the role of reflection in leadership learning. *Journal of Leadership Education, 11*(2).

Wiborg, E. R. (2020). *A critical discourse analysis of leadership learning* (Publication No. 28022412) [Doctoral dissertation, Florida State University]. ProQuest.

Wilson, S. (2008). *Research is ceremony: Indigenous research methods.* Fernwood Publishing.

Wren, J. T. (1994). Teaching leadership: The art of the possible. *Journal of Leadership Studies, 1*(2), 73–93.

Wiborg, E. (2018). Coalescing communities: The call for critical leadership pedagogy in leadership education. In K. L. Guthrie & V. S. Chunoo (Eds.), *Changing the narrative: Socially just leadership education* (pp. 305–320). Information Age Publishing.

Wiborg, E. R. (2020). *A critical discourse analysis of leadership learning.* Available from Dissertations & Theses @ Florida State University - FCLA; ProQuest Dissertations & Theses Global. (2447509036). https://login.proxy.lib .fsu.edu/login?url=https://www.proquest.com/dissertations-theses/ critical-discourse-analysis-leadership-learning/docview/2447509036/ se-2?accountid=4840

Williams, T. O. (2016). Internalization of dominance and subordination: Barriers to creative and intellectual fullness. In K. L. Guthrie, T. Bertrand Jones, & L. Osteen (Eds.), *Developing culturally relevant leadership learning (No. 152). New directions for student leadership* (pp. 87–94). Jossey-Bass.

Yosso, T. J., Smith, W., Ceja, M., & Solórzano, D. (2009). Critical race theory, racial microaggressions, and campus racial climate for Latina/o undergraduates. *Harvard Educational Review, 79*, 659–691.

Zimmerman-Oster, K., & Burkhardt, J. (1999). Leadership in the making: Impact and insights from leadership development programs in U.S. colleges and universities. *Journal of Leadership Studies, 6*(3–4), 50–66.

APPENDIX

Overview of Questions Provided

Operationalizing Culturally Relevant Leadership Learning, pages 241–248
Copyright © 2021 by Information Age Publishing
All rights of reproduction in any form reserved.

CRLL Constructs	Personal Development	Professional Development	Co-Curricular Program Development	Co-Curricular Implementation	Academic Program Development	Academic Implementation	Theoretical Frameworks	Research Methods
Identity	• How do your past experiences with leadership contribute to your current approach to understanding students' leadership identity? • What role do you feel your social identities play in how you have conversations on culture and leadership?	• In what ways do you consider your social identities with your professional leadership educator identity? • How will you use tools, intentional emergence pedagogy, in instructional and assessment strategies?	• How will you incorporate identity development as a learning outcome for all co-curricular programming? • What reflective strategies will be used to support students' answers to "Who am I?" • How can you incorporate a life story approach to help all learners see themselves already in the work of leadership?	• In what ways will you support students in acknowledging, reflecting, and honoring their salient identities? • How will you incorporate leadership identity development in student leader trainings? • How is identity foundational to co-curricular leadership learning opportunities you design?	• How can identity be presented as a socially constructed concept throughout the curricula? • How will identity be integrated in all areas of the curricula? • In what ways will leadership identity development be explored and infused with salient social identities?	• In what ways will you share your personal identities with students? • How will you use tools, such as the Model of Multiple Dimensions of Identity (MMDI) (Jones & McEwen, 2000), in instructional and assessment strategies? • How will identity be integrated throughout the course rather than a "one and done" topic?	• How can identity and positionality be presented a socially constructed concepts throughout the research process? • How will positionality be negotiated in all areas of the research process? • In what ways will leadership identity development be researched while centering minoritized social identities?	• How can positionality statements be written to address biases and power dynamics throughout the research process? • How will leader identity be negotiated in respect to research design and culturally relevant research methods? • In what ways can counternarrative methods be centered in culturally relevant ways?
	• What does cultural competence mean to you?	• How will identity be integrated throughout professional development opportunity for the purpose of reflection and self-work?						
Capacity	• Reflect on your own capacity for leadership?	• What reflection and professional development strategies will be used for you and other leadership educators you work with to practice considering CRLL and anti-racism frameworks?	• In what ways will individual leadership learning plans be incorporated for capacity development of student leaders?	• What activities, role playing, simulations, case studies, or games will be used for students to practice deconstructing complex problems?	• How will the curricula be scaffolded to best develop competencies needed for leadership?	• What instructional strategies will be used for students to practice deconstructing complex problems?	• How will leadership theoretical and conceptual frameworks be critiqued and analyzed through a culturally relevant leadership learning lens?	• How will traditional research methods be critiqued through a culturally relevant leadership learning lens?

(continued)

CRLL Constructs	Personal Development	Professional Development	Co-Curricular Program Development	Co-Curricular Implementation	Academic Program Development	Academic Implementation	Theoretical Frameworks	Research Methods
Capacity (continued)	• Who, what, and when contributed to building your leadership capacity?	• How will professional development outcomes center your own capacity development for engaging with diverse students?	• For semester long programs, how can you intentionally scaffold learning for maximum capacity development?	• How will students be supported when engaging across differences?	• In what ways is reflection integrated throughout the curricula to assist students' development of this skill?	• How will engaging across differences be developed throughout the course?	• In what ways is reflection integrated throughout the research process to assist the research in interrogating their own identity?	• In what ways can traditional understandings of culture be integrated throughout the research methods?
	• How can you continue to grow your capacity for cultural competence and culturally relevant leadership?	• How will you develop an ongoing process to assess your evolving capacity to facilitate and engage in culturally relevant leadership learning?	• How will engaging across differences be integrated in all programs?	• How will diverse students be represented in capacity development in your programs?	• How will authenticity and self-awareness be at the heart of the curricula?	• How will course learning outcomes center capacity development of diverse students?	• What strategies will you employ in order to center identity and self-awareness through the research process?	• What strategies can researchers adapt that are rooted in culturally relevant research approaches?
Efficacy	• What resistance to social justice issues and frameworks have you experienced teaching and facilitating leadership education?	• How can professional development opportunities center more diverse voices and experiences?	• How do you redefine leaders beyond only holding positions?	• How are diverse voices and experiences represented and modeled intentionally?	• In what ways will issues of power and dominance be deconstructed and examined?	• How are diverse voices and experiences represented and modeled intentionally?	• In what ways will issues of privilege and structural inequities be deconstructed and examined in the leadership process?	• In what ways will dominant narratives be disrupted by socially just research methods?
	• How is resistance contributed to your own confidence when leading topics on diversity and social justice?	• How can professional development redefine who you and other leadership educators consider can be leaders and what leadership is with a socially just lens?	• During student leader trainings, in what ways will you deconstruct and examine internalized subordination and dominance?	• What reflective aspects of a program will support students' belief in their ability to be a leader?	• How will topics of adaptive leadership be explored to sharpen learners' belief in the ability to lead?	• How will this course redefine who can be leaders and what leadership is beyond positional?	• How will topics like deviant practice be explored in leadership learning research?	• How will counternarratives of minoritized educators and learners be explored in leadership learning research?

(continued)

CRLL Constructs	Personal Development	Professional Development	Co-Curricular Program Development	Co-Curricular Implementation	Academic Program Development	Academic Implementation	Theoretical Frameworks	Research Methods
Efficacy (continued)	• How did you navigate the resistance? What would you have done differently?	• What assessment strategies will be used to assess your own professional development ongoing growth?	• In what ways will you create opportunities for students to reflect on what they believe they can do to enact positive change?	• How will your program redefine leadership to being socially just?	• In what ways will students' own positionality on various social issues be explored in order for them to develop their sense of being able to enact change?	• What assessment strategies will be used to honor diverse voices and experiences?	• In what ways will leadership educators' own positionality intersecting social identities be explored in order for them to develop their sense of researcher identity?	• In what ways will current research and theories be interrogated and critiqued in literature reviews and theoretical frameworks explored in order for them to develop their sense of researcher identity?
Historical Legacy of Inclusion/Exclusion	• What culture(s) do you consider yourself a member of? • What is the history of your cultures' legacy of inclusion/exclusion in society? In higher education? In leadership?	• What histories need to be acknowledged in order to center an anti-racist framework for leadership education? • How can leadership educator professional development be redesigned and not center historically white learning environments?	• From examining the historical legacy of your program, department, division, and university surrounding values of diversity and inclusion, how do you need to redesign your programming? • How is the history of your institution examined in your leadership learning programs? Do you acknowledge the land you use? Why are buildings named after specific people?	• How will you include land acknowledgement statements in your programs? • How will historical narratives of diverse leaders and followers be used in the learning of leadership?	• In what ways will your institutional history be explored and connected to leadership learning? • In addition to institutional history, how will opportunities to confront the legacy of inclusion and exclusion in higher education and leadership be discussed?	• Will you include a land acknowledgement statement in your syllabus? What will this statement include? • How will your classroom be redesigned from historically white learning environments?	• In what ways will your context and environmental history be explored and connected to the theoretical and conceptual framework guiding the research? • In addition to history and environmental context, how can theoretical frameworks confront the legacy of inclusion and exclusion in leadership education research?	• Whose ideas of leadership are represented in current leadership theories? • In what ways can context and environmental history be centered throughout the research methods?

(continued)

CRLL Constructs	Personal Development	Professional Development	Co-Curricular Program Development	Co-Curricular Implementation	Academic Program Development	Academic Implementation	Theoretical Frameworks	Research Methods
Historical Legacy of Inclusion/Exclusion (continued)	• In what ways have you perpetuated historical legacies of inclusion and exclusion personally and professionally?	• How will historical narratives of minoritized leadership educators be used in leadership educator professional development opportunities?	• What historical leaders do you present as archetypes in your programs? Do they hold diverse identities?	• In what ways will your program challenge dominant ways of leading (and being)?	• How will concepts of power, privilege, and oppression be discussed historically throughout the curricula by exploring it in different contexts?	• How will historical narratives of diverse leaders and followers be used in the learning of leadership?	• How will concepts of socially just leadership education be discussed historically throughout the research design in different contexts?	• How can disrupting and naming dominant approaches to research methods confront the legacy of inclusion and exclusion in leadership education research?
Compositional Diversity	• What is your process in understanding your own social identities? • In what spaces do you hold minoritized identities?	• Have you done an audit of identities represented as leadership educators in your professional context? If so, what can you determine from who is represented as leadership educators?	• What is your process in considering speakers, panelists, and facilitators? Are diverse identities represented?	• From an audit of identities represented in your programs, what can you determine from who is participating?	• Throughout the curricula, will diverse authors be included in required course content?	• Have you done an audit of identities represented in your classes? If so, what can you determine from who is taking your courses?	• How will minoritized experiences be explored through leadership learning research?	• How does who has access to formal leadership education determine the research findings of leadership education research?
	• How are individuals who hold minoritized identities centered in your pedagogy or work as a leadership educator?	• How will who is included or excluded from being identified as a leadership educator be addressed?	• How are diverse individuals represented (or not represented) in student government and other student organizational leadership positions?	• How will individuals with diverse race, class, gender, and sexuality be acknowledged, honored, and invited to contribute to the program?	• Will the demographics of instructors and teaching assistants align with institutional, local, state, national, and global demographics?	• How will who is included or excluded from academically based course be addressed?	• Will research participant identities align with the environmental contexts being explored in the research questions?	• How can research recruitment methods be more inclusive and culturally relevant?

(continued)

CRLI Constructs	Personal Development	Professional Development	Co-Curricular Program Development	Co-Curricular Implementation	Academic Program Development	Academic Implementation	Theoretical Frameworks	Research Methods
Compositional Diversity (continued)	• How do your identities align with institutional, local, state, national, global demographics?	• How will race, class, gender, and sexuality be acknowledged and honored in the professional development space and contribute to the ongoing learning of leadership educators?	• Do student affairs staff demographics align with institutional, local, state, national, global demographics?	• In what ways are your programs interrogating diversity beyond simple numbers of people?	• How can curriculum be developed to include all perspectives, even those whose are not in attendance?	• How will race, class, gender, and sexuality be acknowledged and honored in the academic space and contribute to the learning environment?	• How can leadership learning research be developed to include more culturally relevant approaches?	• How can leadership learning research be more inclusive of researchers who hold minoritized identities?
Psychological Dimension	• What language is used in your syllabi or program materials you design and what messages do these send? • How do you incorporate diverse perspectives in your own work?	• How will space be created for you and other leadership educators to reflect on your own journey in leadership education? • What opportunities will you create for yourself and your colleagues to confront differing worldviews from both content and cultural perspectives?	• What language is used in your marketing materials and what messages do these send? • Are diverse students included in decision making process for co-curricular programming?	• How will space be created for participants to reflect on their leadership learning? • How will students be supported in confronting differing worldviews from both content and process perspectives?	• How will courses situate students as equity-minded leaders who are empowered to act inclusively? • In what ways will opportunities for learners' cognitive dissonance be intentionally included in curricula?	• How will space be created for learners and instructors to reflect on their leadership learning? • What opportunities will be provided for students differing worldviews from both content and process perspectives?	• How can leadership educators also be scholar-activist who are empowered to center socially just research outcomes? • In what ways can leadership learning researchers constantly frame their positionality statements in identity, capacity, and efficacy?	• How can researchers continue to educate themselves on critical methods and culturally relevant approaches to research methodology? • How can your epistemological approach be more culturally relevant?

(continued)

CRLL Constructs	Personal Development	Professional Development	Co-Curricular Program Development	Co-Curricular Implementation	Academic Program Development	Academic Implementation	Theoretical Frameworks	Research Methods
Psychological Dimension (continued)	• How do your internal and external beliefs show up in your work as a leadership educator?	• In what ways will you and other leadership educators be challenged to consider and confront the cultural realities that resist necessary change?	• How will participants be invited into the program by both internal and external beliefs?	• In what ways will students be challenged to consider and confront the cultural realities that resist necessary change?	• How is critical reflection integrated throughout courses?	• In what ways will students be challenged to consider and confront the cultural realities that resist necessary change?	• How is socially just reflection integrated throughout the research process?	• How can research reflexivity be guided with prompts that are rooted in CRLL?
Behavioral Dimension	• How do you model leadership learning as a self-work and personal development process for leadership learners?	• In what ways will behaviors of being a leadership educator be redefined to include and center more minoritized leadership educators?	• How do you model leadership learning as a liberatory process throughout your programs?	• How are your programs including diverse leaders' ways of being?	• How will opportunities for learners' reflection on their own cultural socialization and engagement with difference be included in the curricula?	• How will ways will behaviors of being a leader be redefined to include diverse individuals?	• How will researchers' reflection on their own leader identity, capacity, and efficacy be included in the theoretical framework?	• How can leadership researchers apply the National Leadership Educators Research Agenda to their modes of inquiry?
	• In what ways can you model for learners to engage across difference in culturally relevant ways?	• How will observations of the behavior of current leadership educators be discussed through professional development?	• In what ways can you authentically support students to engage across difference?	• In what ways is reflection being modeled as a critical strategy for all leadership learning?	• In what ways will your program have theory as foundational, but be centered in practice of diverse individuals?	• How will observations of the behavior of current leaders be discussed throughout the course?	• In what ways will your research be grounded in a socially just theoretical foundational and center minoritized individuals?	• How can researchers constantly answer for themselves, "what makes this research design culturally relevant?"
	• How can you engage in critical reflection to unlearn and relearn culturally relevant approaches to leadership learning?	• How will critical reflection be used both as a professional development strategy as a self-work strategy?	• How do we engage in critical reflection to unlearn and relearn ways to dominate ways of knowing, being, and doing?	• How are your programs interrogating current leader's behaviors?	• How will all experiences be included, and elitism be eradicated from the curricula?	• How will critical reflection be used both as an instructional strategy and an assessment of learning strategy?	• How can oppressive systems be addressed and navigated through the research design?	• How can culturally relevant approaches be more explicit in the research design?

(continued)

CRLL Constructs	Personal Development	Professional Development	Co-Curricular Program Development	Co-Curricular Implementation	Academic Program Development	Academic Implementation	Theoretical Frameworks	Research Methods
Organizational Structural Dimension	• How will you interrogate your own complicity within organizations and structures that perpetuate inequities for some groups?	• How will anti-racist pedagogy and intentional emergence pedagogy be integrated throughout professional development curriculum to challenge dominate ways of being a leadership educator?	• How will you interrogate student organizational positions and how those positions are selected?	• What tools will be utilized, such as critical feminist pedagogy (hooks, 1994), to break down hierarchies between facilitator and students, in the program structure?	• How can your courses be developed or redesigned to challenge the traditional dominant ways of leading?	• How will critical pedagogy be integrated throughout curriculum to challenge dominate ways of being?	• How can leadership education research approaches be redesigned to challenge the traditional dominant ways of inquiry?	• How can leadership education train reviewers to critique studies framed from traditional and dominant ways of inquiry?
	• In what ways can you continuously interrogate your role in the leadership identity, capacity, and efficacy for learners?	• In what ways will relevant depictions of leadership educator across social identities, social locations, and organizations be integrated into all aspects of professional development?	• In what ways will development of identity, capacity, and efficacy be integrated into organizational leader trainings?	• How will students be encouraged to use criticality in their own student organizational structures?	• In what ways will the curriculum be developed with criticality in mind?	• In what ways will relevant depictions of leaders across social identities, social locations, and organizations be integrated into the structure of the course?"	• In what ways will the theoretical framework and research design be developed with CRLL in mind?	• How can leadership development be made accessible in meaningful ways outside of higher education?
	• What role will you play in generative practices centered on socially just outcomes for organizational structures in leadership education?	• What opportunities will be created for discussion regarding current societal contexts?	• How will generative practices be intentional in student organizational structures?	• How will space be integrated into programs for tough conversations about oppressive structures?	• How will feedback on courses' cultural relevance be intentionally collected and incorporated into future curriculum revisions?	• What opportunities will be given for discussion regarding current oppressive practices in higher education?	• How can research peer debriefing and triangulation be more culturally relevant?	• What does the practice of civic leadership look like, and how might this inform civic leadership development and research outcomes?

About the Authors

Cameron C. Beatty (he/him/his) is an assistant professor in the Educational Leadership and Policy Studies Department at Florida State University. Cameron teaches courses in the undergraduate leadership studies program and the higher education graduate program, as well as conducts research with the Leadership Learning Research Center. Cameron's research foci includes exploring the intersections of gender and race in leadership education, leadership development of Students of Color on historically White college campuses, and understanding experiences of racial battle fatigue for Black and Latinx students. In 2019, Cameron co-edited a monograph titled: *Critical Considerations for Race, Ethnicity and Culture for Fraternity and Sorority Life* (Jossey-Bass, 2019). Cameron also co-authored the book, *Engaging in the Leadership Process: Identity, Capacity, and Efficacy for College Students* (Information Age Publishing, 2021), with Kathy L. Guthrie and Erica R. Wiborg. He is a scholar passionate about deconstructing race, systemic racism, and hegemonic masculinity in postsecondary education environments. Cameron is a 2020–2021 McKnight Junior Faculty Fellow with the Florida Education Fund. He recently received the FSU Inclusive Teaching and Mentoring Award. Cameron was named a 2018 ACPA (American College Personnel Association) Emerging Scholar designee. Prior to joining the faculty at Florida State University, Cameron was an assistant professor at Salem State University in the higher education student affairs program. He was also previously the coordinator and lecturer for the leadership studies program at Iowa State University, where he was not only responsible for

Operationalizing Culturally Relevant Leadership Learning, pages 249–250
Copyright © 2021 by Information Age Publishing
All rights of reproduction in any form reserved.
249

the administration of the certificate program, but also directed the Global Leadership Study Abroad Program to Sweden and the Vermeer International Scholarship Program. Cameron has professional experience in fraternity and sorority advising, campus programming boards, and supervising academic peer mentors.

Kathy L. Guthrie (she/her) is an associate professor of higher education at Florida State University. In addition to teaching in the higher education program, Kathy also serves as the director of the Leadership Learning Research Center and coordinates the Undergraduate Certificate in Leadership Studies, which are both partnerships between the College of Education and the Division of Student Affairs. Prior to becoming a faculty member, Kathy served as a student affairs administrator for 10 years in various areas including campus activities, commuter services, community engagement, and leadership development. Kathy's research focuses on leadership learning, socially just leadership education, online teaching and learning, and professional development for student affairs professionals specifically in leadership education. Kathy has developed and taught both undergraduate and graduate courses in leadership and higher education. Kathy has authored/co-authored over 45 refereed journal articles and book chapters, and co-edited four monographs in the New Directions series. She co-authored *The Role of Leadership Educators: Transforming Leadership* (Information Age Publishing, 2018) and *Thinking to Transform: Reflection in Leadership Learning* (Information Age Publishing, 2019); and co-edited *Changing the Narrative: Socially Just Leadership Education* (Information Age Publishing, 2018) and *Shifting the Mindset: Socially Just Leadership Education* (Information Age Publishing, 2021). She has received awards including FSU Transformation through Teaching Award, Graduate Faculty Mentor Award, ACPA Contribution of Knowledge award and honored as an ACPA Diamond Honoree and NASPA Pillar of the Profession. Guthrie has served on several editorial boards and is currently the associate editor of the *New Directions for Student Leadership* series (Wiley). Kathy has worked in higher education administrative and faculty roles for over 20 years and loves every minute of her chosen career path. Kathy enjoys spending time with her daughter and husband, where all three of them are affectionately known as Team Guthrie.

About the Contributors

Dr. Alan Acosta (he/him) has worked in the higher education profession for over 14 years, training students and professionals on adjudicating student conduct cases, managing student crises, and helping create a welcoming campus community. He believes in the importance of helping college students to become ethical, inclusive global leaders.

Bailey P. Albrecht (they/them/theirs) is the assistant director for adventure education at Bradford Woods–Indiana University. They find passion in incorporating student leadership and identity development in outdoor education. Bailey received their bachelors from Texas A&M University, and their masters from Texas State University.

Dr. Amena O. Anderson (she/her/hers) is assistant professor of practice and assistant director of West Virginia University's ADVANCE Center. Her research centers on leadership for social justice change within academia enacted by academics.

Dr. Jennifer M. Batchelder (she/her/ella) identifies as a Chicana/Latina. She is a graduate of the Florida State University Higher Education program. Her research interest involves the study of generativity (guiding the next generation) and leadership development for Latin* college students. As a research assistant, Jennifer served as an instructor for the Undergraduate Certificate in Leadership and contributed to research on leadership programs.

Operationalizing Culturally Relevant Leadership Learning, pages 251–259
Copyright © 2021 by Information Age Publishing
All rights of reproduction in any form reserved.   **251**

Mac Benavides (he/him) is a graduate teaching assistant in the Staley School of Leadership Studies at Kansas State University where he teaches a class encouraging his students to explore topics of power and privilege in leadership activity at the personal and systemic levels. Mac received a Master of Arts in Educational Administration from the University of Nebraska and is currently a student in the leadership communication doctoral program at Kansas State University. His research and practice centers around global and domestic intercultural learning, leadership education, and creating inclusive and equitable learning environments at institutions of higher education.

Adrian L. Bitton (she/her) is currently a doctoral student in the higher education and student affairs program at The Ohio State University. She earned her MA at the University of Maryland and BA at the University of Richmond. She held several leadership educator positions in student affairs prior to pursuing her PhD. Her research interests include the intersections of identity and leadership, leadership efficacy, and socially just leadership education.

Brittany Brewster (she/her) is a doctoral student at Florida Student University in the higher education program. Her research explores the experiences of underrepresented populations in higher education, with a special interest in Black women. Her research seeks to refine policies and practices to strengthen the pathway to the professoriate.

Destiny Caldwell (she/her) is the program coordinator for the Machen Florida Opportunity Scholars program at the University of Florida. She is also finishing her master's degree in higher education at FSU. Destiny's research interests center on exploring opportunities for culturally relevant education and advancing resources for marginalized students.

Sayrar Chansomebath (she/her/hers) received a Master of Arts in Educational Administration from the UNL. She is currently a graduate program coordinator for the Department of Anthropology and Program in Middle East/South Asia Studies at the University of California, Davis. As a student affairs professional, her passion lies in intercultural and student development, equity and access, and student retention.

Jessica Chung (she/her) serves as the curriculum and instruction coordinator for the undergraduate leadership minor at the University of Minnesota Twin Cities. She has spent years studying and practicing leadership education and development pedagogies to better serve all students through course curriculum and instructor training. Her hope is for every student to see how their own unique gifts are, in fact, leadership. She is endlessly fascinated by the intersection between leadership and art.

Dr. Vivechkanand S. Chunoo (he/him) is an assistant professor of agricultural leadership, education, and communication at the University of Illinois at Urbana–Champaign. He is invested in changing dominant narratives in leadership and shifting the mindset of education toward justice and equity.

Michael Cobden (he/him/his) is the head of Wellbeing (counseling, disability, mental health, and faith) at the University of West London. He has extensive experience of working in both higher education and further education in England, United Kingdom. Michael is an active member of the London Higher Taskforce for Tackling Racism in Higher Education in the United Kingdom as well as also being a member of the AimHigher London Disability Working Group which supports students with disabilities to access and succeed in higher education.

Dr. Jasmine D. Collins (she/her) is assistant professor of agricultural leadership, education and communications at the University of Illinois at Urbana–Champaign where she teaches organizational and community leadership courses and studies the impact of sociological factors on college student experiences and developmental outcomes.

Lauren R. Contreras (she/her) is the program coordinator for the CWC Leadership Scholars Program at the DU. Lauren is also a PhD student and graduate research and teaching assistant in the higher education department at the Morgridge College of Education at the DU.

Audrey Cooper (she/her) graduated from Florida State University in 2020 with a Bachelor of Science in information, communication, and technology and the undergraduate certificate in leadership studies. She became exposed to the university's leadership learning program through her involvement with the Panhellenic Association at Florida State University.

Brittany Devies, MS, (she/her) is a doctoral student at Florida State University studying higher education. Brittany is a graduate assistant for the Leadership Learning Research Center and a lead instructor for the undergraduate leadership studies certificate. Her research interests include the intersections of gender and leader identity development, CRLL, and the experiences of women in higher education.

O'Juan D. Edwards (he/him/his) is a PhD student in the higher education program at Florida State University. O'Juan has served as a leadership educator to underrepresented populations at PWIs for several years.

John Egan (he/him/his) is a leadership educator at Georgia Southern University and received his EdD in educational leadership from Georgia Southern University and his MS in kinesiology with a concentration in sport management and policy from the University of Georgia. He currently serves as the literature review coordinator for the SLPKC. They partnered together to facilitate the SLPKC Anti-Racism Book Club.

Onyedikachi Ekwerike (he/him) is a PhD candidate in the leadership communication doctoral program at Kansas State University. His research interests focus on nonprofit and social change leadership.

Dr. Jesse R. Ford (he/him) is an assistant professor of higher education at the University of North Carolina at Greensboro. As a critical scholar, his program of research uses culturally responsive frameworks to explore the influences of race and gender on the educational experiences of underrepresented populations in academia. Jesse earned a bachelor's degree in history from Coastal Carolina University and a master's degree in higher education and student affairs. He holds a PhD in higher education from Florida State University.

Christine Hernandez (she/her/hers) is the director for the Office of Student Engagement at Whittier College and is awards chair for the Student Leadership Knowledge Community. She received her bachelor's degree from California State University, Fullerton and a master of science in education from the University of Pennsylvania.

Tess Hobson (she/her) is a graduate teaching assistant in the Staley School of Leadership Studies at Kansas State University where she teaches a course about inclusive leadership called Culture and Context in Leadership. She received a master's degree in college student development and a graduate certificate in social justice education from Kansas State University, and is now pursuing a PhD in student affairs and higher education at K-State. Her research interests revolve around the power of storytelling as a pedagogy in developing students' capacity to practice inclusive leadership.

Pei Hu (she/her) is an international doctoral student in the Higher Education program at Florida State University. Her research interests focus on academic leadership programs and international student leadership development. Currently, she serves as a graduate assistant for the Leadership Learning Research Center, responsible for conducting leadership research projects and teaching in the Undergraduate Certificate in Leadership Studies. Pei received her bachelor's degree in Chinese Literature and

Linguistics from Jianghan University in China and obtained her master's degree in Higher Education at Florida State University.

Cassandra R. Kepple (she/her) is a doctoral student in the higher education program at Florida State University. Cassandra works as a research assistant studying how colleges can best support students with autism as well as best advising practices in higher education. Cassandra's research interests revolve around specific programming on college campuses that help ensure success for diverse student populations.

Dr. Lori E. Kniffin (she/her) is the assistant director of the Institute for Community and Economic Engagement at UNC Greensboro where she also earned her PhD in educational studies with a concentration in cultural foundations. Her research interests include collective leadership development, civic leadership, and critical leadership studies. She is an assistant professor of leadership studies at Fort Hays State University.

Adam Kuhn (he/his/they/them) is director of student engagement at the University of Toronto. Adam is also working on his PhD in higher education at the Ontario Institute for Studies in Education where he researches postsecondary experiences of Queer students.

Sharrell Hassell-Goodman (she/her) is a PhD candidate at George Mason University pursuing a degree in higher education with a concentration in women and gender studies and social justice. Sharrell has taught courses in the School of Integrative Studies on identity, social justice, and social science research. Her current research interests are first-generation college students, Black women in higher education, social justice advocates in higher education, identity and leadership, and critical participatory action research.

Julie LeBlanc (she/her) is a doctoral candidate in the higher education program at Florida State University. She works in the Leadership Learning Research Center as an instructor for the undergraduate certificate in leadership studies program. She has over 7 years of experience designing community engagement and leadership education programs.

Yang Li (she/her) is a PhD student in the higher education program at Florida State University. She earned her MS in the global higher education program at Educational Leadership and Policy Analysis Department from the University of Wisconsin–Madison. Yang currently serves as a graduate assistant in the Center for Global Engagement (CGE) and her main work at CGE is to assess programs related to international students' campus experience and involvement. Her current research interest lies in student success, especially international students' success in U.S. higher education.

Sherrina S. Lofton is a doctoral student in the Higher Education doctoral program and an Academic Advisor at Florida State University. She holds a bachelor's in finance and real estate and a master's in career counseling from California State University, Northridge. Sherrina's research focuses on the transition experiences of collegiate and professional athletes.

Dr. Linnette R. Lopez Werner (she/her/hers) has been teaching leadership in higher education since 2001 and served as the director of the undergraduate leadership minor at the University of Minnesota for 13 years before taking on a new leadership role at Hamline. She now serves as an associate dean at Hamline University, where she oversees graduate programs in education and leadership, legal studies, and creative writing.

Dr. Antron D. Mahoney (he/him/his) is the visiting assistant professor in gender and sexuality studies, specializing in Black sexualities, at Davidson College in Davidson, NC. He investigates the intersections of social movements and theories of race, gender, and sexuality to understand how Black gender ideology is formed in relation to 20th and 21st century social movements in the United States and the African diaspora. His primary focal points include Black feminist and queer praxis, U.S. higher education, leadership, and media studies.

Marissa P. Mainwood (she/her/hers) is a doctoral student in the higher education program at FSU. Her interests include student leadership development, international education, and online learning. Marissa is currently employed in the FSU College of Business as the student engagement coordinator.

Juan Cruz Mendizabal (he/him/his) is the assistant director for leadership education and development at Appalachian State University. Juan facilitates cocurricular leadership programs and teaches in the leadership studies minor.

Dr. Lisa Bardill Moscaritolo (she/her) is vice provost for Student Life at the American University of Sharjah in the United Arab Emirates and the secretary-general for the International Association of Student Affairs and Services. Lisa has been teaching for Purdue Global University, formerly Kaplan University, for over 15 years and teaches classes in leadership and management for the School of Business and Information Technology. She has served on several writing teams on the internationalization of student affairs/service practice and research.

Carlos Ordonez (he/him) serves as national director, Student Health and Wellbeing at Tec de Monterrey. He is a multilingual professional, a lifelong learner, passionate about well-being, intercultural communication, conscious leadership, diversity, equity, and inclusion. He wants to see students overcoming the different challenges they face in life and flourishing as human beings.

Dr. Julie E. Owen (she/her) is associate professor of leadership studies at the School of Integrative Studies, George Mason University, where she coordinates the leadership studies major and minor, and is affiliate faculty with the higher education program, and with women and gender studies. Owen has authored over 30 publications, including *We Are the Leaders We've Been Waiting For: Woman and Leadership Development in College* (Owen, 2020a).

Dr. Erin Sylvester Philpot (she/her) is an assistant director in leadership development and community engagement in the FSU Center for Leadership and Social Change. She has nearly a decade of experience as a student affairs practitioner and has a passion for graduate student development and the identity-informed leadership education. Erin received her MEd from the University of South Carolina and is a proud two-time Florida State Alumna where she received her bachelor's and doctorate.

Dr. Darren E. Pierre (he/him/his) is a lecturer in the Office of Global Engineering Leadership in the A. James Clark School of Engineering at the University of Maryland-College Park. Darren's teaching is focused on college student development, student affairs profession, and leadership within higher education. He carries years of experience as a university administrator, a leader within the field of higher education, and a contributor to many entity groups affiliated with higher education.

Dr. Kerry L. Priest (she/her) is an associate professor in the Staley School of Leadership Studies and Leadership Communication Doctoral Program at Kansas State University. Her interdisciplinary scholarship focuses on leadership identity, professional development, and critical, community-engaged methods for collective leadership development.

Riccardo Purita (he/him/his) is a third-year doctoral student in the higher education program at Florida State University. His research interests include social class identity, college experiences of low-income students, and college promise programs.

Dr. Avani Rana (she/her/hers) is the director of leadership programs at The College of New Jersey. She received her bachelor's degree in political science from Douglass College, Rutgers University, master of arts in higher education administration from New York University, and her EdD in education, culture and society from the Graduate School of Education at Rutgers University. Dr. Rana is the outgoing chair of the Student Leadership Knowledge Community.

Aliah Mestrovich Seay (she/her/hers) is a licensed clinical marriage and family therapist and works as both an instructor at the Staley School of Leadership Studies and an extension specialist (Culture and Communication Skills Development) for the Department of 4-H Youth Development at Kansas State University. With over 20 years of cumulative experience in K–12, higher education, and the not-for-profit sectors, Aliah's professional and research interests involve intercultural coaching and training techniques that focus on cultural identity development, listening, mindfulness, and finding innovative ways to engage with difference differently.

Josephine Shikongo is a second-year PhD student in the educational leadership and policy studies program at Oklahoma State University. Her research interests include leadership, academic capitalism, entrepreneurship, endowments funds, and public policy. She is also a certified accountant.

Dr. Dorsey Spencer, Jr. (he/him) is the dean of students at Colgate University in Hamilton, NY, where he oversees a significant portion of the students cocurricular and extracurricular experiences at the institution. He has published several book chapters on undergraduate Black men and leadership learning and created a Black male leadership course at a previous institution.

Dr. AdriAnne Yvette Archie Sternberg (she/her) is a native of Louisville and currently resides in Nashville, TN where she serves as the associate dean and director of leadership development at Belmont University. AdriAnne has over 15 years of educational leadership experience, teaching and training in both the for profit and nonprofit sectors. She enjoys all types of music, playing outdoors, and spending time with her husband and son.

Dr. Leonard Taylor (he/him/his) is an assistant professor of Higher Education Administration at Auburn University. He holds a PhD in organizational leadership, policy and development from the University of Minnesota—Twin Cities. Leonard's research related to leadership education is focused on using critical theories to rethink and advance leadership practice(s), and leadership education curriculum and pedagogy.

Dr. Trisha Teig (she/her) is the faculty director of the CWC Leadership Scholars Program and a teaching assistant professor for the Pioneer Leadership Program at the DU. As a leadership educator, her teaching and research focus on critical feminist implementations of leadership to address and dismantle systemic inequalities and enact positive, equitable change.

Dra. Maritza Torres (she/her/hers/ella) is the assistant director for LEAD scholar's academy at the University of Central Florida. Maritza teaches, advises, and facilitates leadership learning and scholarship to undergraduate and graduate students. Maritza's research centers on Latina undergraduate leader identity development, CRLL, and identity-based leadership courses. Maritza is a coauthor of *Thinking to transform: Reflection in leadership learning* and contributed to *Changing the narrative: Socially just leadership education.*

John Weng (he/him/his) serves as the assistant director for Asian student administration at University of California San Diego and a lecturer for the University of San Diego, Department of Leadership Studies, where is also pursuing his doctorate in leadership studies. He is passionate about leadership education and leadership development which informs his teaching, practice, and scholarship.

Dr. Erica R. Wiborg (she/her) is a graduate of the Higher Education PhD program at Florida State University. She is a critical, qualitative scholar passionate about deconstructing systemic racism, the sociohistorical influences of race and racism, and hegemonic whiteness in higher education. Erica's overall research focus is within curricular and cocurricular student engagement. Previously, Erica served as a research assistant in the Leadership Learning Research Center and worked full-time as a program coordinator in the Center for Leadership and Social Change at Florida State University, where she coordinated college student development programs focused on the outcomes of leadership, social justice, identity, diversity, and community engagement.

Dr. Aoi Yamanaka (she/her/hers) is an assistant professor and associate director of academic services in the School of Integrative Studies at George Mason University, where she teaches courses on social justice and global leadership. Aoi's current scholarship focuses on social justice issues in higher education, cultural leadership, and civic engagement in a diverse environment.

Made in United States
Orlando, FL
27 January 2023

29092744R00157